Simply Fish

SIMPLY FISH
Jenny Baker

illustrated by Madeleine Baker

MAGNA BOOKS

First published in 1988
by Faber and Faber Limited
3 Queen Square London WC1N 3AU

This edition published
1993 by Magna Books.
Magna Road, Wigston,
Leicester, LE18 4ZH,
produced by the Promotional
Reprint Company Limited, UK

Printed in Hungary

ISBN 1 85422 438 7

Contents

Acknowledgements

First I want to thank ROBIN BRUCE, academic and man of Billingsgate, who knows so much about fish, whose name should not just be in capitals but emblazoned in lights, for giving me so much help and encouragement, remaining unruffled from my first unannounced phone call to finding himself roped into reading and vetting the entire manuscript. For introducing Robin to me, my grateful thanks to Dr Humphrey Greenwood of the British Museum (Natural History) and also for all the help he gave me sorting out the fish of the Seychelles, including lending me his own reference books and talking enthusiastially for hours even though he was about to embark that week on a three-month expedition to Africa. Also I must thank him for lending other books as reference guides for the illustrations. Thank you to my daughter Madeleine for doing all the illustrations and putting up with me introducing new fish right up to the last minute. I wish to thank many other people who gave me help and guidance: the fishmongers who answered all my endless questions, cheerfully cleaned and gutted and sold me lots of delicious fish; all sorts of people in the industry such as Chris Newnes and Jack Shiels, who put me right about Zanders and lent me a book on St Peter's fish; Chris Leftwich, the Inspector to the Worshipful Company of Fishmongers for the information about the regulations regarding the sale of certain fish and for his interest; Denys Bradfield of the National Federation of Fishmongers, Middlesex (you can contact him if you're searching for a fishmonger in your area or trying to find where to buy a particular fish; he may be able to help you). My thanks, too, to the various bodies who gave me help such as the Seafish Industry Authority; the Atlantic Salmon Trust; the Shellfish Association of Great Britain; Scottish Salmon Information Service; British Trout Association and the Universities Federation for Animal Welfare. Then of course I must thank my family for putting up with all the experiments and with me for being rather distracted a lot of the time; and many friends for talking about fish, lending me books, swapping stories and recipes. Finally for all the endless drafts, the getting up early in the morning and staying up late at night, I really must extend my more than grateful thanks to my ever faithful Amstrad PCW8256.

Introduction

Simply Fish is more than a cook book. It's a book designed to help you find out more about fish, how to identify them and sort out their names; when and where to buy them; how much to buy and what to ask the fishmonger, as well as explaining how to prepare them and giving you cooking ideas and recipes. It covers fish and shellfish that you will find at the fishmongers and also those fish that might be presented to you by an angler. In it are all the familiar fish you've known since your childhood, plus exotic fish imported from abroad and others caught round our coasts which may be new to you.

How many times have you decided to try something different, perhaps looked up a new recipe and settled on a particular fish before setting out, only to find the fish wasn't there? On the slab are a whole range of others, many with familiar names but a few quite unknown to you. Whilst you wait in the queue, you find yourself longing to try one of these, then realize you aren't sure how much you need or how to go about preparing and cooking it. So you stand there dithering until you find yourself buying the same old standby, or worse, fleeing, empty-handed.

I have written this book especially for moments like these. A book to use there and then, on the spot, to be leafed through to find the answers to those questions you don't dare to ask. Questions like, what is that fish? where does it come from? how much do I need to buy? will you fillet it for me? how do I cook it? A book to use at the fishmonger as well as in the kitchen.

How to use this book

The fish are arranged from A–Z so they are instantly accessible. Each is self-contained, with its own set of information, illustration, cooking ideas and recipes; but because many fish can be treated similarly, there are also cross-references to other fish and recipes. Each fish is set out like so:

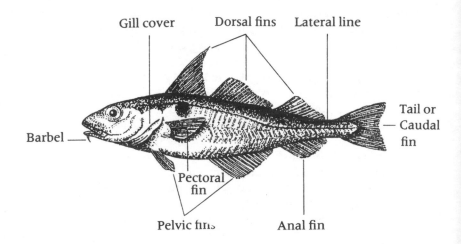

NAME followed by alternative names and other related fish.

Habitat Showing whether sea or freshwater and which areas the fish is likely to come from.

Pros and Cons Relevant to flavour, price, etc.

Size In most cases the marketable length.

Description Distinguishing features, colour, etc.

How sold	Whether whole fish, fillets, steaks, etc.
Qty per person	A guide to how much to buy for an average serving; this obviously must depend on individual appetites but you'll soon know whether to adjust the amounts up or down slightly.
Ask fishmonger	What special requirements for that fish, such as filleting, etc.
Availability	Seasons, areas, type of shops, etc.
Notes	Relevant facts of interest peculiar to that particular fish.
Preparation	What you need to do to prepare the fish for cooking.
Cooking ideas	Suggestions to give you ideas, followed by specific recipes.

At the end of the book I have included a section called 'Fish Medley' which covers recipes like Bouillabaisse or the freshwater Matelote which use a selection of different fishes; another section explains all the basic ways of cooking fish such as grilling, baking, etc.; there is a section on butters and sauces which includes all those mentioned in the recipes, and another on the techniques of preparing fish, covering cleaning, boning, filleting, etc. I have also included a list of handy gadgets and a page showing comparative weights and temperatures. Throughout the book I have used two measuring systems, metric and our own more familiar system. Use whichever you feel happier with. Quantities are really a guide; recipes should be treated as something flexible, more a means of inspiration than a set of hard and fast rules. Recipes are for four, unless otherwise stated.

Buying fish

The choice in your fishmonger's is as dependent as the fish themselves on weather and season so it is often impossible to go shopping already having made up your mind. Your particular fish may not be available, or there may be other fish on the slab which are fresher and more exciting. So be prepared to choose when you get there.

The signs of freshness

	Good signs	Bad signs
EYES	Full and bright	Dull and sunken
BODY	Firm and springy	Limp and spongy
SKIN	Glistening	Dull and dry
GILLS	Bright red	Dull or grey
SMELL	Of the sea	Strong and fishy*

The eyes are the most important clue. Fish can be washed to get rid of bad smells and the gills artificially coloured but the eyes cannot lie.

Keeping fish fresh
Buy if possible on the day you want to cook it. Unwrap it and put it in a plastic bag and keep it in the fridge. If you plan to keep it until the next day, it will deteriorate less if you surround it with ice. Handle it with care; fish bruises easily.

* Sometimes cartilaginous fish (Skate, Dogfish and Shark) smell of ammonia; this will disappear on cooking.

Your fishmonger

There are fishmongers who really know their fish and others who buy and sell fish as if they were so many bags of potatoes. A good fishmonger displays his fish on ice, not just on a refrigerated counter. He understands the principles of keeping fish fresh, ice being the ideal medium for maintaining it at a constant temperature. He handles his fish with care. Fish are easily damaged so if you see boxes being thrown about, you'll know you have a careless fishmonger. Your good fishmonger will know about his fish and come up with ideas on how to cook it. He will offer to clean and scale it for you and won't look aghast if you ask him to bone or fillet it. After all, it's part of the job, so don't be afraid to ask him to do it; you don't expect to pluck a chicken, or cut lamb into chops. Cherish him. Be nice to him. Smile rather than frown anxiously. Remember his task is made harder by a public who have largely forgotten all they knew about fish. Tell him of your successes and give him your recipes so he can hand tips on to other customers. Equally, report your failures and don't be afraid to complain if he's sold you something below standard. Above all make him believe that you are interested in fish, in trying new ones, in buying fresh ones and that you just aren't impressed by being fobbed off with fillets of this or that or fish sold under placatory aliases like rock salmon or rock fish.

Some notes on the fish industry

If you go to a fishmarket like Billingsgate early in the morning, you will find it teeming with business. Stalls are piled high with boxes of every imaginable kind of fish all packed in ice; there are baskets full of crabs and lobsters, trays of prawns, tubs filled with clams and oysters, cockles and mussels. There are live eels and jellied eels; fish as familiar as cod and as exotic as octopus. The floor is awash. Porters hurtle down the gangways between the stalls, pushing their laden trolleys at breakneck speed, somehow just missing sending everything flying like so many skittles. There are more varieties of fish at Billingsgate than at any other market in Europe, a great hubbub of selling, bustle and mateyness. Talk to almost any of the merchants and you find a person with great individual character, full of enthusiasm and hopeful for the future. There are signs of a revolution taking place with exciting changes in the industry and a public at last becoming more interested in buying fresh fish.

The enormous range is due to the wealth of fish and shellfish caught around our coasts as well as those imported from all over the world. The market is responding to our more sophisticated tastes created by holidays abroad and to the demand of people whose cultures originate in places like the Caribbean, Africa, India, countries of the Mediterranean, the Middle and Far East. The development of farming and cultivation techniques means that salmon, trout, carp, St Peter's fish, mussels and oysters are far more plentiful and no longer only available at certain seasons. Experiments in these techniques continue with other varieties such as bass, sea breams, turbot, scallops and prawns. Increased supplies of these farmed fish will offset the reduction in availability of some wild fish due to tougher laws on minimum sizes, closed seasons and fishing quotas. It's worth considering the harm that certain snobbish attitudes towards fish farming can cause; if, for example, we insist on eating only wild salmon, not only will we destroy the new and courageous salmon farming industry but we will exhaust the supply of wild salmon itself.

Fish and shellfish are there for us to enjoy; all that is needed is for us to respond to the challenge by buying them *fresh* and being flexible and a bit courageous in our choices. Worth encouraging are fishmongers, market stalls and supermarkets who display fish as whole fish on the slab surrounded with ice and have staff who know what they are talking about. Fishmongers themselves could consider being more adaptable, perhaps staying open late one evening at the end of the week to fit in with people's shopping patterns. Fish with a sell-by date sold pre-packed, whether whole or cut into fillets or steaks, are really second-best and should be treated as such; useful when there is no other alternative. Although they freeze reasonably well, frozen fish and shellfish do not compare with fresh in flavour and quality and are best thought of as store-standbys.

Most fish and shellfish are not cheap, yet we still expect that they should be. In the bad old days of the past, cheap fish depended upon cheap labour. It is a labour intensive industry with many stages to get the fish from the boats to the fishmonger's slab. The fishermen do a job that is as dangerous and as physically demanding as it ever was but at least they are better rewarded; good reason for not begrudging paying the price. If we do, we shall see more and more of our best fish going to the Continent, where it is much in demand and appreciated and where they are quite prepared to pay for it. That marvellous seafood platter you enjoyed in France is more than likely composed of shellfish bought from our country!

So, let's rally to the barricades and ensure the success of the revolution. Buy fish fresh!

Fish from A–Z

ABALONE, *see* **ORMERS**

ALBACORE, *see* **TUNA**

ALLIS SHAD, *see* **SHAD**

ALLISON TUNA, *see* **TUNA**

Anchovy

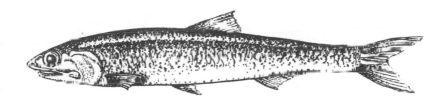

ANCHOVY — *related to:* HERRING, SARDINE (PILCHARD) and SPRAT

Habitat Mediterranean and other European seas, Indian and Pacific oceans.

Pros and Cons Fresh anchovies are rare as they are very soft and fragile and do not transport easily. So if you ever get the chance, perhaps on holiday, snap them up to experience their strange, somewhat bitter flavour. Buy fillets of anchovies in cans or jars to add flavouring to some of the blander fishes, as well as to make such famous Mediterranean specialities as anchoïade.

Size 10–15 cm (4–6 ins).

Description	The slender, compressed body is olive-green or blue with silvery sides. It has a snout-shaped head with a receding lower jaw giving it the appearance of a chinless wonder.
How sold	Fresh: whole fish, by weight. Preserved: filleted, salted and canned in oil; or packed in jars.
Qty per person	Fresh: 175–200 g (6–7 oz).
Availability	Anchovies whole or filleted are sold canned in oil, or in different sauces, and are fairly easily obtainable. You may sometimes find them packed in salt in jars, especially on the Continent.
Notes	Most of the catch is cleaned and beheaded before being packed into barrels in salt to be left to ripen over a period of from 3 to 18 months, during which time they turn from silver to a sombre red.
Preparation	**Fresh:** To clean, snap off the heads, which will come away with most of their innards. They are so soft they can be filleted with the finger nail. Wash and dry with kitchen paper. **Canned and in jars:** If you find them too salty (those in jars are particularly so), soak them for 15–30 minutes in milk or water. If whole, split them and remove the backbone.
Cooking ideas	**Fresh anchovies** can be deep fried like whitebait, baked or grilled, prepared *en escabèche* or simply split and marinaded for 24 hours in lemon juice. You can use recipes for sardines. **Preserved anchovies** can be used like bacon to add flavour to other fish as well as meat and poultry or as the basis of some marvellous, simple dishes. Or use to flavour vinaigrette, mayonnaise or butter (*see* Sauces).

Fresh Anchovies baked as in Naples (or use sardines or sprats)
Heat oven to Gas 6/400°F/200°C. Behead and tail fresh anchovies and arrange like the spokes of a wheel in a round, oiled oven dish. Sprinkle with olive oil and if you like add a layer of sliced tomatoes.

Add salt and pepper, cover with a handful of fresh breadcrumbs mixed with chopped parsley and dribble over some more olive oil. Bake for 15 minutes.

Anchoïade

There are many different versions of anchoïade, from a thick paste for spreading on bread to a hot or cold sauce in which to dip *crudités* (raw vegetables). This can be simply a bowl of celery, which is traditionally eaten in some areas of Provence and Languedoc on Christmas Eve as part of *le Gros Souper* (which is supposed to be a fast but is in fact a feast); or at any time of the year with a whole assortment of seasonal vegetables, the dish becoming a complete meal with the addition of halves of hard-boiled eggs.

Canapé à l'anchoïade

1 can anchovy fillets
4 cloves garlic, finely chopped
olive oil
pepper
1 teaspoon fennel seeds (optional)
French bread

Chop and pound the garlic to a paste (a pestle and mortar comes in handy here, or you can use a food processor). Add the anchovy fillets and pound again. Gradually add sufficient olive oil, drop by drop, beating well until you have a thick paste. Add pepper to taste. Heat oven to Gas 7/425°F/220°C. Spread the paste on slices of French bread, sprinkle with fennel seeds, and put into the oven for 5–10 minutes.

Céleri à l'anchoïade

1 can anchovy fillets
1 or 2 heads of celery
¼ pint olive oil
dash of wine vinegar
black pepper

Separate the stalks of celery, remove stringy bits and to make them really crisp soak for one hour in cold water.

Crush anchovy fillets with a fork, put them into a bowl standing in a saucepan of hot water over a low heat. Gradually beat in the olive oil. Add the vinegar and some black pepper. Keep warm until ready to eat. Put the anchoïade in the centre and let everyone dip in their pieces of celery.

Crudités à l'anchoïade

Prepare a variety of raw vegetables, cutting them into pieces to be picked up in the fingers. Arrange them on a large flat dish with the anchoïade in a bowl in the centre. Your selection might include four or five of the following: fennel, chicory, celery, lettuce hearts, tiny new broad beans still in their shells, cauliflower, tomatoes, mangetout, mushrooms, cucumber, carrot, green or red peppers, radishes, watercress with a garnish of hard-boiled eggs cut in half.

Elisabeth's Anchovy croissants

Simple appetizers using bought puff pastry.

Heat oven to Gas 7/425°F/220°C. Roll out some puff pastry until it is quite thin. Divide into squares, the sides of which are the length of an anchovy fillet. Cut the squares in half to form triangles. Cut each fillet in half lengthways, and roll up each in a pastry triangle. Brush each roll with beaten egg and twist into a crescent shape, pressing the two points together. Bake 10–12 minutes until golden.

Salade niçoise

A dish for high summer, succulent and fresh made with raw vegetables dressed simply with olive oil.

1 can anchovy fillets
6 tomatoes, cut in quarters
1 clove of garlic
1 large green pepper, finely chopped
150g (6 oz) new broad beans
1 bunch spring onions, chopped
handful of black olives
4 hard-boiled eggs (optional)
salt, pepper
fresh basil or parsley, chopped
4–6 tablespoons olive oil

Sprinkle the quartered tomatoes with salt and set aside to drain some of their moisture. Cut the garlic in half and rub the cut side over a wide salad bowl. Put in the green pepper, broad beans and spring onions. Cut the anchovy fillets lengthwise into fine strips (you can use shredded tuna as well if you wish). Add the black olives, and hard-boiled eggs cut in quarters, a little salt and freshly milled black pepper. Top with the tomatoes, sprinkle with chopped basil or parsley and the olive oil.

Tapenade

This mixture of anchovies and black olives comes from Provence. It is delicious as a spread or you can use it to stuff hard-boiled eggs. It is made by stoning 100 g (4 oz) black olives, chopping them finely, adding a chopped clove of garlic, 2 anchovy fillets, 2 tablespoons capers. Crush them all together in a mortar or food processor, but not too finely. Gradually add olive oil, drop by drop as if making a mayonnaise, until you have a soft paste. Finish it off with a few drops of brandy or marc if you like.

ANGLER-FISH, *see* **MONKFISH**

ARBROATH SMOKIES, *see* **HADDOCK, SMOKED**

ARCTIC CHARR, *see* **CHARR**

ATLANTIC BONITO, *see* **BONITO**

ATLANTIC MACKEREL, *see* **MACKEREL**

BALLAN WRASSE, *see* **WRASSE**

BAMBOOFISH, *see* **BREAMS, SEA**

Barbel

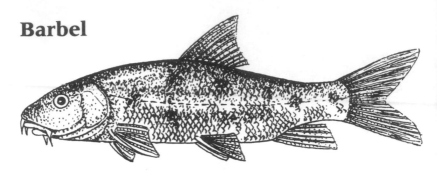

BARBEL — *same family as:* BREAM, CARP, GUDGEON and TENCH

Habitat
Close to beds in deep, swift-running rivers in Central and Eastern England as well as on the Continent.

Pros and Cons
A fish the angler in your family might bring back, it's a fine fighter but is bony and needs plenty of additional flavouring.

Size
Usually around 25–38 cm (10–15 ins).

Description
Slender muddy-green or sandy-brown body with a pale belly. The head is long with leathery, fleshy lips and 4 barbels; the dorsal fin has a spine with an edge like a saw. Scales are small.

Qty per person
Allow 225–275 g (8–10 oz) of whole, ungutted fish.

Preparation
To lose its muddy flavour, ideally the fish should be allowed to swim around in fresh water for at least half an hour – in the bath perhaps? Otherwise trim, scale and clean and, if it is a female, make sure you remove the roe (which is poisonous), though the soft roe of the male can be put back inside (*see* page 282). Rub the fish inside and out with a mixture of salt and vinegar, allow 1 teaspoon of each to every 450 g (1 lb) of fish. Then soak for 30 minutes in acidulated water (2 tablespoons

vinegar, 1 teaspoon salt to every litre [1¾ pints] water). Rinse and dry.

Cooking ideas   Large fish can be baked, smaller ones are best grilled or fried *à la meunière* and served with a butter or sauce; choose one which is highly flavoured with something like anchovy, mustard, shallots, capers, etc. (*see* Sauces). Or cook with other river fish *en matelote* or in a freshwater bouillabaisse.

Baked Barbel
Heat oven to Gas 4/350°F/180°C. Lay the prepared fish in a well-buttered oven dish, score it on both sides two or three times. Season with salt, pepper, parsley, chopped shallots, mushrooms, and bacon or anchovy fillets. Cover with fresh breadcrumbs. Sprinkle over lemon juice and a glass of dry white wine. Bake 30 minutes, basting often.

Barracuda

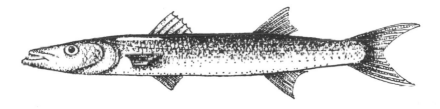

BARRACUDA or BECUNE, Caribbean BECHINE

Habitat   Mediterranean and tropical and warm temperate seas.

Pros and Cons   Imported in very limited numbers most of which find their way to restaurants. It has delicious white flesh, so worth buying if you ever have the chance, though it will be expensive.

Size   Usually around 30–40 cm (12–16 ins).

Description	The long narrow body with small scales is silvery gold with a dark back, pale sides and dark stripes. It has a pointed snout with a protruding lower jaw filled with savage teeth.
How sold	Whole fish or steaks.
Qty per person	Allow 225–275 g (8–10 oz) of whole, ungutted fish. Steaks: 175–200 g (6–7 oz).
Ask fishmonger	If buying whole fish, to clean, trim and scale.
Availability	From the more enterprising fishmongers mainly in London and the SE.
Notes	Of the several species of barracuda, it is the small ones which make good eating. All are ferocious fish, not unlike the pike in appearance; the French name is *brochet de mer* (Sea pike). Not only are large barracuda feared by swimmers and fishermen but some are actually poisonous.
Preparation	Whole fish should be cleaned, trimmed and scaled; otherwise wash and wipe dry.
Cooking ideas	Grill or fry steaks marinaded with olive oil, lemon juice, salt and pepper, serve with a tomato sauce or raïto sauce. Or bake and make into kebabs and grill over charcoal. Whole fish may be poached and served with a sauce.

Baked Barracuda steaks
Heat oven to Gas 4/350°F/180°C. Oil a shallow oven dish. Sprinkle the steaks with salt and pepper and put them in the dish with chopped spring onions, dill and parsley. Lay slices of lemon on top. Pour over a medium can of Italian tomatoes, crushing them with a fork. Squeeze over the juice of a lemon, add a handful of green or black olives. Bake 20–25 minutes.

Poached Barracuda
Lay steaks, or whole fish scored two or three times on either side, in a shallow china or glass dish. Squeeze over the juice of 1 or 2 lemons, add a piece of finely chopped ginger, a clove of chopped

garlic, 2 or 3 sprigs of fresh thyme (or use 1 teaspoon dried), pepper and a whole red chilli. Leave 30 minutes. Poach in a *court bouillon* (*see* poaching section, page 300). Serve with a tomato or raïto sauce.

Bass

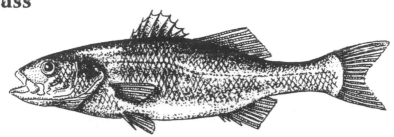

BASS – *also known as:* SEA BASS or SALMON BASS; *related distantly to:* GROUPERS

Habitat	From southern North Sea, English Channel through to Mediterranean.
Pros and Cons	This is a delicious, though expensive, fish with tender, white flesh. It is much prized on the Continent and becoming increasingly popular here.
Size	32–70 cm (13–28 ins).
Description	Similar to but more thickset than the salmon. Body is blue-grey with silvery sides and a shimmering white belly. There is a black spot on the spiny gill covers. It has serrated scales on body and head, a forked tail and spiny rays on the first dorsal fin.
How sold	Whole fish, sometimes steaks.
Qty per person	Allow 225–275 g (8–10 oz) whole fish ungutted. Steaks: 175–200 g (6–7 oz).
Ask fishmonger	If buying whole fish, to clean, trim and scale, though if you are poaching it, scaling can be omitted.

Availability	From the more enterprising fishmongers, all year and especially from areas around southern England and western Ireland. Bass is a favourite amongst the Chinese, so look out for it in shops run by them.
Notes	Popular since Roman times, bass is prized on the Continent and is beginning to find favour here, especially in the restaurant trade. Restricted catches and heavy demand mean the price is high, though farming techniques are being developed, which means they should become more plentiful in the future. They are unrelated to salmon but similar in shape, hence the misnomer salmon bass. They are predators with voracious appetites and on menus you come across them under their French nickname of *loup de mer* (Sea Wolf).
Preparation	Must be cleaned, trimmed and scaled if the fishmonger hasn't already done so. If poaching whole omit the scaling as the skin is quite delicate and you can remove the whole skin when the fish is cooked. Wash inside and out; if cooking whole make sure the gills have been removed. Wipe dry with kitchen paper.
Cooking ideas	Bake whole, stuffed or not, following recipes for the sea breams; steam using the recipe for Rabbitfish on page 186; or it is delicious poached like salmon and eaten with a sauce, perhaps a *beurre blanc* or hollandaise or *maître d'hôtel* butter, or as in Provence, a *pistou*; or serve cold with one of the sauces for cold fish such as mayonnaise, walnut horseradish sauce, gribiche, *pommade verte*, tartare or aïoli. Grill or fry small bass *à la meunière*, or cook *en papillote*; trout recipes are suitable. Steaks are good grilled.

In Provence they grill bass over a barbecue of dried fennel stalks and vine shoots, both of which are sold very cheaply in bundles in the local supermarkets, or gathered by wandering through the vineyards and surrounding areas. Not a practical proposition for us and although fennel does grow wild in this country, care must be taken properly to identify it, similar looking plants being less edible and some rather poisonous. You can achieve something of the same flavour by baking a bass on a bed of Florentine fennel.

Bass baked with fennel

sea bass, either 1 whole or small ones weighing in total about 1 kilo
  (2¼ lbs)
2 tablespoons olive oil
1 onion, chopped
450 g (1 lb) root fennel, cleaned and sliced
juice of 1 lemon
salt, pepper
handful fresh chopped parsley
lemon slices

Heat the oven to Gas 4/350°F/180°C. In a wok or frying pan, heat the olive oil, when it is hot add the chopped onion, cook several minutes until golden. Add the finely sliced fennel and let it soften over a moderate heat. Season with the lemon juice, salt, pepper and parsley. Butter or oil a shallow oven dish, make a bed of half the fennel and onion. Score the fish two or three times on each side and lay on top. Put slices of lemon on top of the fish, cover with remaining fennel. Bake 20–30 minutes, covered loosely with foil. Baste two or three times. Check after 20 minutes by slipping a skewer into the thickest part of the fish. If the flesh flakes and comes away easily it is done, otherwise continue the cooking a little longer. You can flame the dish by heating a tablespoon of brandy plus 1 teaspoon fennel seeds in a ladle, light it and pour over just as you bring the fish to the table.

This is lovely with a sauce *rémoulade* or *pistou*.

Bass baked in foil with ginger

The Chinese love sea bass and cook it flavoured with ginger. Heat oven to Gas 6/400°F/200°C. Score the fish on both sides. Lay it on a piece of oiled foil. Add some chopped spring onions, chopped garlic, a thin slice of root ginger finely chopped, dash of soya sauce, salt, 1 teaspoon sugar and a good sprinkling of olive oil. Bake 30–40 minutes. Serve with wedges of lemon or lime and garnish with spring onions. This recipe can be used for steaks as well as whole fish and is equally successful with fish such as carp or freshwater bream, sea bream, turbot, monkfish, snapper or dogfish. Gauge cooking time according to the size of the fish, allowing 20 minutes for steaks, longer for whole fish.

BAUDROIE, *see* **MONKFISH**

BECHINE, *see* **BARRACUDA**

BECUNE, *see* **BARRACUDA**

BELONS, *see* **OYSTERS**

BIG EYE, *see* **CARANGIDS**

BIG-EYE TUNA, *see* **TUNA**

Billfish

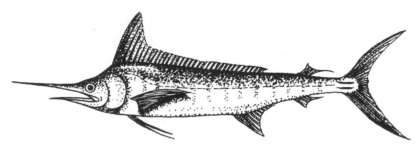

BILLFISH – a group name for a variety of fish which includes SAILFISH and MARLIN; *related to:* MACKEREL and TUNA

Habitat	Temperate and warm seas.
Pros and Cons	Sailfish and marlins have firm, meaty flesh which can be tough so is best when grilled or barbecued. They are imported from the Seychelles or other tropical areas, so won't be cheap.
Size	Usually around 1–1½ metres (3–5 feet), although they can all grow to double this size.
Description	Bodies are spindle shaped, usually with dark, steel-blue backs, and all have the characteristic bill-shaped snouts. The sailfish has a high dorsal fin which gives it its name.
How sold	Steaks or cutlets.
Qty per person	150–200 g (5–7 oz).
Ask fishmonger	For a middle or top cut; tail end will be less meaty and drier.
Availability	Enterprising fishmongers mainly in London and the SE, especially in shops or markets popular with Caribbeans.
Notes	These are the highly prized game fish that Hemingway made his own; the marlin is popular in the Caribbean, where it is nicknamed White or Big Daddy.
Preparation	Wash steaks and dry with kitchen paper.
Cooking ideas	Because the flesh is meaty it is ideal for grilling or barbecueing or cooking *en papillote*. Whatever method you choose, it's a good idea to marinade it first. Swordfish recipes are suitable.

Marinade for Billfish or Marlin

Put the steaks in an oven dish and marinade in the juice of 1 lemon, a clove of chopped garlic, 2 or 3 chopped anchovy fillets, pepper, 2 or 3 tablespoons olive oil and herbs such as a bayleaf, parsley and oregano; or use rosemary and thyme. Or use one of the marinades on pages 299–300.

Grilled steaks
Marinade for 1–2 hours then grill or barbecue as on pages 298–300, basting frequently with the marinade. Serve with a vinaigrette-based sauce, caper cream sauce, *pistou* or aïoli.

En papillote
Marinade for 1–2 hours. Heat oven to Gas 5/375°F/190°C. Lay the steaks on pieces of oiled foil large enough to make parcels. Add some finely sliced spring onion and chopped tomato and pour the marinade on top. Put a slice of lemon on each. Wrap the foil loosely, making sure none of the juices can escape. Bake 15–20 minutes.

BLACK SCABBARD FISH, *see* **SCABBARD FISH**

BLACK SEA BREAM, *see* **BREAM, BLACK SEA**

BLACK SOLE, *see* **SOLE**

BLOATER, *see* **HERRING, SMOKED**

BLUE-FIN TUNA, *see* **TUNA**

BLUE-GREEN PARROTFISH, *see* **PARROTFISH**

BOGUE, *see* **BREAMS, SEA**

Bonito

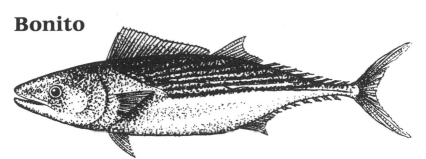

BONITO – *same family as:* MACKEREL and TUNA; other species on sale are the ATLANTIC BONITO and the STRIPED BONITO

Habitat N Atlantic, Mediterranean, Black Sea, Indo-Pacific.

Pros and Cons A fine meaty fish with light flesh with a texture rather like chicken.

Size Up to 70 cm (28 ins).

Description Slender, spindle shaped body with steel blue back, slatted with 5–10 oblique brownish blue stripes, belly and sides are silvery white. Strongly keeled tail with finlets.

How sold Whole fish or cutlets or steaks.

Qty per person Allow 200–225 g (7–8 oz) whole, ungutted fish. Steaks: 150–200 g (5–7 oz).

Ask fishmonger For middle or top cut rather than tail end which is much bonier. If buying whole fish ask him to clean, scale and trim.

Availability From the more enterprising fishmongers, often frozen.

Notes Bonito compares to the highly rated kingfish or king mackerel. It is more delicate than tuna. Most is canned and sold as skipjack tuna.

Preparation Whole fish must be cleaned and trimmed if the fishmonger has not already done so. Frozen fish should be allowed to thaw slowly. The fish is often frozen ungutted so if buying steaks or a piece, care must be taken to remove every vestige of the black entrails lurking near the bone or the taste will be bitter; use the point of a knife, and if necessary rub with salt and lemon juice. Let the fish soak for 10–15 minutes in acidulated water (2 tablespoons vinegar, 1 teaspoon salt to 1 litre [1¾ pints] of water). Drain and dry with kitchen paper.

Cooking ideas   It is good baked or braised, the cooking time being a little longer than for softer fleshed fish. Steaks are good marinaded with chermoula (*see* page 300) and grilled or braised, or cut up and used for kebabs. Recipes for tuna or kingfish are suitable.

Bonite basquaise – Bonito steaks braised with aubergine, peppers and tomato
4 steaks of bonito weighing about 200 g (7 oz) each
flour for coating
1 onion, chopped
4 tablespoons olive oil
2 cloves garlic, chopped
3 or 4 anchovy fillets, chopped
1 chilli, chopped
1 green or red pepper, roughly chopped
1 aubergine, cut in cubes
1 tablespoon tomato purée
1 medium can Italian tomatoes, drained
salt, pepper
thyme, sweet basil, bayleaf
1 lemon, sliced
Heat oven to Gas 6/400°F/200°C. Season the steaks with salt and pepper, coat them in flour. Heat 2 tablespoons olive oil in a wok or frying pan and fry the steaks on both sides for 3 or 4 minutes until golden. Remove. Throw out the oil. Put 2 more tablespoons of oil in the pan and when it is hot, add the chopped onion, let it soften over a medium heat for a few minutes, then add the garlic, anchovy fillets and the chilli. After 2 or 3 minutes, add the green or red pepper and aubergine. Let them soften, stirring frequently, then add

the tomato purée and the drained tomatoes. Crush them up and add salt, pepper and herbs, Lower the heat and let the sauce simmer for 5–10 minutes. Lay half the sauce in a shallow oven dish, put the steaks on top and put the slices of lemon on them. Cover with the remaining sauce. Put a sheet of foil loosely on top and put into the oven for 45 minutes. Serve with rice.

Baked Bonito en papillote with garlic and fennel

You can use a whole fish, a piece of fish or steaks for this recipe. If using whole fish or a piece, score it two or three times on either side. Marinade it for 30 minutes in a glass or china dish with slivers of garlic, chopped anchovy, 1 teaspoon crushed fennel seeds, a chopped dried chilli, thyme, lemon juice and 4 tablespoons olive oil. Heat oven to Gas 6/400°F/200°C. Lay the fish on a piece of foil (steaks on individual pieces), pour over the marinade, fold foil into a loose parcel and bake. Allow 15–20 minutes for steaks and up to 45 minutes for a whole fish.

BOURGEOIS, *see* SNAPPERS

BREAM, EMPEROR, *see* EMPERORS

Bream, Freshwater

BREAM, FRESHWATER – *same family as:* BARBEL, CARP, GUDGEON, ROACH and TENCH

Habitat
Favours sluggish waters in lowland rivers, canals, reservoirs and lakes in eastern England, southern Scotland and on Continent.

Pros and Cons
This angling fish doesn't excite fishermen or gourmets. It has no fight in it, not much flavour and is very bony.

Size
Usually around 30 cm (12 ins) but can be double this size.

Description
The colour of the deep compressed body with its large scales and slimy skin varies with age and habitat from leaden blues to muddy greens, the sides and belly are bronze and the fins charcoal. The head is small, the eyes protrude and the lips are rounded and pursed.

Qty per person
Allow 225–275 g (8–10 oz) of whole, ungutted fish.

Availability
Hardly ever on sale, though you might come across it in London and the SE, mainly in Jewish or West Indian shops.

Notes   This is a greedy fish which grubs around in the mud searching for worms and weeds. A. F. Magri MacMahon in *Fishlore* remarks on how the bream reminds him of all those people who wear the label 'Important' but who, he implies, are really no more than pompous windbags. So what do you do when presented with a bream by the fisherman who has caught it?

Preparation   To get rid of its muddiness, ideally it should be allowed to swim around for a while in fresh water. Otherwise, trim, and scale with care because the scales are really quite sharp. Clean and remove the gills. Rub the fish inside and out with a mixture of salt and vinegar, allow 1 teaspoon of each to every 450 g (1 lb) of fish. Then soak for 30 minutes in acidulated water (2 tablespoons vinegar, 1 teaspoon salt to every litre [1¾ pints] water). Drain and dry well with kitchen paper.

Cooking ideas   It can be baked, braised, stuffed, grilled or cooked *en matelote* with other freshwater fish. Follow recipes for carp, or other members of its family. Or bake like bass in foil with ginger (*see* page 13). Whichever method you choose, add plenty of strong flavourings such as garlic, bacon, anchovies, herbs like rosemary or oregano and serve with strongly flavoured sauces or butters.

Breams, Sea

BREAMS, SEA, known as PORGIES in America

There are many species of sea bream, the two most likely to be found on sale are the BLACK (page 23) and the RED (page 25), both of which are caught off our coasts. Other breams are being imported in small numbers, some from the Mediterranean, others from Africa. Many are snapped up by restaurants but some are sold by fishmongers especially in and around London. Those from the Mediterranean include:

BAMBOOFISH or SAUPE 20–35 cm (8–14 ins); an intensely round dun-yellow fish, with broad, vertical stripes looking like the stems of bamboos.

BOGUE are small, olive yellow fish with silver bellies, around 20–35 cm (8–14 ins). You might find them in shops run by Greek Cypriots.

DENTEX, known as DENTÉ in France, can grow to 1 metre (39 ins). Adult fish are an overall dull red with 4–6 canine teeth, the males have a large bump on their foreheads. They make good eating.

GILT-HEADED BREAM, known as DAURADE in France, considered by many to be the finest of all sea breams, are found mainly in the Mediterranean, although very occasionally they have been caught off our SW coast. They grow up to 60 cm (24 ins).

PANDORA, known as PAGEOT ROUGE in France, are often sold under their Greek name of LITHRINI. They are around 25–40 cm (10–16 ins) and rose pink in colour and have firm flesh.

SEA BREAM or COUCH'S SEA BREAM known as PAGRE COMMUN in France and RED PORGY in America. Grows to around 75 cm (30 ins).

Other breams are being imported from North and West Africa such as COQ ROUGE, SAR, which is similar to black sea bream, and GROS YEUX, which is similar to red sea bream.

Cooking ideas Large sea breams are good stuffed, baked or braised. Smaller ones may be grilled or fried. Follow recipes for black or red sea breams on the following pages. Or prepare small ones *en escabèche* as they do in Nice with bogues. Follow the recipe on page 211 but flavour with coriander, juniper berries and marjoram.

Bream, Black Sea

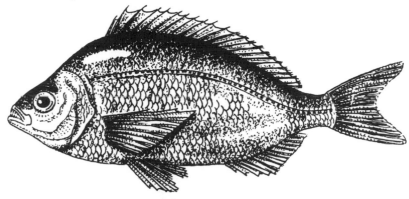

BLACK SEA BREAM, or OLD WIFE

Habitat	European Atlantic area.
Pros and Cons	This is a delicious fish with white and delicate flesh; don't be put off by the rather mournful appearance.
Size	22–40 cm (9–16 ins).
Description	The oval compressed and scaly body wears widow's weeds of shimmering grey-brown chequered with darker grey and ochre. It has a small mouth and teeth, big black eyes and spiny fins.
How sold	Whole fish.
Qty per person	Allow one 225–275 g (8–10 oz) whole fish ungutted.
Ask fishmonger	To clean, scale and trim, removing gills.
Availability	June to February in the south of England.
Notes	This fish is fairly disregarded by most and consequently it is quite cheap when you can find it. Its nickname 'Old Wife' refers only to its appearance; the flesh is sweet and tender especially if it is marinaded before being cooked.

23

Preparation	Clean, scale and remove gills if the fishmonger hasn't done so. Wash and dry with kitchen paper.
Cooking ideas	Good grilled or fried after marinading for 1 or 2 hours in lemon juice. Or poach in a *court bouillon* and serve with a sauce.

Grilled Black Sea Bream with tomatoes

4 black sea bream
pepper, salt
3 tablespoons olive oil
1 teaspoon each of dried thyme, fennel seeds and crushed chillies
juice of 2 lemons or limes
4 medium-sized tomatoes
1 clove garlic cut in slivers
thyme
salt, pepper
olive oil and lemon wedges

Clean and score the fish two or three times on either side. Season inside and out with salt and pepper and marinade them for 1–2 hours, using a shallow glass or china dish, in the olive oil, herbs and lemon juice, turning them once during this time.

Whilst the grill is heating, prepare the tomatoes, cut them in half, cut a cross in the centre of each and press slivers of garlic inside, dust with thyme, season with salt and pepper and sprinkle with olive oil.

Grill the fish as on page 298, brushing them at intervals with the marinade. At the same time grill the tomatoes. Serve with lemon wedges.

Fried Black Sea Bream

Marinade the fish as in the previous recipe, but instead of the thyme, fennel and chillies, push sprigs of rosemary and slivers of garlic into the slits where the fish has been scored. When you are ready to fry them, roll them in flour and fry in olive or peanut oil, allowing 4 or 5 minutes on each side. Serve with a tomato or creole sauce or a flavoured butter and lemon wedges.

Dorade grise à l'aïoli – Black Sea Bream with aïoli

Ask the fishmonger to fillet the fish for you and to give you the head, bones and trimmings. These you add to a *court bouillon* (page 301). When you are ready to eat, poach the fish (*see* page 300) and serve with a bowl of aïoli and new potatoes.

Bream, Red Sea

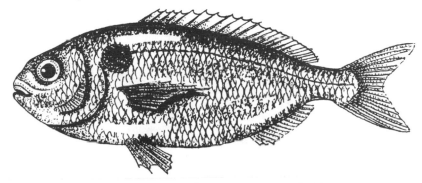

RED SEA BREAM known as DORADE in France

Habitat	Atlantic and Mediterranean as well as imported from North Africa and South America.
Pros and Cons	The flesh is white and delicate and is delicious flavoured with herbs and spices. Not very cheap as many are imported but spectacular as a centrepiece for a party.
Size	Up to 50 cm (20 ins).
Description	The oval, compressed body with its tough scales and spiky fins varies from rose-grey to pinkish with silvery sides. It has large eyes and a dark smudge behind the gill covers.
How sold	Whole fish.
Qty per person	Allow 225–275 g (8–10 oz) whole, ungutted fish.
Ask fishmonger	To clean, scale and trim and remove the gills if you are cooking a whole fish. Or ask him to cut into steaks or fillets. Head and trimmings can be used for stock or the soup pot.

Availability   All year, though supplies are limited to the more specialist fishmongers.

Notes   This is an excellent fish even if not quite as splendid as some of the Mediterranean sea breams, though they do benefit from being eaten in the special atmosphere evoked by gnarled olive groves and sun-drenched vineyards. Efforts are being made to perfect farming techniques, so hopefully this and other sea breams will eventually be more widely available and less expensive.

Preparation   Fish must be cleaned, scaled and trimmed and the gills removed if you are cooking whole. Wash it well inside and out and dry with kitchen paper.

Cooking ideas   Whole fish benefit from being marinaded before cooking and are good baked, stuffed or grilled. Enhance the flavour with bacon, anchovies, garlic and herbs such as fennel or rosemary. Grill steaks or make kebabs, soaking them for an hour or two in a chermoula or harissa marinade (pages 299–300). Cook fillets like sole or plaice. Follow recipes for other sea breams or those for bass, snappers, groupers or emperors. Or make couscous, page 69.

La Daurade ou Pageot au four

A Provençal recipe for gilt-headed or pandora breams which is simple and delicious and can be used for other sea breams. Score the fish two or three times on either side and insert slivers of garlic and fennel seeds in the slits. In the cavity put a sprig of rosemary and one of thyme. Squeeze over the juice of a lemon and leave to marinade for 1 hour. Heat oven to Gas 4/350°F/180°C. Put the fish into an oiled oven dish and along its length lay alternating slices of lemon and tomato. Add salt and pepper. Moisten generously with olive oil and pour over a glass of white wine. Bake for 20–30 minutes depending on the size of the fish, basting two or three times.

Red Sea Bream braised with tomato, rosemary and anchovies
1 red sea bream (or other sea bream) of about 900 g (2 lbs)
4 fillets of anchovy (or use rashers of unsmoked streaky bacon,
   chopped)
thyme, rosemary
juice of 1 lemon
pepper
olive oil
1 leek or onion, chopped
2 or 3 tomatoes, chopped (or one medium can, drained)
2 cloves of garlic, chopped
salt
1 tablespoon tomato purée
2 tablespoons dry white wine or vermouth
Score the fish two or three times on either side, chop half the
anchovies (or bacon) into small pieces and insert these slivers into the
slits, sprinkle with thyme and rosemary, the juice of a lemon and
some pepper and leave to marinade for 1 hour. In a wok or frying
pan, heat 2 tablespoons olive oil, add the leek or onion, the remaining
anchovies (or bacon) and let them cook over a medium flame for a
few minutes before adding the tomatoes and garlic. Stir in the tomato
purée, add salt and pepper and simmer for about 15 minutes until it
has all softened to a purée.
   Meanwhile set oven to Gas 4/350°F/180°C. Add the wine or
vermouth to the sauce. Put the fish on a piece of oiled or buttered foil.
Pour over the sauce. Make the foil into a parcel, and bake for about
40 minutes.

Brill

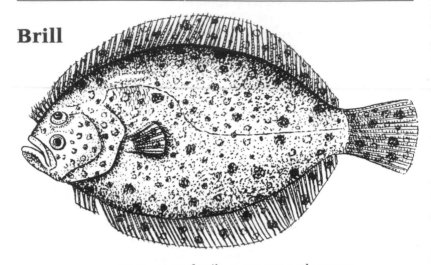

BRILL – *same family as:* TURBOT and MEGRIM

Habitat	European seas.
Pros and Cons	This is the middlebrow member of its family, smaller, not quite so expensive and almost as fine as turbot; lighter and more delicate than megrim.
Size	Around 35 cm (14 ins) but can grow to double this size.
Description	Left-facing flat fish with an almost circular body, the eyed side is a translucent grey-brown with myriads of dark and pale freckles. Scales are smooth and there are no bony tubercles.
How sold	Whole fish or fillets. Sometimes steaks.
Qty per person	Allow 175–225 g (6–8 oz) whole fish, gutted. Fillets: 150–175 g (5–6 oz). Steaks: 175–200 g (6–7 oz).
Ask fishmonger	If you don't want to cook the fish whole, ask him to fillet it and give you the head and trimmings for stock or soup. He will also remove the dark skin if you want, although this is easily removed after cooking.

Availability	All year from specialist fishmongers; most abundant in spring and autumn.
Notes	Brill is popular in the restaurant trade which makes it scarce in the shops and pushes up the price.
Preparation	Wash the fish inside and out and pat dry with kitchen paper. The dark skin which is tough can be removed before or after cooking, the blind-side just needs to be scraped with the blunt side of a knife.
Cooking ideas	Best cooked on the bone, either baked or poached in a strong *court bouillon* and served with perhaps a hollandaise or béarnaise sauce or flavoured butter. Small brill or steaks can be fried or grilled. Fillets can be fried *à la meunière* or baked *en papillote* and served with a sorrel sauce or a purée of spinach. Recipes for sole, turbot, dab, or flounder are all suitable.

The following recipe is very simple and a little unusual as it uses red rather than white wine.

Brill à la fermière
1 brill weighing around 800 g (1¾ lbs)
50 g (2 oz) butter
1 onion, chopped
salt and pepper
175 g (6 oz) mushrooms, sliced
150 ml (¼ pint) red wine
kneaded butter made with 25 g (1 oz) each of flour and butter
Heat oven to Gas 4/350°F/180°C. Heat a wok or frying pan and add half the butter; when it sizzles put in the chopped onion, and cook over a medium heat until soft. Cut two or three slits lengthwise along the dark skin of the brill (to prevent it curling during cooking) and season it on both sides with salt and pepper. Butter a shallow oven dish, lay the onion on the base, put the fish on top. Lay the sliced mushrooms over the fish, pour over the red wine and dot with the rest of the butter. Cover lightly with foil and put into the oven and cook 20 minutes, or until the fish comes away from the bone when tested with a skewer. Strain the liquid into a small

saucepan, bring to the boil and add the kneaded butter bit by bit, whisking to incorporate it and thicken the sauce. Pour over the fish and put back into the oven for a few minutes more to glaze.

Brill au poivre
4 brill steaks
4 teaspoons green peppercorns
flour to coat
50 g (2 oz) butter
2 tablespoons half or single cream

Crush peppercorns and press into the steaks. Coat in flour. Fry in hot butter and a little oil (*see* page 295). Remove fish from the pan and stir the cream into the buttery juices. Pour over the fish and serve with lemon wedges.

Brill with watercress
1 brill weighing around 900 g (2 lbs) divided into fillets but ask
  fishmonger for head, bones, trimmings
court bouillon
1 bunch watercress
25 g (1 oz) butter
150 ml (¼ pint) double cream
1 teaspoon tomato purée
salt, pepper
2 egg yolks

Make a *court bouillon* (*see* page 301), adding the fish head, bones and trimmings to it. Let it cool and strain. Remove leaves from the watercress and chop, melt the butter in a saucepan and add half the leaves, let them soften over a low heat. Remove them from the pan and set aside. Lay the fish in your poaching pan, cover with the *court bouillon* and bring slowly to the boil, as soon as it boils lower the heat and simmer for 3 minutes. Remove pan from heat. Measure 300 ml (½ pint) of the poaching liquid, put it into the pan you used for the watercress and boil it hard to reduce by about one third. Lower the heat, stir in the cream and tomato purée and taste to check seasoning, if necessary add more salt and pepper. Off the heat, stir in the egg yolks and return to a very low heat. Keep stirring and as soon as the sauce thickens and coats the back of the spoon, remove from the heat. Add softened watercress. Carefully remove fish from poaching liquid and put on a hot dish, cover with the sauce and garnish with remaining watercress.

BROCHET DE MER, *see* **BARRACUDA**

BROWN SHRIMP, *see* **SHRIMPS**

BROWN TROUT, *see* **TROUT**

BUCKLING, *see* **HERRING, SMOKED**

CACATOIS, *see* **PARROTFISH**

CALAMARI, *see* **SQUID**

CAPITAINE BLANC and ROUGE, *see* **EMPERORS**

Carangids

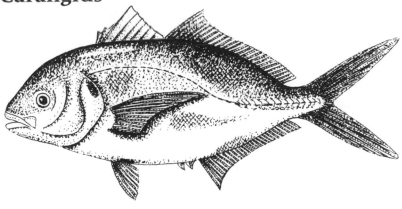

CARANGIDS – *see also* HORSE MACKEREL
Several species are imported, some fresh others
frozen, under such names as JACKS, SCADS, CARANGUE,

KING CARANGUE (sometimes called KINGFISH), YELLOW-
TAIL, RAINBOW RUNNER, POMPANO, CREVALLY and TREVALLY

Habitat Mediterranean, Atlantic, Red Sea and Indo-Pacific depending on species.

Pros and Cons These are oily fish with tasty though slightly coarse flesh. They are imported fresh as well as frozen. They are not tunas (their flesh is paler and milder in flavour) although some fishmongers label them as such. You can recognize them by their distinctive lateral keeled scales or scutes.

Size From around 25–100 cm (10–39 ins) depending on species.

Description Most have a very bold lateral line which looks like a row of neat surgical stitching ending in a ridge of bony spurs. It curves deeply around the sickle-shaped pectoral fin. Finely scaled bodies are compressed, colours vary through greys, blue-greens with paler gilded sides and belly.

How sold Whole fish, steaks or pieces.

Qty per person Allow 225–275 g (8–10 oz) whole, ungutted fish. Steaks or pieces: allow 175–200 g (6–7 oz).

Ask fishmonger To scale, clean, trim (and remove gills if you are cooking whole fish); or if you prefer, to fillet it or cut into steaks. If you are buying just a piece or steaks, ask for a middle or top cut, rather than the tail which tends to be dry and bony.

Availability Often in shops patronized by Caribbeans. Most are imported, some fresh, others frozen from as far away as New Zealand. The Atlantic related horse mackerel is dealt with on pages 127–8.

Notes In the Seychelles and the Caribbean the numerous species enjoy a high reputation with many local names, those of the West Indies being wonderfully descriptive such as Goggle-Eyed Jack, Round Robin, Big Eye. This species includes the RAINBOW RUNNER, a renowned food fish sold here in limited quantities, and the POMPANOS, famous in both Americas and some Mediterranean regions.

Preparation If frozen, defrost and if necessary, scale, clean and trim, making sure all traces of intestines, blood and any blackness are removed; if necessary use salt to rub it all away. Wash fish and dry with kitchen paper.

Cooking ideas Whole fish may be baked; smaller ones grilled; steaks are good grilled or baked; fillets can be baked, or fried; recipes for bonito, tuna or mackerel may be used. These are oily fish and go well with tart flavours.

Trevally or other Carangids baked with cucumber stuffing
This is based on a Caribbean recipe.
1 fish weighing 700–900 g (1½–2 lbs)
pepper, salt
1 red chilli, chopped (or teaspoon chilli powder)
1 clove of garlic, cut into slivers
1 thin slice of root ginger, cut in slivers
2 lemons or limes
olive or peanut oil
1 onion, chopped
1 tablespoon soya sauce
1 tablespoon sunflower seeds
100 g (4 oz) breadcrumbs
½ cucumber, peeled and chopped
1 teaspoon dried thyme
1 tablespoon fresh parsley
2 tablespoons yoghurt
Score the fish two or three times on either side and season inside and out with salt, pepper and chilli. Put slivers of garlic and ginger into the slits. Squeeze over the juice of 1 lemon or lime. Set aside for 30–40 minutes.

Heat oven to Gas 6/400°F/200°C. Heat 1 tablespoon of oil in a wok or frying pan and fry the onion over a medium heat, until beginning to colour. Remove from the heat and mix in the soya sauce, sunflower seeds, breadcrumbs, cucumber, thyme, parsley, salt, pepper and the yoghurt. Cut a piece of foil large enough to wrap the fish, oil it lightly. Put the fish in the middle and fill the cavity with the stuffing, spread any that is over on the top of the fish. Sprinkle some oil over the top, or dot with butter. Lay remaining lemon or lime cut in slices along the length of the fish. Fold the foil over to make a loose parcel and bake for 30–40 minutes.

CARANGUE, *see* **CARANGIDS**

CARAPAU, *see* **HORSE MACKEREL**

Carp

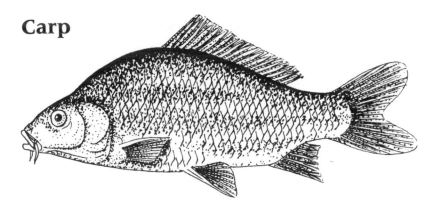

CARP – *same family as:* BARBEL, BREAM, GUDGEON, ROACH and TENCH

Habitat Warm, densely weedy ponds, lakes, canals, sluggish streams and rivers. Also farmed on Continent, especially in Eastern Europe.

Pros and Cons A prized angling fish, though those marketed are farmed. It has firm, delicate flesh which needs strong seasonings.

Size Usually around 30–40 cm (12–16 ins) but can grow to more than double this size.

Description The colour of the humped back varies according to species from golden yellow to a watery mixture of grey-greens or charcoal browns. The scales, which are large and tough, can be all over, or few and very large as with the mirror carp, or in the case of the leather carp, none at all. It is distinguished from other freshwater fish such as bream by its two pairs of barbels.

How sold Whole fish.

Qty per person Allow 225–275 g (8–10 oz) whole, ungutted fish.

Ask fishmonger To trim, scale and clean, removing gills and the spleen behind the head.

Availability From enterprising fishmongers all year but more especially between October and March.

Notes Those lovely, free Chinese brush paintings of fish often represent the carp, not surprisingly as it originated in the East. It is highly esteemed in central Europe and forms part of the Christmas and New Year fare in Germany. Depending on the region, it is eaten with a sauce made either from horseradish and capers, or more outlandishly from gingerbread and red wine. One of the coin-like scales of the mirror carp kept for a year is said to preserve your luck. Carp also features in Jewish cookery and the Chinese like to eat it with a sweet and sour sauce.

Preparation If the fishmonger hasn't prepared it, first remove the fins, which are very sharp. The scales are quite tough; you will find it easier to shift them if you plunge the fish for a few seconds into boiling water. If you're going to poach the fish, you need not scale it, but can simply remove the skin when the fish is cooked. Clean out the fish, making sure you remove gills, spleen and gall sac at the back of the head, otherwise it will be bitter. Rub it inside and out with salt and vinegar, 1 teaspoon of each for every 450 g (1 lb) weight. If your fish is not a farmed one but caught by an angler, to remove all traces of mud follow the instructions for freshwater bream (page 21). Dry it well with kitchen paper.

Cooking ideas May be baked, stuffed, braised, poached or cooked *en matelote*. Small carp can be grilled or fried and served with sorrel sauce or a flavoured butter. Or bake like bass in foil with ginger (page 13), or steam as for rabbitfish (page 186).

Grilled small Carp

Score the fish two or three times on either side and rub with lemon juice, season with salt and pepper. Grill (*see* page 298), basting often with a mixture of oil and lemon juice. Garnish with watercress, lemon wedges and serve with grilled or stuffed tomatoes.

Carpe farcie d'Auvergne – Baked stuffed Carp

1 carp weighing about 1 kilo (2 lbs)
1 tablespoon oil
1 onion, chopped
1 clove garlic, chopped
100 g (4 oz) mushrooms, chopped
cup of breadcrumbs plus 3 or 4 tablespoons
1–2 tablespoons chopped parsley
salt, pepper
1 egg, beaten
1 tablespoon white wine or lemon juice
white wine or lemon juice to moisten
25 g (1 oz) butter or oil
Heat oven to Gas 4/350°F/180°C. Make the stuffing by heating the oil and cooking the onion until soft over a medium heat. Add garlic and mushrooms and continue cooking until the mushrooms are reduced. Off the heat add the cup of breadcrumbs, parsley, salt, pepper, egg and the white wine or lemon juice. Mix well and stuff the fish. Put it in a buttered shallow oven dish, moisten with white wine or lemon juice, dot with butter or sprinkle with a little oil. Bake 30 minutes, basting from time to time. Sprinkle over the 3 or 4 tablespoons breadcrumbs and put back in the oven for a further 5–10 minutes to turn golden and crisp.

Carp roe is a delicacy. Poach it 3 or 4 minutes in salted water. Drain and dry. Roll in seasoned flour and fry in sizzling butter. Have ready a hot serving dish, squeeze over plenty of lemon juice and garnish with chopped parsley.

Carp braised with red wine and gingerbread
1 carp weighing about 1 kilo (2 lbs)
1 onion, finely chopped
2 shallots, chopped
100 g (4 oz) gingerbread, cut in small pieces
salt, pepper
juice of 1 lemon
glass red wine
Heat oven to Gas 4/350°F/180°C. In a buttered oven dish, make a layer of the onion, shallots and gingerbread. Score the prepared fish and lay it on top. Season with salt and pepper, lemon juice and pour over the red wine. Cover the dish with foil and cook in the oven for 30 minutes.

CARPETSHELL, *see* CLAMS

Catfish, Freshwater

The freshwater catfish is extensively farmed in America and farming is beginning in Belgium and elsewhere, some being imported here.

Pros and Cons   Not yet very common, but may become more so. Tends to be rather watery, so needs plenty of flavouring but still interesting to try.

Size   From around 25–38 cm (10–15 ins).

Description   Scaleless fish, with a flattened belly, broad head and long barbels like cat's whiskers; the thick, slimy skin is covered with a mucus which makes the fish look dirty, which in fact it isn't.

How sold   Whole fish.

Qty per person   Allow 225–275 g (8–10 oz) whole, ungutted fish.

Ask fishmonger   To clean and remove gills.

Availability   Mainly specialist fishmongers.

Notes   In America large quantities of this fish are bought by one of the big hamburger chains who sell it battered with chips.

Preparation   Must be cleaned and gills removed.

Cooking ideas   Follow recipes for St Peter's fish, trout, carp, adding generous amounts of flavourings such as bacon, anchovies, herbs, etc.

Catfish, Sea

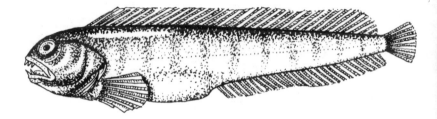

CATFISH, SEA or WOLFISH — *also known as:* WOOF OR SEA WOLF; usually sold as ROCK TURBOT or ROCK FISH, sometimes as ROCK SALMON

Habitat   N Atlantic.

Pros and Cons   This is one of those fish whose appearance is likely to give us the vapours, so you won't see it complete on the slab. It feeds on crabs, sea urchins and other molluscs, grinding them up with its teeth and so has a delicious flavour and is comparatively cheap.

Size   Can grow to over 1 metre (39 ins).

Description   All you will see are the fillets sold under one of its aliases. It's a pity; it's an impressive creature with its tabby stripes and rounded head displaying a mouthful of teeth, and a shape like a baseball bat frilled with fins.

How sold	Fillets, either fresh or frozen; sometimes whole fish. SMOKED CATFISH is also sometimes sold and is said to rival SMOKED SALMON.
Qty per person	Fillets: 150–175 g (5–6 oz). Whole fish: allow 225–275 g (8–10 oz).
Ask fishmonger	To reveal this fish's true identity, see page 76.
Availability	Widely available all year.
Preparation	Nothing to do but wash and wipe it dry with kitchen paper.
Cooking ideas	The flesh is firm and has been compared to veal. Whole fillets can be baked like monkfish (*see* recipe for gigot de mer, page 153). Excellent fried and served with *beurre noir* (page 289), or grilled with green peppercorns. Use recipes for cod or tuna, braise with vegetables, or cook in a curry sauce following the recipe for garfish on page 95, or make kebabs.

Baked Catfish with tomatoes and green peppers

675 g (1½ lbs) catfish fillets
olive or peanut oil
1 leek, sliced
1 clove of garlic, chopped
1 green pepper, roughly chopped
3 or 4 tomatoes, chopped
1 tablespoon tomato purée
1 teaspoon soya sauce
thyme, basil, bayleaf
juice of 1 lemon
salt
1 teaspoon chilli powder
handful of fresh breadcrumbs
Heat oven to Gas 6/400°F/200°C. In a wok or frying pan heat 2 tablespoons of oil. When it is hot add the leek and stir fry for several minutes, add garlic, green pepper and tomatoes and continue cooking for 3 or 4 minutes. Stir in the tomato purée and soya sauce. Add herbs and lemon juice, salt and chilli powder. Lay the fish in an

oiled shallow oven dish, add the sauce and top with the breadcrumbs. Sprinkle with oil and put in the oven for 15–20 minutes.

Grilled Catfish with green peppercorns
Marinade the fish in oil, lemon juice, salt and 1 tablespoon of crushed green peppercorns for an hour. Grill as on page 298, brushing frequently with oil.

CAVALLA or **CAVALLY,** *see* **CARANGIDS**

Charr

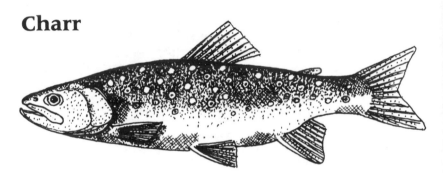

CHARR or ARCTIC CHARR – *also known as:* CHAR; *same family as:* SALMON and TROUT

Habitat   Mountain lakes in UK and Europe; in Arctic regions it spends its life in the seas and like its cousin the salmon migrates to fresh water to spawn and breed.

Pros and Cons   A rare treat to be absolutely snapped up if you are ever offered one. Flesh is white or pink depending on the fish's diet and very delicate.

Size   Usually around 25–30 cm (10–12 ins) but can grow to double this length.

Description   Streamlined with a blue-green back with paler sides speckled with pinkish red or orange spots. The belly is brilliant red. Narrow tail stalk with forked fin.

How sold	Whole fish.
Qty per person	Allow 225–275 g (8–10 oz) whole, ungutted fish.
Availability	Occasionally sold in lakeland areas from May to September; a related species is also imported from France, where it is being cultured and is sometimes to be found in specialist fishmongers.
Ask fishmonger	To clean, scale and remove gills.
Notes	Charr is most famous in the Lake District, especially around Windermere, where it used to be sold potted in special dishes decorated with fish. Nowadays, you might find one of these dishes sold as a rarity in an antique shop. You may be offered charr in restaurants in the area or find it in the Swiss or French Alps, where it is romantically called *Omble* or *Ombre chevalier*, Shadowy Knight.
Preparation	If necessary clean, scale and remove gills. Wash and dry with kitchen paper.
Cooking ideas	May be grilled, fried, baked *en papillote*. Follow recipes for trout.

Potted Charr (or use salmon, trout or smoked salmon)
Break cooked charr into small ½ cm (¼ in) pieces. Mix with an equal weight of lightly salted, softened butter. Season with pepper, pinch of mace and nutmeg. Put into pots and chill. If you plan to keep it for any length of time seal the top with clarified butter (*see* page 296).

CHICKEN HALIBUT, *see* **HALIBUT**

CHINCHARD, *see* **HORSE MACKEREL**

Clams

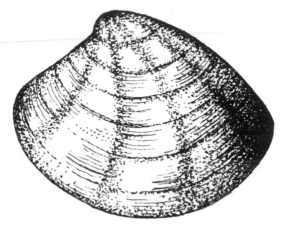

CLAMS – several species available in Britain

Habitat   Coastal waters.

Pros and Cons   There are a variety of clams which are becoming increasingly available and the price varies considerably. They are as interesting as mussels and some prefer them to oysters.

Size   CARPETSHELL (French: PALOURDE) Up to 8 cm (3¼ ins).
HARD CLAM or QUAHOG Up to 13 cm (5 ins).
RAZOR-SHELL Up to 12 cm (4½ ins).
VENUS SHELL (French: VERNI) Up to 7 cm (2¾ ins).
WARTY VENUS (French: PRAIRE) Up to 7 cm (2¾ ins).

Description   Clams are double-shelled bivalves, some quite smooth whereas others are ridged; they resemble stones on a beach, some being dull, others shiny as if just dipped in seawater. They are almost round with the exception of the RAZOR-SHELL, which is long and curved like a cut-throat razor and open at both ends. Colours vary from the yellow, brown or white of the CARPETSHELL; dull greys and browns of the HARD CLAM; brown of the RAZOR-SHELL; brown tinged with pink and red of the VENUS SHELL; and grey, white or brown of the WARTY VENUS.

How sold Individually or by weight, depending on size: also canned, and these are useful to add flavour to fish soups.

Qty per person Depends on size: large ones: 6–12: allow 225 g (½ lb) of small ones.

Ask fishmonger To check none are damaged or open.

Availability All year with the exception of very hot or very cold weather, mostly from specialist fishmongers or direct from fishmarkets. The hard clam or quahog is cultivated around Southampton waters and the Isle of Wight, so possibly from local outlets, though most are exported.

Notes Clams are not very much appreciated in this country whereas they are very popular in France, along the Brittany and Normandy coasts as well as the Mediterranean. You may come across tellins which are similar and known in the trade by their French name of *venus*. Of the three species available two are native to the British Isles, but the hard clam or quahog originated in America; there's a romantic but probably apocryphal story that it migrated to Portsmouth and Southampton waters via the great ocean liners. Whatever the truth, quahogs are now commercially exploited in that area with most being exported to France or back to the USA.

Preparation Wash and scrub, make sure they are closed and discard any that are open.

Cooking ideas Clams, like oysters, are best treated simply, leave the chowders to your visits to America. Although they can be eaten raw like oysters, they are not subject to the same regulations of purification, so are best cooked. Follow recipes for mussels or eat them with pasta. Don't overcook or they will be tough.

Clams with pasta

Make a tomato sauce, following the recipe on page 292. Scrub the clams and add at the end of the cooking time, letting them cook just until they open. Serve with shell pasta. Or if you prefer, steam open the clams in a pan with just a little water. Take them out of their shells and add them to the sauce just long enough to heat them through; eat with spaghetti.

Palourdes farcies – Stuffed Carpetshells (or use hard clams)

48 carpetshells
4 cloves garlic, chopped
2 shallots, chopped
handful chopped parsley
100 g (4 oz) unsalted butter, softened
salt, pepper
3 tablespoons double cream
lemon juice
100 g (4 oz) breadcrumbs

Crumple a piece of foil and lay it in the base of a grill pan to support the clams. Mix together the garlic, shallots, parsley, butter, salt, pepper, cream and lemon juice. Heat the grill. Put clams into a large pan over a high heat with no extra liquid and steam them open. As they open, remove from pan with a slotted spoon. When they are cool enough to handle (use a cloth to hold them), remove the shallower half shell. Fill the others with the butter mixture, dust with breadcrumbs and put under the grill for about 3 minutes. Eat with plenty of French bread.

Vernis à l'arlésienne

Use venus shells or other small clams, allowing 1 kilo (2 lbs) for 4 people. Make a sauce by mixing a tablespoon of mustard, 1 of vinegar and 4 of olive oil, salt and pepper (shake them together in a screw top jar, or mix them in a bowl using a whisk). Put the clams in a large pan with a handful of chopped parsley, 2 chopped cloves of garlic and 50 g (2 oz) butter. Cover and put on a high heat to open the clams. As soon as they have opened take them out and put into a hot, deep dish and pour over the mustard sauce. Eat at once, using fingers and have napkins handy.

COALFISH, *see* COLEY

Cockles

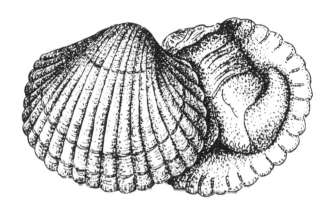

COCKLES

Habitat   Sandy seashores and mudflats.

Description The double heart-shaped shell with its radiating ribs comes in various shades of browns, mud yellows, dirty whites or pinks or even blues.

How sold   They are usually sold ready cooked and free of shells, most often in jars in either vinegar or brine. Those in brine are preferable, as the others taste of nothing except vinegar. They are sold on stalls at the seaside. In France you may see them on sale as *coque* or the related dog cockle as *amande de mer.*

Notes   Abandoned cockle shells litter sandy beaches, but the living molluscs bury themselves beneath the sand, and are gathered at low tide. Stand near the edge of the sea and look out for small jets of water squirting out of the sand – the cockles are siphoning the water for air. Digging them out is almost impossible, because as fast as you dig, so they bury themselves deeper.

Preparation   There are all sorts of restrictions in this country governing the sale of live cockles. If you ever do have to handle them, slosh them about in a bucket of water and then, to purge them of impurities, they must be soaked for several hours in salted water. Finally rinse them either under running water or in several changes of water to get rid of all traces of sand and mud.

Cooking ideas   Although fresh cockles can be eaten raw, in France they are nicknamed 'Poor Man's Oysters', it is not advisable in these days of pollution. Steam them open like mussels or follow recipe for stuffed clams (*see* page 44).

Cod

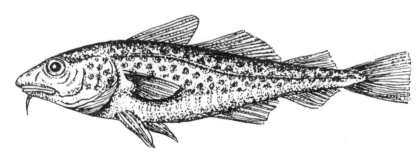

COD – *same family as:* COLEY, HADDOCK, HAKE, LING, POLLACK and WHITING

Habitat   N Atlantic and North Sea.

Pros and Cons   With its firm, flaky flesh, cod is a simple everyday sort of fish and it's a great shame it has become so expensive.

Size   Usually around 30–100 cm (12–39 ins).

Description	The long, tapering body is sandy brown or grey-green with darker speckles, it has silvery sides and belly and a barbel on its chin.
How sold	Whole, fillets, steaks or cutlets; also SALTED, page 51, and SMOKED, page 54; young cod are sold as CODLING and are far and away superior to the steaks and fillets of the larger fish; look out for cheap COD LUGS (trimmings) for soup; COD'S ROE is also sold often ready-cooked or smoked (*see* page 50).
Qty per person	Fillets: 150–175 g (5–6 oz). Steaks or cutlets: 175–200 g (6–7 oz). Allow 225–275 g (8–10 oz) of whole, ungutted fish.
Ask fishmonger	For the best flavour, ask for a cut from the head end, although it will be less tender than that from the tail.
Availability	All year but best late autumn and winter.
Notes	Most of the catch comes from deep-sea trawlers and it is frozen on board. Sometimes local fishermen sell inshore cod at some of the main fishing ports and these are really quite special.
Preparation	Deep sea cod is cleaned on board, but you may have to clean and trim a freshly caught codling. To counteract the wateriness of cod, dry it well with kitchen paper and leave to marinade for an hour sprinkled with lemon juice and salt. Drain away the moisture which will have exuded and wipe well. This is a trick worth using when defrosting frozen steaks or fillets.
Cooking ideas	Grill or bake in foil; makes good fish and chips; or cook with strong flavourings such as tomato, garlic, red or green peppers, cheese. Cook it in a curry sauce, following recipe for garfish on page 95. Or make couscous, page 69. CODLING are delicious poached, grilled or fried. You can use recipes for other fish in its family, as well as those

for salted cod, in which case remember to add salt to the recipe. Or recipes for dogfish, catfish, monkfish.

Cod with tomatoes, black olives and onions
4 cod steaks
2 tablespoons olive oil
1 onion, chopped
1 clove garlic, chopped
1 medium can of Italian tomatoes
bayleaf, thyme, oregano
glass dry white wine, vermouth or juice of 1 lemon
handful black olives
salt, pepper
chopped parsley to garnish
In a wok or casserole, heat 2 tablespoons of olive oil and cook the chopped onion until soft. Add the garlic, tomatoes, bayleaf, thyme and oregano, a glass of wine, vermouth or lemon juice. Let it bubble and reduce. Add salt, pepper and simmer uncovered for 15 minutes. Add the cod steaks and olives and cook covered on a very low heat for 5–10 minutes until the fish is opaque. Serve garnished with parsley.

Baked Cod fillets
4 cod fillets
1 onion, finely chopped
1 tablespoon chopped parsley
1 tablespoon chopped chives
100 g (4 oz) mushrooms, sliced
salt, pepper
handful soft breadcrumbs
75 g (3 oz) grated cheese
oil
1 small carton half or single cream
Heat oven to Gas 5/375°F/190°C. In a buttered dish put a layer of chopped onions with the parsley and chives. Lay fish on top and surround with sliced mushrooms. Add salt, pepper and sprinkle with breadcrumbs and grated cheese, dribble over a few drops of oil. Bake for 10 minutes, pour in the cream. Leave until the top bubbles and browns, 5–10 minutes.

Cod steaks in white wine with rosemary
4 cod steaks
3 tablespoons olive oil
1 onion, finely chopped
1 clove garlic, finely chopped
1 stick celery, finely diced
1 tablespoon parsley
1 teaspoon dried rosemary
flour to coat
salt, pepper
2 glasses dry white wine
sprigs of rosemary to garnish
Heat oven to Gas 5/375°F/190°C. Heat olive oil in a frying pan and when it is hot add chopped onion, garlic, celery, parsley and rosemary. Dip steaks in flour and add to the pan, frying them quickly on either side, just to seal. Season with salt and pepper. Put into an oven dish, pour over 2 glasses dry white wine. Bake 20–30 minutes, basting two or three times. Serve garnished with sprigs of rosemary.

Cabillaud dieppoise – Cod with mussels
550–700 g (1¼–1½ lbs) cod fillets
½ kg (1 pint) mussels
150 ml (¼ pint) water
pepper
kneaded butter made from 25 g (1 oz) each of butter and flour
1 small carton double cream
juice of 1 lemon
salt
handful of chopped parsley
Scrub and clean the mussels and put them into a large pan with the water and some pepper. Put over a high flame, bring to the boil and cook over a fierce flame until the mussels open. Take them out and shell them but keep the liquid, which will have increased with the water exuded from the mussels. Put the fish into a shallow pan, strain over the mussel liquid and bring just to the boil, lower heat and poach the fish for 2–3 minutes. Measure 300 ml (½ pint) of the cooking liquid into a saucepan, bring to the boil, add the kneaded butter in pieces, stirring until it thickens. Lower heat and stir in the cream. Add the mussels. Put the fish on to a hot dish. Add the lemon

juice to the sauce, check for seasoning, if necessary adding more salt and pepper, and pour over the fish. Dust with parsley.

Fresh cod's roes are sold by weight in pairs covered by a connecting membrane. If they are not already cooked, add them to salted, boiling water, keeping them intact in their membrane, and simmer for about 10 minutes. Drain them and leave to get cold. They can then be thickly sliced (about 1 cm [½ in]), coated in seasoned flour and fried in butter or oil until crisp. Eat them with a strongly flavoured sauce such as caper, mustard or Creole.

Smoked cod's roe are first salted, before being washed and smoked. They should be dark red and firm and pink in the middle. You can eat them as they are, thinly sliced with lemon juice and lots of brown bread and butter. Or make your own *poutargue*, which is guaranteed to put you off for ever from the widely available shocking-pink mixture masquerading as the Greek *taramasalata*, from which this southern French version was devised. Authentically it should be made with the roe of the grey mullet, but smoked cod's roe is an honourable substitute.

Poutargue
100 g (4 oz) smoked cod's roe
200 g stale French bread, crusts removed
juice 2 lemons
8 tablespoons olive oil
Skin the cod's roe. The skin is paper thin, to remove it easily dip in boiling water for a few seconds, like skinning a tomato. Put the roe in water and leave to soak 1 hour to remove some of the salt.

Soak the bread in water for a few moments and squeeze it dry. Put the roe and the bread into a blender. Mix. Add oil and lemon juice alternately, a tablespoon at a time, mixing until you have a thick, pale mixture. If you have no blender, pound bread and roe in a mortar, and beat in oil and lemon juice. For a lighter result, use curd cheese instead of bread.

Cod, Salted

Pros and Cons Cod, dried and heavily salted to preserve it, was distributed throughout Catholic Europe as a cheap way of providing fish on Fridays and fast days for the common people. True to form, they proceeded to create lots of tasty ways to cook it. Because of our abundance of fresh cod, we never took it very seriously, but nowadays it is becoming something of a cult. Being strange and unfamiliar, it seems to encompass all the mystique of foreign holidays and there's a feeling almost of ritual in the long soaking and preparation that is quite unconnected with mundane, fresh cod. It is indispensable in such Mediterranean dishes as brandade and aïoli garni but, dare I say it without being heretical, you could use fresh cod in some of the other recipes. Don't expect it to be cheap and you must plan ahead, allowing up to two days in which to soak it.

How sold In fillets, which should be thick and white; if they are thin and yellow, they are probably old and very dehydrated and will be stringy and tough.

Qty per person 150–175 g (5–6 oz) – go for a middle cut, and not the fins or tail end, which will be bony and sparse.

Availability Most likely to be found in delicatessens run by Greeks, Italians, Portuguese, Asians or West Indians. Take care when buying, as it can be dehydrated and tough and may be coley or ling rather than cod.

Preparation Soak for 36–48 hours, changing the water at least six times; the longer you soak it, the less salty it will be.

Cooking ideas Salt cod is famous in such dishes as aïoli garni and brandade and is used in dishes all over southern

Europe as well as in the Caribbean, using flavourings like tomatoes, garlic, peppers, black olives, etc.

Morue catalane

This dish comes from the Roussillon, that area of France to the west
of the Camargue. Allow 450–675 g (1–1½ lbs) of salt cod. Soak and
poach the cod in fresh water, bringing it to the boil and let it barely
simmer for 8–10 minutes. In a wok or frying pan, heat 2 tablespoons
olive or peanut oil and lightly brown two chopped onions, add two
green or red peppers cut in slices and a clove of garlic, chopped. Let
it all soften and add a large can of tomatoes. Bring to the boil, add
pepper, thyme, basil, bayleaf. Divide the fish into portions, add to
the pan, lower the heat and cook gently for 15 minutes. Serve with
garlic bread.

Morue en raïto

This is part of the traditional Christmas Eve supper in Provence, but
it is equally good at any other time of the year. Prepare a raïto sauce
(page 292). Cut the soaked cod into pieces about 10 cm (4 ins)
square. Dry them and fry quickly in olive oil, 2–3 minutes on each
side. Drain them on greaseproof paper and then put them into the
sauce and simmer gently for 10 minutes, uncovered. Add capers
and/or olives just before serving.

Aïoli garni

This famous dish of the Midi turns the Friday salt cod into a feast.
Aïoli is the sauce with which it is served and *garni* refers to the
abundant garnish of vegetables etc., which surround the fish. You
need a day in high summer, preferably one when it is too hot to sit
in the sun, so you set your table under the shade; if this is a trellis of
vines so much the better. Invite a handful of special friends all of
whom adore garlic and make sure you have plenty of light red or
rosé wine cooling in the refrigerator. For the feast you should allow
150–175 g (5–6 oz) soaked cod per person. Put it into a pan of fresh
water (add no salt) and bring slowly to the boil. As soon as you see
the first bubble, turn off the heat, cover and set aside whilst you
prepare eggs, vegetables and aïoli. Hardboil 1 egg per person. Prepare
a variety of vegetables leaving some raw to add crispness and lightly
cooking others so as to preserve their individuality – choose from

potatoes, cauliflowers, fresh fennel, French beans, carrots, leeks, artichokes, radishes, peppers, what you will. Finally put the fish on a platter, surround it with the quartered eggs and the vegetables. In the Midi the dish would be garnished with small grey snails, mussels and perhaps pieces of lightly poached squid; instead use unshelled prawns or shrimps. Serve with a large bowl of aïoli (page 286) and lots of French bread.

Brandade

This is a creamy purée of salted cod, olive oil and milk, flavoured with garlic, that makes a wonderful starter to a meal. It is a speciality of Nîmes, in the heart of Languedoc. Made in the traditional way, it takes time and energy, so if you have neither to spare, make the food processor do some of the work. Don't feel ashamed, your French counterpart probably buys it in a jar in the local supermarket.

450–675 g (1–1½ lbs) salt cod
150–275 ml (5–7½ fl oz) olive oil
150–275 ml (5–7½ fl oz) milk
1 tablespoon lemon juice
1 clove garlic, chopped
pepper, nutmeg
salt if necessary

Poach the prepared salted cod in fresh water, letting it barely simmer for 8–10 minutes Set aside for a further 10 minutes, then take it out of the pan and remove any bones. Leave the skin, it not only helps the flavour but being gelatinous will contribute to the success of the operation. Put the cod, bit by bit, into the food processor and blend until smooth, taking care that there are no lumpy pieces. You will end up with a white purée flecked with black. If you have no processor, you could use a mincer. If you have neither use a mortar and pestle (or a bowl and wooden spoon) to crush the fish, hence the need for time and energy. Put the fish into a saucepan on the edge of the heat source (or use a double saucepan, the lower half containing simmering water), the secret being to avoid overheating the mixture. Warm the olive oil and milk to blood heat in two separate saucepans (dip your finger in, you should be able to count to ten before you pull it out), allowing 150 ml (5 fl oz) of each for every 450 g (1 lb) of fish. Begin to add olive oil to the fish purée, drop by drop, beating with a wooden spoon or whisk, as if making a mayonnaise. When you have added about a spoonful, add some milk in the same way. Continue to add oil and milk, alternately, until you have a thick mixture like mashed potato. Season with lemon juice, a chopped clove of garlic, pepper and nutmeg. (If you have a disaster and the oil begins to separate, put it all into the processor and blend, or into a bowl and beat it really hard.) Taste and, if you think it necessary, add a little salt. Put into a warm bowl and bring to the table. Eat with slices of French bread, sprinkled with olive oil and toasted at the top of a hot oven (or serve with toast or fried squares or triangles of bread).

Morue en bouillabaisse

This is a simple everyday dish but one of the best ways of using salted cod. Follow the method for bouillabaisse on page 271, omitting all the other kinds of fish. Add 5–6 medium sized potatoes cut in quarters to the boiling bouillon, boil rapidly and when they are half cooked, add the soaked, salted cod cut in slices and boil a further 5–10 minutes. Check the seasoning, put the fish in a dish, the soup in a tureen, serve with French bread toasted in the oven and a bowl of rouille.

Cod, Smoked

Pros and Cons   There's not a lot to be said about smoked cod; it is far and away inferior to smoked haddock and most on sale has not been smoked at all but dipped in brine, coloured with tartrazine and finally dipped in a solution which gives it a smoky flavour. It is tough, stringy and salty.

Genuine smoked cod is pale yellow and is likely to be found only from a fishmonger who does his own smoking. Follow recipes for smoked haddock (*see* pages 113–15).

Coley

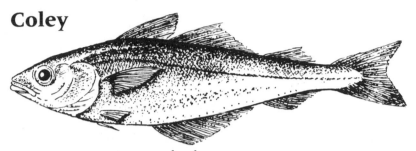

COLEY – *also known as:* SAITHE or COALFISH; *same family as:* COD, HADDOCK, HAKE, LING, POLLACK and WHITING

Habitat N Atlantic.

Pros and Cons My mother-in-law's cat turned up her nose at everything but coley. She wasn't a fool. Coley may look a rather grubby pink, but cooked it turns pristine white and though it may be a little coarse, it's a marvellous standby for lean days and far cheaper than cod or haddock.

Size 30–100 cm (12–39 ins).

Description Long, tapering body, charcoal-coloured tinged with olive green or black, sides and belly silvery white. Tail fin is forked. Has teeth and no barbel.

How sold Usually in fillets (sometimes under that blanket misnomer of rock salmon). SMOKED COLEY is sometimes sold – treat like smoked salmon, it's saltier but much cheaper.

Qty per person Fillets: 150–175 g (5–6 oz). Allow 225–275 g (8–10 oz) whole fish, ungutted.

Availability Widely available, all year.

Notes In Ireland and Scotland, whole young coley are highly valued and have many local names. However, it is the adult fish, kept on ice, that is found elsewhere on the slab, usually laid out in ready-cut fillets.

Preparation   Fillets should be washed and any blood or blackness removed. Like cod, coley can be watery; to counteract this pat it dry with kitchen paper and marinade it for an hour sprinkled with lemon juice and salt. Drain any moisture and dry again.

Cooking ideas   Use instead of haddock in recipes for baking or braising; or cook in curry sauce like garfish on page 95; good in stews, soups or fish pies.

Coley with anchovies, tomatoes and mushrooms

4 coley fillets
2 fillets anchovy, chopped
1 tablespoon olive oil
1 onion, chopped
1 tablespoon tomato purée
2 tomatoes, chopped
100 g (4 oz) mushrooms, chopped
½ teaspoon oregano
½ glass white wine (or use lemon juice)
salt, pepper
2 or 3 tablespoons fresh breadcrumbs
oil
lemon juice and parsley
Heat oven to Gas 4/350°F/180°C. Heat oil, fry chopped onion and anchovy fillets. Stir in tomato purée. Put into an oven dish, lay the fish fillets on top. Cover with the chopped tomatoes, mushrooms, oregano, wine (or lemon juice), salt and pepper. Sprinkle with breadcrumbs and a little oil. Bake 15–20 minutes. Take from oven, add a squeeze of lemon juice and some chopped parsley.

COMMON CRAB, *see* **CRAB**

COMMON EEL, *see* **EEL**

COMMON PRAWN, *see* **PRAWNS**

Conger Eel

CONGER EEL

Habitat	Coasts of N Europe and Mediterranean.
Pros and Cons	Meaty, robust, firm flesh with few bones and not very expensive. Don't confuse it with the slim, freshwater eel, which is sweeter and more delicate.
Size	70 cm–2.7 m (28 ins–9 ft).
Description	The thick, scaleless, serpentine body varies according to habitat from dark grey-brown to black with a lighter belly. Dorsal fin runs almost its entire length.
How sold	Cutlets or steaks, usually about 2.5 cm (1 in) thick or in large pieces for roasting. Also SMOKED.
Qty per person	175–200 g (6–7 oz).
Ask fishmonger	For a piece from middle or upper end (the tail end is full of spiky bones, although it would be useful for soup). Beg the head to use in soups or to add flavour to a bouillabaisse.
Availability	Widely available, best March to October; found locally caught in fishmongers around the coast of Devon and Cornwall.
Notes	The conger eel is nicknamed Evil-Eye by anglers, who have great respect and admiration for this powerful and ferocious fish.

| *Preparation* | Wash and wipe the steaks dry with kitchen paper. The skin is tough but can most easily be removed once it is cooked. |
| *Cooking ideas* | Good stewed or braised in cider or wine, can be grilled or cooked *en matelote*. A piece can be roasted whole, or it can be cut in cubes and made into kebabs. Suits robust flavours such as garlic, tomatoes, peppers; or use in soups or as part of a bouillabaisse. Recipes for this and the freshwater eel are not interchangeable. |

Conger Eel with cider and onions
4 conger eel steaks
2 tablespoons olive oil
1 onion, chopped
flour for coating
cider
salt, pepper
thyme, parsley, bayleaf
sliced apples (allow 1 apple per head) or baked sweet potatoes
Heat oven to Gas 6/400°F/200°C. Heat the olive oil in a wok or frying pan and cook the chopped onion over a medium heat until soft. Dip fish steaks in flour and add to the pan, brown quickly on each side. Put into a shallow ovenproof dish, pour over the cider, just sufficient to come halfway up the dish. Season with salt and pepper, thyme, parsley, and a bayleaf. Bake 15–20 minutes, basting after 10 minutes. Eat with slices of apple fried gently in a little butter or baked sweet potatoes.

La matelote à la normande
Matelote is a stew usually made with freshwater fish, but this version uses conger eel.
4 conger eel steaks about 2½ cm (1 in) thick
2 tablespoons olive or corn oil
200 g (8 oz) small whole pickling onions
100 g (4 oz) mushrooms
2 or 3 shallots or 1 onion, chopped
2 or 3 cloves garlic, crushed
1–2 tablespoons Calvados (or use brandy)

salt, pepper
300 ml (¼ pint) cider or red wine
kneaded butter made from 25 g (1 oz) each of flour and butter
cayenne pepper
chopped parsley
Skin and remove bones from the eel and cut in even-sized pieces, rinse and pat dry with kitchen paper. Heat the oil in a wok or saucepan and add the whole small onions and cook until they are golden. Add chopped mushrooms and when they are softened, remove them and the onions and set aside. Add the finely chopped shallots or onion with the crushed cloves of garlic and cook a few minutes without browning. Put the pieces of conger eel on top, let them heat a few moments before flaming with the Calvados or brandy. Add salt, pepper, cider or red wine, small onions and mushrooms and cook gently, uncovered, for 15–20 minutes. Put the fish on to a dish and keep warm. Thicken the sauce by adding the kneaded butter in small pieces, stir until the sauce is smooth, let it reduce for a few minutes, add a little cayenne. Pour the sauce over the fish and dust with parsley. Eat with garlic bread.

Congre à la safranado – Conger Eel with saffron
This recipe comes from the region of Toulon and Var in Provence.
4 conger eel steaks
4 tablespoons olive oil
2 onions, chopped
2 tablespoons brandy
2 cloves garlic
1 tablespoon tomato purée
thyme, parsley
saffron
salt, pepper
1 medium can Italian tomatoes
Heat the oil in a pan and cook the chopped onion until it is golden, remove and set aside. Cook the fish steaks over a medium heat for two or three minutes, turning them over. Flame with the brandy. Add cooked onions, garlic, tomato purée, herbs, few strands of saffron, salt, pepper and the tomatoes. Simmer for 15–20 minutes.

Roast Conger Eel
Roast as gigot de mer on page 153.

Congre au riz – Conger Eel with rice
4 conger eel steaks about 2½ cm (1 in) thick
2 tablespoons olive or peanut oil
1 onion, chopped
1 clove garlic, chopped
1 teaspoon turmeric
1 medium can Italian tomatoes
salt, pepper
1½ cups rice
sufficient water plus the liquid from the can of tomatoes to make up
  3 cups
Heat oil in a saucepan and gently cook the onion for a few minutes
until soft, add chopped garlic and the turmeric. Drain the tomatoes,
saving the liquid. Add tomatoes to the pan, then the salt and pepper
and the rice. Mix well. Add the liquid from the tomatoes and the
water. Bring to the boil. Lay the fish on top. Cover the pan, lower
the heat and cook very gently for 20 minutes.

Conger Eel, Smoked

Pros and Cons	It is expensive but you don't need much. The eels are gutted, dipped in brine and hot smoked, so they are cooked. The skin should be black and glistening, not burnt, and the flesh should be creamy. Also sold in fillets.
Ask fishmonger	Best bought from a fishmonger who smokes his own; ask for a freshly cut piece (pieces lying on the slab could be dry and will cost as much), if possible avoid the tail end which is bonier.
Qty per person	Allow 50 g (2 oz) per head.
Preparation	Peel off skin, cut in chunks or fillets.
Cooking ideas	Eat just as it is with plenty of lemon juice or horseradish sauce and brown bread and butter. Or make into pâté, *see* recipe for bloater paste, page 125), or add to scrambled eggs.

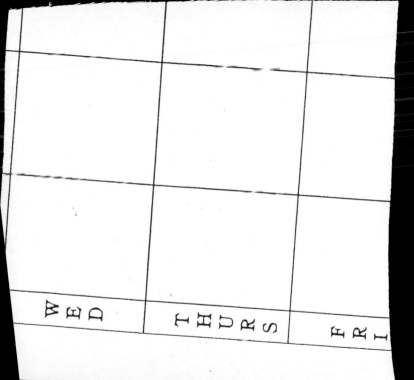

	WED	THURS	FRI

COQ ROUGE, *see* **BREAMS, SEA**

CORAL TROUT, *see* **GROUPERS**

CORDONNIER BRISANT, *see* **RABBITFISH**

COUCH'S SEA BREAM, *see* **BREAMS, SEA**

Crab

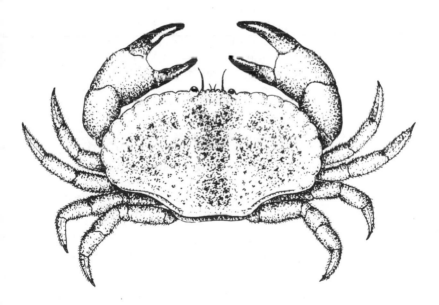

CRAB – *also known as:* COMMON CRAB or EDIBLE CRAB

Habitat   European coastal waters.

Pros and Cons   Crabs are fairly cheap and just as much a treat as the more expensive shellfish. Preparing your first crab may seem a bit daunting but once you've got to grips with it, you'll find all it needs is time and if you have no time just set everyone to work at table.

Size Minimum legal size is 11.5 cm (4½ ins) but usually beween 14–20 cm (5½–8 ins) across.

Description The large curved shell is usually a mottled brown with tones of pink, violet or yellow. The body meat is brown, that of the claws and legs is white.

How sold Whole, either live or ready cooked. Some people absolutely insist you must buy your crabs live, but if you are far from the sea, it seems unnecessarily cruel to be such a stickler and to condone the practice of letting them linger out their last days cramped in a fish tank. If you are buying a live crab, make sure it has been kept in cool conditions and is quite sprightly. Otherwise buy them ready cooked from a reliable fishmonger, *making sure they are freshly cooked.* You can even buy them ready-dressed which means no work for you, but you'll pay double the price and the crab meat will probably be over-liberally laced with breadcrumbs.

Sometimes you may come across soft-shell crabs, probably frozen, which are a different species (shore crab) and are imported; they are specially reared and marketed just as they shed their shell before the new shell has hardened. (It's illegal to sell our native crabs in this fashion.)

Qty per person Allow a crab of around 450 g (1 lb); 2 people can feed off one weighing around 800 g (1¾ lb).

Ask fishmonger If you have a preference for a male or female crab, tell him. Male crabs contain more white meat than the female, which has smaller claws and a higher proportion of brown meat. It's really a matter of your own preference which you buy. To tell the difference, have a look at the tail flap; the male's is narrower and more pointed than that of the female. Ask him to let you feel the weight, which should seem heavy for its size; give it a shake, there should be no sound of water rattling; both claws should be intact and you should avoid a cracked or holed shell. If you are buying a live crab, ask him to tie the claws to avoid a nasty nip when you get home.

Availability   All year but best April to December.

Notes   Several species of crab are found round our coasts but in this country we tend only to eat the common or edible crab, exporting the others to the Continent, where they are more appreciated. These include the shore crab, velvet and spider crabs.

Preparation   If your crab is not already cooked, you will have to overcome your soft-hearted feelings and kill it yourself. If crabs are plunged into boiling water they can shoot their claws so fishmongers generally drown them first in desalinated water. The only really humane way is to turn it on its back and stab it using an awl which should be at least 26 cm (10½ ins) long. There are two nerve centres which must be pierced, the first in a vent behind the tail and the other at a point behind the head. For the novice, it's not easy to be sure you can locate these two weak points but if you contact the Universities Federation for Animal Welfare, 8 Hamilton Close, South Mimms, Potters Bar, EN6 3QD, they will send you a leaflet which sets it out very clearly. (It also includes the humane way to kill a lobster.) Otherwise try and get a demonstration from an expert or buy your crabs ready cooked.

Cooking ideas   Put the uncooked crab into boiling water liberally seasoned with salt, 3 tablespoons to every litre (1¾ pints). Secure the lid and boil, allowing 10 minutes for every 450 g (1 lb). Set aside to cool.

Crab has such a sweet and tasty meat, that there's not much point exhausting yourself producing an elaborate sauce in which to swamp it.

Either dress it in the traditional manner, or let everyone tackle their own; or if you want it hot, serve it simply au gratin.

Dressing a crab for the table

The crab must be boiled. Let it cool but prepare it whilst it is still warm, you'll find it easier.

Give yourself time, sit down at the table. Have a wooden mallet or rolling pin, a teaspoon, oyster knife, pair of kitchen shears, a skewer and two bowls – one for the white meat, the other for the brown.

1.   Lay the crab on its back with the head towards you, hold it in one hand and with the other break off the two claws and the eight legs, twisting them backwards. Extract all the meat from the claws and legs, using the mallet or rolling pin to crack the shells (hold them in the palm of your hand whilst you rap them, they'll be less likely to splinter into lots of small pieces) and use the skewer to release the stubborn bits.

2.   With the tail piece towards you, twist off and discard the tail flap. Use the point of a knife to loosen round the centre portion (which held the legs), then twist the knife to prise this central piece apart from the main shell and split it in half with a heavy knife; use a teaspoon and a skewer to scoop out all the meat from all the crevices and remove the meat in the outer shell. Everything is edible except the baglike stomach sac near the mouth, gills and grey-green lungs known as deadman's fingers. Remove the brown meat found under the inner rim, putting it into a separate bowl from the white meat. Discard any rubbery dark-red bits which are the beginning of a new shell.

3.   Break away the underside of the shell as far as the dark line running close to the edge; it breaks off quite naturally. Wash out the shell, dry with kitchen paper and oil lightly.

4.   Season the brown meat with salt, pepper, a dash of vinegar and a little olive oil and mix in 1 tablespoon of fresh breadcrumbs. Arrange around the sides of the shell.

5.   Flake the white meat, add salt and pepper and a spoonful or two of mayonnaise made with a mild flavoured oil like sunflower and fill the centre of the shell. Garnish with parsley. Vary the flavouring by adding chopped herbs and capers, shallots or spring onions and mixing a little mustard with the mayonnaise.

Crab au naturel

If you're not trying to impress anyone, this is really quite the best way of eating crabs and it's how they do it in lots of restaurants in France. Just make sure you are with friends you really like and give each one a cooked crab to themselves, get rid of the inedible bits in the kitchen (*see* 2 above). Set the table with forks, skewers, nutcrackers, whatever you have in the way of picking instruments, some home-made mayonnaise, a bowl of watercress, fresh bread, lots of butter, lemon wedges, cayenne pepper, finger bowls, napkins plus a bottle or three of lightly chilled wine. Just warn everyone not to try and crack the claws with their teeth, it can result in expensive dental repairs.

Crab au gratin

Prepare individual crabs for each person following stages 1–3 above. Mix the brown and white meat together and for each crab mix in ½ teaspoon mustard, a dash of Worcester sauce, squeeze of lemon juice, salt, cayenne pepper and 1 tablespoon curd cheese. Moisten with beaten egg or a little milk. Put the mixture into the shells or into individual dishes. Sprinkle over some breadcrumbs mixed with parsley and dribble over some olive or peanut oil. Heat oven to Gas 4/350°F/180°C and bake for 10 minutes. Serve with lemon wedges and a garnish of watercress.

CRAWFISH, *see* **LOBSTER, SPINY**

Crayfish, Freshwater

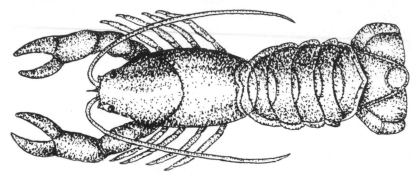

CRAYFISH, FRESHWATER (This name is also sometimes used for the SPINY LOBSTER or CRAWFISH, *see* LOBSTER, SPINY)

Habitat Freshwater lakes, ponds or streams in UK, Europe and elsewhere.

Pros and Cons Delicately flavoured freshwater crustaceans, unfortunately very expensive and rare.

Size 7½–10 cm (3–4 ins).

Description Living they are a greeny-brown becoming shocking pink or deep red when cooked.

Features A rather thickset diminutive version of a lobster.

How sold Whole, usually live.

Qty per person 6–8 depending on recipe.

Availability Rarely in this country except from the most enterprising fishmongers; they are widely sold in France as *écrevisses*, where you will see them displayed live on market stalls or in fishmongers.

Notes Our wild, native crayfish have almost entirely succumbed to a virulent plague due to pollution. Some fish farms rear a close relation, the American signal crayfish, and supplies are sent to London fishmarkets, although most will find their way to restaurants or to France. Others are imported live from Turkey and these might be sold by enterprising fishmongers.

Preparation Rinse before cooking, *see* below. Wild crayfish need de-veining, which means removing the black thread of the intestines found under the centre tail section; use a pointed knife to ease it out. Cultivated crayfish may already be clean.

Cooking ideas They can be simply poached in a flavoured *court bouillon* then served hot or cold with the stock – *écrevisses à la nage*. Everyone pulls them apart at table, discarding legs and shells. The tail meat is succulent and tasty as is the meat from the head. You can use the discarded shells to make crayfish butter, which can be used to add flavour to fish sauces.

To cook live crayfish
Boil 3 litres (5½ pints) of water with 2 tablespoons salt. Or use a *court bouillon*. Plunge in the crayfish, bring back to the boil and let it bubble for 4 minutes. Remove the fish and drain. When cool enough to handle, you can shell them and remove the intestines; or let everyone do their own at table.

Beurre d'écrevisses – Crayfish butter (or use prawn or shrimp shells)
Put the discarded shells into a food processor and mix till finely crushed, or use a mortar and pestle. Add 100 g (4 oz) softened butter and mix to a cream. Put into a saucepan over a low heat and let the butter slowly melt, stirring constantly. When the butter begins to show flecks of foam, strain it through a fine mesh into a bowl. Put into the fridge to set. You can use this butter as an accompaniment to grilled fish or as a base for fish sauces.

CRAYFISH, *see also* **LOBSTER, SPINY**

CREVALLE JACK, *see* **CARANGIDS**

CREVALLY, *see* **CARANGIDS**

Croakers

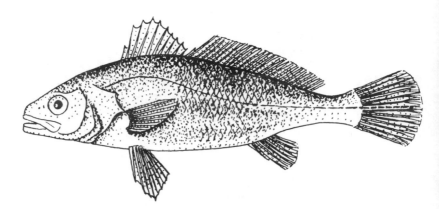

CROAKERS — *also known as:* DRUMS; includes YELLOW CROAKER and the Mediterranean MAIGRE and OMBRINE

Habitat   There are many species living in tropical or temperate seas, some in estuaries, others in big river systems; those sold here are likely to be imported from SE Asia, or occasionally from the Mediterranean.

Pros and Cons   Croakers sold here will usually be frozen, and are sometimes sold as frozen snappers; they are quite cheap but are inclined to be insipid so need plenty of added flavourings; a few fresh maigres come from France.

Size   Around 40–60 cm (16–24 ins).

Description   Perch-like fish, the first dorsal fin is about half the length of the second; the lateral line continues on to the tail fin. There may be barbels on the chin or pronounced pores on lower jaw. They are generally a dullish yellow or grey and some have stripes or bars.

How sold	Whole fish; sometimes steaks.
Qty per person	225–275 g (8–10 oz) whole, ungutted fish. 175–200 g (6–7 oz) steaks.
Ask fishmonger	To clean, scale, trim and remove gills. Ask if it is fresh or frozen.
Availability	Probably in shops and markets patronized by Chinese, Indians or Caribbeans.
Notes	Most croakers on sale are frozen but sometimes you may come across the French maigre or perhaps in the South of France, the related ombrine. Croakers are so called because of the noise they make as a means of communication by vibrating their swim bladder; they sound like so many frogs.
Preparation	Must be scaled, cleaned and trimmed and gills removed.
Cooking ideas	Poach and eat with a well-flavoured sauce; or steam like rabbitfish (*see* page 186), or use recipes for snapper. Grill steaks after first marinading (*see* pages 299–300 for marinades); or make a couscous; or cook like garfish in curry sauce (*see* page 95).

Couscous

This dish really calls for a *couscousier*, which consists of a specially shaped pot in which the vegetables and fish (or meat) are cooked together, over which stands a steamer holding the couscous (a fine grain rather like semolina made from refined wheat). It comes from N Africa but has been adopted by the French and this recipe is based on one given to me by Monique, the grandaughter-in-law of Madame Boeuf. Failing a *couscousier*, use a normal saucepan with a colander on top, if necessary lining it with a piece of muslin so that the grains cannot slip through.

4 croaker steaks (or use steaks of other fish such as snapper, grouper, grey mullet, sea bream, cod, redfish or hake)
4 tablespoons olive oil
2–3 courgettes cut in pieces
1 medium can of Italian tomatoes
2 green or red peppers, deseeded and cut in pieces
3 cloves of garlic, chopped
2 or 3 onions, chopped
salt
2 teaspoons harissa
450 g (1 lb) couscous
50 g (2 oz) butter, cut in pieces
50 g (2 oz) raisins
2 cups cooked chickpeas (or use 1 can)

Into the pot put the olive oil, the courgettes, tomatoes, peppers, garlic, onions, salt and 1 teaspoon harissa; just cover with water. Bring to the boil, lower heat and cover.

Put the couscous into a bowl and cover with water, add ½ teaspoon salt; leave it for about 10 minutes when it will absorb the water and swell in volume. Put it into the steamer and stand this over the pot containing the vegetables. Put the lid on top and cook for 45 minutes. After this time, empty the couscous into a bowl and mix in the butter with a fork and add the raisins. Put back into the steamer. Add the chickpeas and the fish to the pot and simmer 20–30 minutes.

To serve, put the couscous into a deep, wide bowl, and arrange fish and vegetables on top, removing them from the pot with a slotted spoon. In a bowl serve some of the cooking liquid as a sauce, and for those who like a hot sauce, mix the remaining harissa with some more of the cooking liquid and serve this in a separate bowl.

CROISSANT, *see* **GROUPERS**

CUCKOO WRASSE, *see* **WRASSE**

Cuttlefish

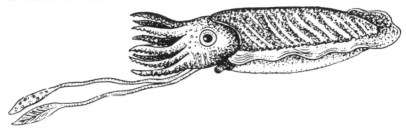

CUTTLEFISH – *also known as:* INKFISH; *related to:* OCTOPUS and SQUID

Habitat   N Atlantic and Mediterranean.

Pros and Cons   Whole cuttlefish are a bit messy but not difficult to prepare and are as tasty as squid, but although they live in abundance around our shores they are rare in shops.

Size   Up to 25 cm (10 ins).

Description   Squat, bee-shaped body in sepia shades of grey or black surrounded by a speckled frill; the arms and tentacles grow from the head. The body contains the flat cuttleshell, familiar as a beak exerciser to those who keep tame birds.

How sold   Whole, by weight; or frozen, cleaned and split.

Qty per person   Allow 175–200 g (6–7 oz).

Ask fishmonger   To order some if he doesn't stock them.

Availability   In summer from specialist fishmongers, most of the catch is exported.

Notes   Inkfish is not just a fanciful nickname. The thick liquid found in the sac inside the cuttlefish's head is the original sepia ink. When sensing danger, this liquid is ejected into the water clouding all the surrounding area and masking the fish's escape.

Preparation	Wash in cold water. Use a sharp, pointed knife and cut the cuttlefish from just below the head to the tail. You'll feel the knife scrape against the cuttle-bone. Gently ease open the slit and extract the bone. Carefully remove the inner membrane and lift out the innards, amongst which you will see the ink sac. Don't break it, or you'll be covered in ink, but lift it out and keep if you are going to use it in your recipe. Cut off the tentacles above the eyes, keep them, but discard remainder of head. Carefully wash the bag of the body, inside and out, making sure you leave no grit lurking. You can cook the cuttlefish whole or chop tentacles, arms and body into smallish pieces.
Cooking ideas	Stew with wine and garlic, tomatoes and onions; the ink can be used to colour the fish in a rather spectacular fashion. Lots of squid recipes can equally apply to cuttlefish, and vice versa.

Seiches à la mode de l'Estaque or Langouste à l'armoricaine des pauvres – (Poor man's spiny lobster)

675–900 g (1½–2 lbs) cuttlefish
675–900 g (1½–2 lbs) tomatoes
3 cloves garlic
1 teaspoon crushed fennel seeds
bayleaf
3 or 4 tablespoons olive oil
salt, pepper
1 glass dry white wine
handful of stoned green olives

Prepare the cuttlefish as above and cut it into small squares, put them into a pan with the tomatoes, roughly chopped. Add garlic, fennel, bayleaf and the olive oil. Season well. Give it all a stir and put it on a medium heat, bring to the boil. Pour over the wine and add the olives. Let the wine evaporate, lower the heat, cover and cook gently for about 45 minutes.

Cuttlefish cooked in its own ink

Prepare the cuttlefish and reserve the ink sacs. Heat 2 or 3 tablespoons olive oil in a wok or pan and fry a chopped onion until soft, then add the squares of cuttlefish, and cook over a low heat for about 10 minutes. Stir in 1 tablespoon tomato purée, 2 finely chopped cloves garlic, a handful of fresh breadcrumbs, a glass of dry white wine, salt and pepper. Stir in the ink from the sacs. Cover and cook over a low heat for 45 minutes. Serve with rice and fried croûtons.

Dab

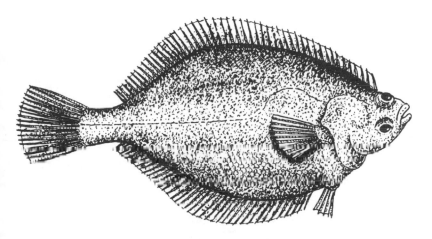

DAB – *same family as:* FLOUNDER, HALIBUT, LEMON SOLE, PLAICE and WITCH

Habitat	European Atlantic.
Pros and Cons	One of the sweetest flavoured and least expensive flat fish. Dabs are often passed off as small plaice, they're easily recognizable because they lack the bony nodules on the head and their dark skin is rough.
Size	15–30 cm (6–12 ins).
Description	Right facing, oval flat fish, sandy brown on eyed-side with paler and darker blotches, often faintly speckled with orange or yellow; the finely toothed scales feel like glasspaper; blind side white. Mouth

is very small, and the lateral line curves deeply around pectoral fin.

How sold	Whole fish or in fillets.
Qty per person	Allow 200–225 g (7–8 oz) whole fish, gutted with head. Fillets: 150–175 g (5–6 oz).
Ask fishmonger	To remove head if you prefer or to fillet. Ask for head for stock. Dark skin can be removed after cooking.
Availability	In season April to February but best June to December. Main catch is in North Sea so is widely available in East Anglia.
Notes	If you suspect the fishmonger is passing dabs off as plaice, don't feel cheated, he is just pandering to our conservatism over our choice of fish, the dab is actually superior. It is shown as *limande* on French menus.
Preparation	Wash the fish and dry with kitchen paper.
Cooking ideas	Delicious cooked whole on the bone either fried in butter and served with tartare sauce, grilled or baked in foil. Or cook fillets with mustard; recipes for plaice and lemon sole are suitable and vice versa.

Dab grilled with chives, fennel and parsley

Mix 50 g (2 oz) softened butter with 1 teaspoon crushed fennel seeds, a handful of snipped chives, 1 tablespoon chopped parsley, juice of half a lemon, salt and pepper. Cut two or three slashes on either side of fish. Spread with the butter and grill as on page 298. Or if you prefer use oil instead of the butter and marinade the fish for an hour or two before cooking. Grill and brush with the marinade.

Limandes à la moutarde – Fillets of dabs with mustard

2 dabs weighing in total about 800 g (1¾ lbs) filleted or 550–675 g
(1¼–1½ lbs) dab fillets
50 g (2 oz) butter
salt, pepper

juice of 1 lemon
1 medium onion or 4 shallots, chopped
4 tablespoons dry cider
1 small carton half or single cream
1 tablespoon Dijon mustard
1 tablespoon chopped gherkins (optional)
Heat oven to Gas 6/400°F/200°C. Put the butter in a shallow oven dish and put it into the oven just until the butter melts, 3–4 minutes. Take it out, lay the fillets in the dish, add salt, pepper and the lemon juice. Put into the oven whilst you prepare the sauce. Put chopped onions (or shallots) and the cider into a small saucepan and bring to the boil. Cook until the cider evaporates. Stir in the cream, and off the heat, add mustard and the optional gherkins. Pour over the fish and return to the oven just to glaze the sauce without letting it brown, 3–4 minutes.

DAURADE, *see* BREAMS, SEA

DEEP-WATER PRAWN, *see* PRAWNS

DENTÉ, *see* BREAMS, SEA

DENTEX, *see* BREAMS, SEA

Dogfish

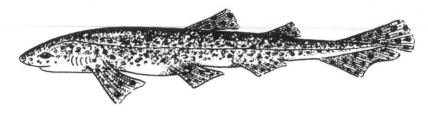

DOGFISH — *also known as:* ROUGH HOUND or LESSER-SPOTTED DOGFISH; usually sold as either ROCK SALMON, ROCK FISH, ROCK EEL, HUSS, FLAKE or RIGG; *related to:* SHARKS and SKATES

Habitat E Atlantic and Mediterranean.

Pros and Cons A wonderfully useful, cheap buy; the close-textured, tasty flesh has no small bones to catch you unawares, there is simply an easily dealt with cartilaginous backbone.

Size 45–75 cm (18–30 ins).

Description Only the pink tinged body and tail-end is sold, ready skinned and trimmed. Dogfish are splendid little sharks, with mouths filled with canine teeth and sandy, freckled skin as rough and tough as sandpaper.

How sold In cut pieces by weight.

Qty per person 175–200 g (6–7 oz).

Ask fishmonger To reveal the true identity of his fish if he is using one of the blanket names like ROCK SALMON.

Availability All year but more abundant from summer to autumn.

Notes Other small sharks, closely related to the dogfish, such as SMOOTH HOUND and SPUR-DOG, are sometimes sold under one of the misnomers listed above. Like other cartilaginous fish (ones with no small bones but a soft backbone of gristle), they are popular in the fish and chip trade and with children. The slight smell of ammonia is normal and will disappear on cooking.

Preparation   Simply wash under running water and pat dry.

Cooking ideas   Good baked, braised, fried, grilled or poached. Serve with sauce *au citron* or black butter. Can be cut into chunks and fried like small eels, or made into kebabs, or battered and deep fried. Use recipes for cod or angler fish. Or bake like bass in foil with ginger (*see* page 13).

Dogfish Moroccan style

675 g (1½ lbs) dogfish
3 tablespoons olive oil
1 onion, chopped
1 clove of garlic, chopped
1 teaspoon each paprika, salt, crushed cumin
½ teaspoon each crushed coriander, black pepper and harissa (failing harissa use a mixture of paprika and red pepper)
1 medium can Italian tomatoes

Heat the oil in a wok or pan, add the chopped onion and cook over medium heat until it is softened and beginning to brown, add garlic, paprika, salt, cumin, coriander, black pepper and the harissa. Stir over the heat and add the can of tomatoes, crushing them a little. Bring to the boil, lower the heat and simmer for 15 minutes. Add the fish and cook it gently, covered, for a further 10–15 minutes.

Dogfish with garlic and green peppercorns

Cut the fish into slices, marinade in lemon juice, salt and pepper for 1 hour. Pat dry and roll in flour. Heat 4 tablespoons olive oil in a wok or frying pan, add a chopped onion, let it soften for a few minutes. Add the fish and a chopped clove of garlic. Let it cook gently, turning it once. When cooked add 1 tablespoon green peppercorns and 2 or 3 tablespoons cream. Stir and serve on rice.

Dolphinfish

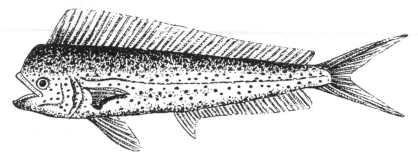

DOLPHINFISH or DORADO, also known by Hawaiian name of MAHI-MAHI

Habitat	Tropical and warm temperate oceans.
Pros and Cons	Dolphinfish are magnificent sporting fish, imported in small quantities from the Seychelles and the Caribbean. They make delicious eating.
Size	Usually around 60 cm (24 ins).
Description	The dingy aspect of the caught fish bears no relation to its living colours of turquoise, yellow and silver. It has a long dorsal fin which sprouts directly behind the domed forehead, a loofah-shapéd body, protruding lower jaw and forked tail like a bandit's moustache.
How sold	Cut pieces and steaks.
Qty per person	Steaks: 175–200 g (6–7 oz).
Ask fishmonger	To buy it if ever he sees it in the market.
Availability	Rarely available in fishmongers, most supplies are snapped up by the restaurant trade. If you see it on the menu, well worth ordering.
Notes	The dolphinfish has no connection with the dolphin, which is not a fish but a mammal. The Spanish and Portuguese name is *dorado* and it is often

known by this name. You may also come across it in Malta and S Italy. Don't confuse it with the French name for the red sea bream – *dorade*.

Preparation Wash and pat dry with kitchen paper.

Cooking ideas Marinade steaks in oil, lemon juice and garlic before grilling, or bake them in foil parcels or braise with vegetables. Fry fillets *à la meunière*.

DORADE, *see* **BREAM, RED SEA**

DORADE ROUGE, *see* **BREAMS, SEA**

DORADO, *see* **DOLPHINFISH**

DOVER SOLE, *see* **SOLE**

DRUMS, *see* **CROAKERS**

Dublin Bay Prawn

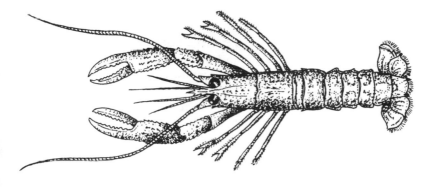

DUBLIN BAY PRAWN – *also known as:* NEPHROPS, SCAMPI, NORWAY LOBSTERS and LANGOUSTINE; *related to:* LOBSTER

Habitat	NE Atlantic and Mediterranean.
Pros and Cons	Live Dublin Bay prawns are fragile and difficult to move around, so are a rare and expensive luxury; you're more likely to find just the tails still in their shells; but most common of all are the bagged, frozen variety sold as scampi.
Size	Whole, legal minimum shell length 25 cm (10 ins).
Description	A diminutive and dainty facsimile of the lobster, with boot-button eyes and stripes varying from pale coral to deep rose, pink or orange red.
How sold	Sometimes whole, live; more often just the tails, fresh or frozen; and frozen, shelled, in packets under their Italian name of *scampi*.
Qty per person	Whole: 4–6 depending on size; frozen tails in shell allow 225–250 g (8–9 oz).
Ask fishmonger	If buying whole Dublin Bay prawns to give you ones with unbroken shells and with the claws intact.
Availability	Season is April to November. Live are rare except perhaps direct from a fish market or an enterprising fishmonger; otherwise look out for the tails, still in their shells. Chinese supermarkets are a good hunting ground.
Notes	Whole Dublin Bay prawns look wholly seductive but are very expensive though three or four would make a splendid garnish for a seafood platter. Shelled, frozen scampi in packets tend to be low on flavour because they will have been frozen when caught, thawed to be shelled, then refrozen to be bagged. Avoid frozen, breaded scampi; fish fingers are a better buy.
Preparation	Rinse live ones and cook in shells; you'll find scissors are handy when removing the shells; discard head and innards and black thread of the intestines.

Frozen tails should be thawed, when they can be cooked as they are, or shelled beforehand, depending on the dish you are preparing.

Cooking ideas Live Dublin Bay prawns need only be rinsed and then dropped into boiling salted water (allow 1 tablespoon per litre). Cook them for two minutes after the water has returned to the boil. Take off the heat and leave five minutes before draining them. Serve whole on their own with a home-made mayonnaise, or as part of a seafood platter. Don't ignore the meat in the claws, it's sweet and very moreish. The tails can be baked in their shells, or shelled and fried in oil with garlic and parsley; or marinaded in lemon juice, salt, pepper, thyme, bayleaf and threaded on skewers with mushrooms and grilled, served with rice cooked with an onion, and coloured with saffron or turmeric. Or cook them in a simple sauce like the scallops on page 214. Most recipes for scallops or freshwater crayfish are suitable.

Langoustines au four – Baked Dublin Bay prawns

Buy the tails in their shells and when they have thawed, split them in half lengthways. Heat the oven to Gas 7/425°F/220°C. To prevent the tails from falling over, put a crumpled sheet of foil on a baking sheet and lay the tails on top. Season them with salt, cayenne, a sprinkling of thyme and marjoram (or oregano). Pour over some melted butter (or use olive oil). Put them in the oven for about 10 minutes.

Fried Dublin Bay prawns

Heat 3 or 4 tablespoons olive oil or butter in a frying pan or wok. Add a chopped clove of garlic, and let it just turn colour but not blacken. Remove it. Add the shelled Dublin Bay prawns and cook over a medium heat for 4 or 5 minutes, shaking them from time to time to turn them and prevent them sticking. Season them with salt, pepper and a squeeze of lemon juice, sprinkle them with parsley and pile into a hot dish. Serve with lemon wedges and a mayonnaise-based sauce like aïoli or tartare or *rémoulade*, and French bread.

EARSHELL, *see* **ORMERS**

ECREVISSES, *see* **CRAYFISH**

EDIBLE CRAB, *see* **CRAB**

EEL, CONGER, *see* **CONGER EEL**

Eels and Elvers

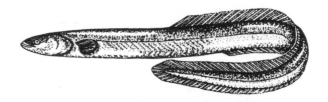

EELS and ELVERS

Habitat   Rivers, ponds, canals and streams of Britain and Europe, as well as being imported during scarce periods from as far away as New Zealand.

Pros and Cons   If you're squeamish, you may not fancy eels or their tiny young, elvers. Overcome your feelings of nicety and you will discover they are rich and tasty delicacies with none of the rough robustness of their distant relative the conger.

Size   Males rarely more than 50cm (20 ins), though females can be double this size.
Elvers are 6–8 cm (2½–3 ins) long.

Description	Slender sinuous body with a long dorsal fin which joins the anal fin through the tail. Mature eels are black, tinged with green or brown with silver sides and belly. Elvers are as thick as a bootlace and transparent.
How sold	Whole and alive by weight. Also SMOKED and JELLIED.
Qty per person	Whole eels: 150–175 g (5–6 oz). Elvers: 100–150 g (4–5 oz). Jellied: 50–75 g (2–3 oz).
Ask fishmonger	To kill and skin whole eels and, if you wish, to chop into sections.
Availability	Eels and jellied eels all year from specialist fishmongers, especially popular in the East End of London. Elvers, February–May, especially around the Severn, and in E Anglia.
Notes	For centuries the eel was regarded as a mysterious creature, spending most of its life in fresh water before disappearing to spawn. Finally it was discovered that the sexually mature eel travelled across the Atlantic to an area south-east of Bermuda. Here in the warmth and depth of the Sargasso Sea, they spawn and die. The eggs hatch into tiny, leaf-shaped larvae with needle-sharp teeth and are carried by the Gulf Stream across the Atlantic towards Europe. Up to three years later, they have developed into little round elvers with red blood and they arrive *en masse* in the estuaries of rivers in Western Europe. Those that are not caught continue their migration to the inland waterways where they spend their lives until they return to their spawning grounds.
Preparation of EELS	The killing and skinning of an eel is not a pleasant job. The dead eel, in the same manner as a beheaded chicken, manifests all the signs of being alive by continuing to writhe and squirm in the most disconcerting way. So if you don't fancy it and don't want to know, just make sure the fishmonger does

it for you. If you have to do it yourself or are able to give the job to some tougher member of your family, the method is as follows.

The eel after first being stunned and trimmed of fins is suspended by a cord tied round its neck. An incision is made around the neck and the thick skin turned over all round like a polo neck collar, the whole skin is then peeled off all in one go, like an elastic stocking. Use pliers if necessary. The head is cut off and discarded. If you need to bone it: slit it along the belly, open it out, press it flat and remove the backbone all in one piece.

Preparation of ELVERS Those in the know take pillowcases in which to bring them home, thus allowing them to breathe. Elvers are slimy. Wash them several times, still in their pillowcase, in a bucket of salted water, wringing them out in between each immersion. Set them aside to drain for several minutes and then empty them into a clean teacloth and rub them vigorously.

Cooking ideas Recipes for eel and conger eel are not interchangeable, the eel is far more delicate. Eels, being very rich, are best grilled, stewed or made into pies. Or use as part of a *matelote* or freshwater bouillabaisse. Elvers are usually deep fried like whitebait or fry them in olive oil flavoured with garlic as in Spain.

Grilled Eel kebabs with mushrooms and tomatoes
Cut eels into 5 cm (2 ins) pieces (they need not be skinned as the grilling will turn the skin brown and crisp) and marinade for at least one hour in 4 tablespoons olive oil, lemon juice and vinegar, chopped clove of garlic, bayleaf, rosemary, salt and pepper. Thread on to skewers with pieces of mushroom, tomatoes and bayleaves. Cook as for kebabs, page 299.

Catigot d'Anguilles
This dish which is a mixture between a soup and a stew comes from the region around Arles and the Camargue and is as famous in its own area as the bouillabaisse is in Marseille and like that dish, it

depends on being cooked over a fierce flame in order that the oil amalgamates with the liquid.

2 or 3 eels weighing in total around 675–800 g (1½–1¾ lbs)
8 tablespoons olive oil
2 onions, chopped
1 medium can of Italian tomatoes
sprig of celery
bayleaf, thyme, 1 red chilli (or ½ teaspoon chilli powder)
5–6 whole cloves of garlic
salt and pepper
300 ml (½ pint) red wine and the same amount of water
croûtons – triangles of bread, fried in oil

Cut the skinned and cleaned eel(s) into slices around 7–8 cm (2½–3 ins) long. In a large, heavy pot heat the olive oil and add the chopped onions. Let them brown and then add the tomatoes, celery, bayleaf, thyme, the chilli and whole cloves of garlic. Add the pieces of eel and let everything cook over a medium heat for 5 minutes, giving a stir from time to time. Add salt and pepper. In another pan put 300 ml (½ pint) red wine and the same amount of water, bring it to the boil and pour into the pot. Let it boil quite fiercely for 20 minutes, then serve surrounded by the croûtons of fried bread.

Jellied Eels

You can buy eels ready jellied in London, especially in the East End, but if you want you can jelly your own. You simply put the skinned eel cut in chunks into a saucepan, add a chopped onion, carrot, stick of celery, a bayleaf, some parsley, salt and pepper and enough water, white wine or cider just to cover. Bring slowly to the boil and simmer covered for an hour. Put the pieces of eel into a small pot or jar. Boil the remaining ingredients together until they reduce by about a quarter, strain the liquid over the pieces of eel and discard the vegetables and herbs. Let it cool when it will form a jelly. Eat with lemon juice and buttered toast. It is very rich and filling.

Eel pie

Heat oven to Gas 6/400°F/200°C. Cut the eels into chunks and roll them in flour. Put in a pie dish with a sliced onion, salt, pepper, herbs such as thyme, parsley and rosemary, add a pinch of nutmeg and if you like two or three hard-boiled eggs cut in quarters. Sprinkle with lemon juice and add a mixture of half water and dry white wine (or cider) to come halfway up the dish. Cover with puff pastry. Brush with beaten egg or milk and bake 30–40 minutes, until the pastry is risen and golden. Eat hot or better cold when it will be rich in jelly.

Elvers fried with garlic
Many of our elvers are exported to Spain, where they are regarded as a great delicacy. They are fried in individual pots from which they are eaten using wooden forks so as not to burn the mouth.

Put the cleaned and dried elvers in a bag containing 3 or 4 table-spoons flour and shake well to coat them. Turn them into a sieve and shake out the excess flour. Heat some olive oil in a wok or frying pan, allowing enough to cover the bottom by about 1 cm (½ in). When it is hot, add 2 chopped cloves of garlic. Let the garlic sizzle and turn golden then remove it. If you let it blacken the dish will be bitter. Add the elvers, as soon as they turn opaque, they are ready. Drain on kitchen paper, sprinkle with a little cayenne pepper and some parsley and garnish with lemon wedges.

SMOKED EEL is delicious sliced and eaten with lemon juice and cayenne pepper.

Emperors

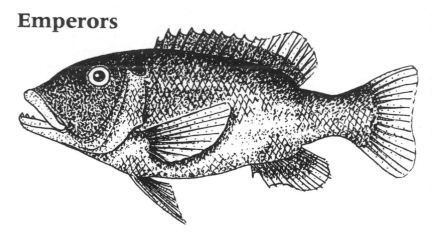

EMPERORS – *also known as:* EMPEROR BREAMS; usually sold under their Creole names of CAPITAINE ROUGE,

CAPITAINE BLANC, LASCAR, MADAME BERRIE or GUEULE
LONGUE

Habitat Tropical Indo-Pacific.

Pros and Cons Emperors are closely related to sea breams and their flesh is very similar. Most have white flesh though that of the Capitaine Rouge is pink. They are also distantly related to snappers.

Size CAPITAINE ROUGE up to 70 cm (28 ins).
CAPITAINE BLANC and LASCAR up to 60 cm (24 ins).
MADAME BERRIE up to 38 cm (15 ins).
GUEULE LONGUE up to 100 cm (39 ins).

Description Emperors have long sloping, perch-like snouts; deep, scaleless cheeks; the first part of the dorsal fin is spiny and the anal fin has 3 spines. Colours vary through reddish browns and silvery greys patterned with spots or bars.

How sold Either whole fish or steaks

Qty per person Allow 225–275 g (8–10 oz) of whole fish, ungutted. Steaks: 175–200 g (6–7 oz).

Ask fishmonger To clean, scale and trim and, if cooking whole, to remove gills.

Availability From enterprising fishmongers especially in London and the SE and in shops and markets patronized by the Caribbean community.

Notes Emperors are not the same family as sea breams, though their flesh is similar, hence their name emperor breams.

Preparation Wash, trim and scale and remove gills if cooking whole, if not already done by the fishmonger. Dry with kitchen paper.

Cooking ideas Whole large fish may be baked or steamed. Grill or fry steaks. Use recipes for sea breams, groupers or snappers.

Stuffed Emperor
1 fish weighing around 1 kilo (2¼ lbs)
2 tablespoons olive oil
1 onion, chopped
3 or 4 anchovy fillets, chopped
1 clove of garlic, chopped
parsley, thyme, oregano
juice of 1 lemon
1 red chilli, chopped (or 1 teaspoon chilli powder)
½ cup breadcrumbs
1 beaten egg
salt, pepper
slices of lemon
lemon wedges and chopped parsley to garnish
Heat oven to Gas 5/375°F/190°C. Heat 2 tablespoons of oil in a wok or frying pan and cook the onion until soft over a medium heat, add the anchovy fillets, garlic, herbs, lemon juice, chilli and breadcrumbs. Mix well, remove from the heat and add the beaten egg. Lay the fish on a large sheet of buttered foil, fill the cavity with the stuffing. Sprinkle some oil over the fish, add salt and pepper, lay lemon slices along the fish and fold over the foil to make a parcel. Bake for 40–50 minutes. Serve garnished with lemon wedges and chopped parsley.

EUROPEAN OYSTER, *see* **OYSTERS**

FINE DE CLAIRE, *see* **OYSTERS**

FINNAN HADDOCK, *see* **HADDOCK, SMOKED**

FLAKE, *see* **DOGFISH**

Flounder

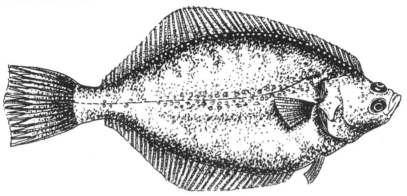

FLOUNDER or FLUKE — *same family as:* DAB, HALIBUT, LEMON SOLE, PLAICE and WITCH

Habitat   N Atlantic and W Mediterranean.

Pros and Cons   A freshly caught flounder is not to be despised especially if you happen to be in Cumbria around Flookburgh, where the catch is prized and they call it Fluke; but flounders like water with low salt content and don't travel very well, the longer they are kept, the more tasteless they become.

Size   Around 30 cm (12 ins).

Description   Right facing oval flat fish with a dark side of drab brown or green with light and dark blotches, sometimes pale orange spots; the blind side is dazzling white; it has spiny prickles along its lateral line and at the base of the dorsal and anal fins.

How sold   Whole fish or in fillets.

Qty per person   Allow 200–225 g (7–8 oz) of whole fish. Fillets: 150–175 g (5–6 oz).

Ask fishmonger   If you prefer to cook the fish skinned, ask him to remove the dark skin; and if you want it filleted, he will do the job for you. If buying fillets, those with dark skin will have more flavour.

Availability Best March to November.

Notes This is the fish in the fairy story who in return for not being caught, granted the fisherman three wishes. The fisherman had obviously never read any fairy stories, or he would have known that he would save himself a lot of trouble if he simply ate the fish.

Preparation Wash the fish and dry it with kitchen paper.

Cooking ideas Grill, fry or braise. Use simple recipes for plaice, brill or sole, remembering to be quite generous with the seasoning.

Grilled Flounder

Marinade the fish in the juice of a lemon with salt, pepper and a generous sprinkling of fresh tarragon or lemon thyme. When you are ready to grill them, heat 100 g (4 oz) butter in a small saucepan, add the juice of a lemon. Grill as on page 298, using the melted butter to baste the fish and pouring any that remains over the cooked fish. Eat with a well-flavoured sauce or butter.

Braised fillets of Flounder

700 g (1 ½ lbs) fillets
2 tablespoons olive oil or butter
1 onion, chopped
1 clove garlic, chopped
1 thin slice of fresh root ginger, chopped or 1 teaspoon dried
2 or 3 tomatoes, roughly chopped
1 green or red pepper, roughly chopped
1 glass dry white wine
salt, pepper
handful of black olives
Heat the oil or butter in a wok or frying pan until sizzling, add the chopped onion, garlic and ginger and cook 2 or 3 minutes. Add the tomato and green or red pepper and cook a few minutes more, stirring. Pour in the white wine and add salt and pepper. Bring to the boil and let it bubble for a few minutes, add salt and pepper,

lower the heat and simmer covered for about 10 minutes. Meanwhile heat oven to Gas 5/375°F/190°C. Lay the fillets in an oiled shallow oven dish, add black olives, pour over the sauce, cover with a piece of buttered paper or foil and bake 10–15 minutes until the fish is just cooked.

FLUKE, *see* **FLOUNDER**

Flyingfish

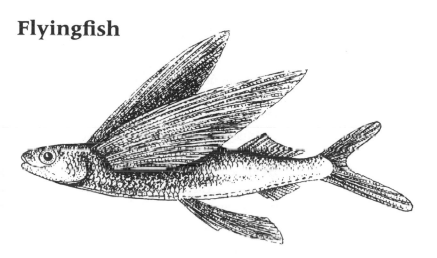

FLYINGFISH

Habitat	Worldwide in warm or tropical waters including Mediterranean and Atlantic.
Pros and Cons	Flyingfish are frozen before being imported so they may not be quite as wonderful as fresh but they are much prized in the Caribbean, especially in Barbados and Tobago and are certainly worth buying if you can.
Size	20–25 cm (8–10 ins).
Description	Iridescent blue-grey slender body with the pectoral fins shaped like wings, a deeply forked tail and silver belly.

How sold	Whole fish and sometimes frozen fillets.
Qty per person	Allow 225–275 g (8–10 oz) of whole, ungutted fish. Fillets: 150–175g (5–6 oz).
Ask fishmonger	To clean and if cooking whole fish to remove the gills; and to trim. If you want it boned, try and persuade him to do it for you.
Availability	Specialist and enterprising fishmongers, especially in shops patronized by Caribbeans or Filipinos.
Notes	Flyingfish feed on crustaceans, hence their delicate flavour. They skim in shoals across the water, their pectoral fins remaining static like the wings of a plane, so that they glide rather than fly. The French with no finesse have given their name for this lovely fish to a particularly loathsome missile – the Exocet.
Preparation	If frozen, allow to thaw slowly. Clean, scale and remove fins. Wash the fish and pat it dry with kitchen paper.
Cooking ideas	Grill, braise or bake; may be fried or poached. Use mackerel recipes.

Creole braised Flyingfish

4 flyingfish weighing about 275 g (10 oz) each before cleaning
2 lemons
salt, pepper
2 tablespoons olive or peanut oil
1 onion, chopped
1 green pepper, roughly chopped
3 or 4 tomatoes, chopped

Bone the fish (*see* page 315) or get the fishmonger to do it for you. Open them out and sprinkle with the juice of one lemon, salt and pepper. Leave for 30 minutes. Heat the oil in a wok or frying pan, add the chopped onion and cook for a few minutes until soft. Add roughly chopped green pepper and the chopped tomatoes. Stir well and squeeze over the juice of the second lemon. Let it simmer for 5 minutes, add the fish, salt and pepper. Cover and simmer gently for 10–15 minutes until the fish is cooked.

Caribbean fried Flyingfish
Allow 1 or 2 fish each depending on their size. Marinade them for 30 minutes with chopped fresh ginger, garlic, salt, pepper, thyme and the juice of a lemon. When you are ready to cook the fish, dip them in flour. Heat enough oil to cover the base of the pan by about 1 cm (½ in); when it is hot, fry the fish on each side for about 5 minutes. Serve dusted with chopped parsley and lemon wedges.

Poached Flyingfish
Marinade the fish for 30 minutes in the juice of a lemon, salt, pepper, chopped garlic, 2 or 3 chopped spring onions. Put fish and marinade into a shallow pan. Pour over a medium can of Italian tomatoes, crushed, and a glass of dry white wine or cider. Bring gently just to the boil, lower the heat and poach the fish very gently for 5–10 minutes.

FROGFISH, *see* **MONKFISH**

Garfish

GARFISH – *also known as:* NEEDLEFISH, OLD WIFE, GREEN-BONE, LONG NOSE, GARPIKE; *related to:* SAURY PIKE, which is similar in shape but has no green bones; cook in the same way

Habitat Mediterranean, Atlantic, Channel, North Sea and Baltic.

Pros and Cons Garfish are incredibly cheap because they have green bones which lots of people find offputting, thinking perhaps the colour means the fish is putrid. In fact the flavour is delicious, quite like trout, though drier.

Size 38–80 cm (15–32 ins).

Description Needle-shaped, elongated body with a brilliant, blue-green back and sides and belly of shimmering silver. It has long pointed jaws with small, sharp teeth.

How sold Whole fish.

Qty per person Allow 225–275 g (8–10 oz) of whole fish, ungutted.

Ask fishmonger To clean and remove the gills; and if you don't want to cook it whole with its green backbone, ask him to fillet it for you.

Availability Not widely available but you may find it from early summer through to August especially from fishmongers off the west coast. Enterprising fishmongers will stock it in London, especially in the East End where it is popular.

Notes It's strange that this fish with its seemingly magical, turquoise-green skeleton is not coveted as something rare and beautiful instead of being rather shunned. Carry it home when you see it and treat it as a prize. For those with a little less spirit of adventure, go for its relation, the saury pike; it has normal coloured bones.

Preparation If cooking whole fish, make sure it is clean and free of blood or blackness and the gills removed. Wash and dry with kitchen paper.

Cooking ideas Bake on a bed of spinach; or cut into steaks, marinade in chermoula, page 300; fry fillets or goujons *à la meunière*. Poach in a curry flavoured sauce, or bake with spinach or cut into chunks and make into kebabs with pieces of bacon, tomatoes and mushrooms, basting frequently and serving with lots of lemon wedges.

Garfish with courgettes in curry sauce – or use cod, coley, hake or haddock
350 g (12 oz) fillets of garfish cut in thin strips about 5 cm (2 ins) long
350 g (12 oz) courgettes
3 or 4 tablespoons olive or peanut oil
2 cloves of garlic, chopped
1 slice of fresh ginger root, finely chopped
a handful of fresh coriander, chopped, or use parsley
1 teaspoon chilli powder
1 teaspoon turmeric
1 teaspoon cumin seeds, ground
1 teaspoon coriander seeds, ground
small can of Italian tomatoes
juice of half a lemon
salt to taste
Cut the courgettes into thin slices, sprinkle them with salt and set them aside to sweat for half an hour. Drain them and pat dry.

Heat the oil in a wok or pan and add the garlic and ginger and let them turn golden, add the courgettes, fresh coriander or parsley, chilli powder, turmeric, cumin and coriander seeds. Toss over a medium heat, then add the can of tomatoes and lemon juice. Bring to the boil, lower the heat and cook until the courgette softens, about 15 minutes. Add the fish, mix well and cook very gently for 3 or 4 minutes until the fish is opaque. Taste and if necessary add a little salt. Serve with rice.

Garfish baked with spinach
garfish weighing about 900 g (2 lbs) in all
450 g (1 lb) spinach (or use frozen spinach)
50 g (2 oz) butter
1 onion, chopped
1 teaspoon flour
salt, pepper, nutmeg
1 lemon plus lemon wedges to garnish
Heat oven to Gas 6/400°F/200°C. Wash the spinach and put into a saucepan with a little salt. Cook over a medium flame until it softens and reduces, about 5 minutes. Drain very well. Melt the butter in a wok or frying pan and cook the chopped onion until it softens and turns gold but does not brown, add the flour followed by the

drained spinach, season with salt, pepper, nutmeg and the juice of half a lemon. Mix well. Take a long strip of foil, longer than the fish. Lay half the spinach mixture in it, lay the fish on top and cover with remaining spinach. Cut the other half of the lemon into slices and lay these along the fish. Wrap the foil loosely around the fish. Lay it on a baking dish and put into the oven, if necessary lifting the parcel at either end, so that it fits. Bake for 15–20 minutes. Serve the fish on a long platter, garnished with fresh lemon wedges.

GARPIKE, *see* **GARFISH**

GILT-HEADED BREAM, *see* **BREAMS, SEA**

GOGGLE-EYED JACK, *see* **CARANGIDS**

GOLDEN MULLET, *see* **RED MULLET**

GOOSE-NECKED BARNACLE – This extraordinary-looking shellfish with its goose-neck stalk topped with a sort of claw-like hoof is rare in this country but immensely popular in Spain and Portugal, where it is called *percebe* and *perceve* respectively. Here you might come across it in a restaurant or a fish market like Billingsgate. They taste totally of the sea.

GRAVLAX, *see* **SALMON, PICKLED**

Grayling

GRAYLING — *same family as:* SALMON and TROUT

Habitat	Favours clear, rapid streams and rivers with sandy or gravelly beds, such as the tributaries of the Severn and the chalky streams of Hampshire.
Pros and Cons	Good angling fish with firm, white flesh which makes delicious eating and rivals that of trout.
Size	30–60 cm (12–24 ins).
Description	Living fish is brilliantly coloured, becomes dull grey on being caught, with stripes of violet tones and silvery sides; young ones are silvery green, the sides spotted with blue. The dorsal fin is high and rounded, there is a small adipose fin near the tail; scales are large, head, mouth and teeth are small.
Qty per person	Allow 225–275 g (8–10 oz) of whole, ungutted fish.
Availability	You won't find grayling in the shops, it is an angling fish caught in summer through to winter.
Notes	Freshly caught grayling smell of thyme. Some say they are superior to trout, but this is hotly disputed by trout fishermen.
Preparation	Persuade your angler to clean, remove gills and scale the grayling as soon as it is caught; otherwise the scales are tough and difficult to remove. You'll find it easier if you dip the fish for a few seconds

into boiling water. Or cook it unscaled and remove skin before eating.

Cooking ideas   Follow recipes for trout. It's delicious poached and served cold with mayonnaise; or cook it *en papillote*, fry or grill it.

Grayling with sorrel

4 grayling
1 tablespoon butter plus 50 g (2 oz)
3 onions, finely chopped
salt, pepper
2 glasses dry white wine
450 g (1 lb) sorrel (or use spinach)
2 teaspoons flour
150 ml (5 fl oz) half or single cream
2 egg yolks
lemon wedges
Heat oven to Gas 6/400°F/200°C. Heat 1 tablespoon butter in a wok or saucepan and add the finely chopped onions. Let them soften but not brown. Spread them over the base of a shallow oven dish. Put the grayling on top, add salt, pepper and pour over the white wine. Put in the oven and as soon as the liquid begins to bubble – check after 5 minutes – cover the dish with a sheet of foil. Leave the oven door open and let the fish continue to cook whilst you prepare the sorrel. Heat the remaining butter in the wok or saucepan, add the cleaned sorrel (or spinach) and let it soften over a medium heat; stir in the flour and let it cook for two or three minutes. Add salt and pepper. Spread the mixture over a serving dish. Lay the fish on top. Cover with the foil to keep hot whilst you pour the cooking juices into the wok or saucepan, let them reduce over a high heat. Reduce heat, stir in half the cream and mix well, then add the rest of the cream, the two egg yolks and heat gently. Don't let it boil. It will thicken like a custard. Pour it over the fish and serve with lemon wedges.

GREAT TREVALLY, *see* **CARANGIDS**

GREATER WEEVER, *see* WEEVER

GREENBONE, *see* GARFISH

GREENLAND HALIBUT, *see* HALIBUT

GREEN WRASSE, *see* WRASSE

GREY GURNARD, *see* GURNARDS

Grey Mullet

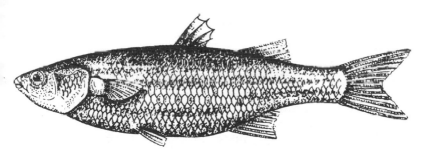

GREY MULLET – no relation to the red mullet. Several species, the most common in British waters is the THICK-LIPPED MULLET.

Habitat   Inshore waters, estuaries of Atlantic and Mediterranean. They are also being cultivated in some bays and shallow lagoons in Mediterranean area.

Pros and Cons   Worth snapping up. Inexpensive and much unappreciated with white and delicious flesh, though can be oily if caught in harbours or bays in populated areas – in which case complain.

Size 32–60 cm (13–24 ins).

Description A long, silvery blue-grey fish with large scales and shaded stripes of greenish greys tinged with pink, giving the effect of diamond-shaped chequers; no lateral line and a first dorsal fin of 4 spiky rays. The mouth of the thick-lipped mullet is very swollen.

How sold Whole fish, or steaks. Most are around ½–1 kilo (1–2 lbs) but can be more than double this size.

Qty per person Allow 225–275 g (8–10 oz) of whole, ungutted fish. Steaks: 175–200 g (6–7 oz).

Ask fishmonger To scale, clean and remove gills if you are cooking it whole but to give you the roe if any; or ask him to cut it into steaks, if you prefer.

Availability All year (best July to October), especially from eastern, southern and south-western coasts and from enterprising fishmongers in London and other areas.

Notes Grey mullet is a favourite on the Continent and in the Middle East but we tend to view it with suspicion. This is to our advantage because the fishmonger sells it at a very reasonable price. In Greece the female roe is used to make taramasalata, although in this country we use smoked cod's roe instead.

Preparation Grey mullet live on plants growing in the mud and have an enormously long gut. Check that the fishmonger has removed all the innards, and rub the cavity with salt to get rid of all blood and blackness, use the point of a knife to clear the stubborn bits. To get rid of any muddy flavour, soak the fish for 30 minutes in acidulated water (2 tablespoons vinegar, 1 teaspoon salt to every litre [1¾ pints] water).

Cooking ideas   Good baked and, because of the large cavity, lends itself to stuffing, add the chopped roe if any; steaks or small whole fish may be grilled; or steam like rabbitfish, page 186. Follow recipes for sea bream, bass or garfish. Or make couscous, page 69.

Grilled Grey Mullet

Score the fish two or three times on either side and fill the cavity with crushed anchovy fillets, chopped parsley and basil. Brush the fish with oil, squeeze over lemon juice and grill as on page 298. You can grill steaks in the same way, or marinade them in chermoula, see recipe below. Serve with a flavoured butter or a sauce like raïto.

Moroccan baked Grey Mullet

The marinade is based on the Moroccan chermoula. You can use it before baking or grilling grey mullet or for other fish such as sea bream, tuna, bonito, swordfish, garfish, snappers or groupers.

2 whole fish weighing about 900 g (2 lbs) in total, or 4 cut steaks
1 teaspoon cumin seeds, crushed
1 whole red chilli, chopped (or 1 teaspoon chilli powder)
2 teaspoons paprika
2 cloves of garlic, chopped
2 tablespoons fresh coriander (or use parsley)
salt
2 tablespoons olive oil
juice of 2 lemons
1 medium can Italian tomatoes
12 black olives

If using whole fish, score them two or three times on either side. Lay them (or the steaks) in a shallow glass or china dish and add the cumin, chilli, paprika, garlic and coriander or parsley rubbing them into the fish. Add salt, olive oil and the juice of 1 lemon. Marinade for about 1 hour. Heat the oven to Gas 6/400°F/200°C. Crush the canned tomatoes, pour them over the fish, add the juice from the second lemon and the black olives. Cover with a piece of buttered paper or foil and bake 25–30 minutes. Test that the fish is done by inserting a skewer into the thickest part, the flesh should lift easily from the bone. If not give it an extra few minutes.

Grey Mullet stuffed and baked in foil
4 small fish or 1 large fish weighing about 1–1½ kilos (2–3 lbs)
1 clove of garlic, cut in slivers
1 onion, finely chopped
50 g (2 oz) unsmoked bacon
chopped roes of the mullet, if any
6 tablespoons breadcrumbs
2 teaspoons capers
50 g (2 oz) mushrooms, chopped
6 black olives, stoned and chopped
1 teaspoon fennel seeds, crushed
1 tablespoon parsley, chopped
2 or 3 tablespoons yoghurt or a beaten egg
olive oil and juice of 1 lemon
Heat oven to Gas 6/400°F/200°C. Score the fish on the outside and insert slivers of garlic into each. Make a stuffing by frying a finely chopped onion and the chopped bacon; off the heat add the chopped roes (if any), breadcrumbs, capers, chopped mushrooms, chopped stoned black olives, fennel seeds and chopped parsley; bind the mixture with 2 or 3 tablespoons yoghurt or beaten egg. Lay the fish on sufficient foil to make a parcel, fill the cavity with the stuffing, spreading any remainder on top. Sprinkle with olive oil and lemon juice. Wrap loosely and bake 20 minutes for small fish, 30–40 minutes for a large fish.

Grey Mullet with courgettes. Or bake it very simply by scoring and seasoning it with salt, pepper and lemon juice. Lay it in a buttered dish (or foil) surround with sliced courgettes. Add parsley, snipped chives, chervil and tarragon. Dot with butter. Cover loosely with buttered paper or foil (or if using foil, wrap it up to make a loose parcel). Bake Gas 6/400°F/200°C for 30–40 minutes depending on size.

GROS YEUX, *see* **BREAMS, SEA**

Groupers

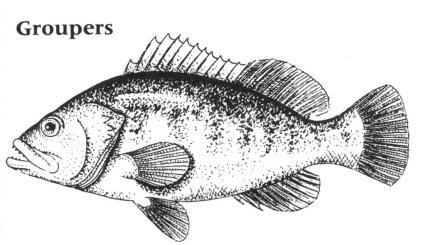

GROUPERS — *also known as:* ROCK CODS; *related distantly to:* BASS. Several species are sold under their Creole names of: VIELLE PLATTE, VIELLE ROUGE, VIELLE MACONDE and CROISSANT or CORAL TROUT.

Habitat   Warm waters of the Mediterranean, Indian Ocean and Caribbean.

Pros and Cons   Groupers are delicious with white, soft flesh similar to bass. Not cheap because they are imported but worth searching out.

Size   Vary from around 25–100 cm (10–39 ins).

Description   The bodies are compressed, oval with strong tails, that of the croissant is crescent-shaped. They have large mouths, serrated scales, spiny gill covers and the first rays of the long dorsal fin are spiny. Colours vary from warm browns, to pale greys, yellowish reds, and orange-red; some are spotted, others barred.

How sold   Whole fish or in steaks both fresh and frozen.

Qty per person   Allow 225–275 g (8–10 oz) of whole, ungutted fish. Steaks: 175–200 g (6–7 oz).

Ask fishmonger	If buying whole fish, to scale, clean, remove gills and the spines in gill covers; or to cut into steaks or fillets.
Availability	Specialist and enterprising fishmongers; look for them in shops and markets frequented by Chinese, West Indians, Greeks and Italians.
Notes	Groupers are popular all over the Mediterranean and you will find them mentioned in cookery books of that region. Of those imported from the Seychelles VIELLE MACONDE is the smallest; VIELLE ROUGE and the CROISSANT or CORAL TROUT are brilliant coral red; whilst the VIELLE PLATTE is the largest and like the giant flat fish halibut and turbot is probably of more interest to the restaurant trade.
Preparation	Wash the cleaned and trimmed fish and dry with kitchen paper, making sure the cavity is clear of blood and blackness. Rub with salt if necessary or use the point of a knife.
Cooking ideas	Can be poached and served hot or cold. Or steam like rabbitfish on page 186. Or bake, stuffed or not; or braise in a sauce; marinade and grill or make steaks into kebabs. Follow recipes for sea bass, sea breams, grey mullet or emperors. Or make couscous, see page 69.

Grouper steaks with paprika and tomato
4 steaks weighing about 175–200 g (6–7 oz) each
salt, pepper
2 tablespoons paprika
juice of 1 lemon
2 tablespoons olive oil
3 onions, finely sliced
1 clove garlic, chopped
1 tablespoon tomato purée
salt, pepper
½ teaspoon oregano
1 medium can Italian tomatoes

4 tablespoons thick yoghurt or sour cream
lemon wedges
Marinade the fish in salt, pepper, 1 tablespoon paprika and the juice
of the lemon. Meanwhile make a sauce by heating the olive oil in a
wok or saucepan, add the sliced onion and let it soften over a low
heat, covered. It will take about 20 minutes. Add garlic, tomato
purée, remaining tablespoon of paprika, salt, pepper, oregano and
the can of tomatoes. Bring to the boil, mix well, lower the heat and
cook uncovered for 15 minutes. Add the fish to the pan, cover and
let it poach very gently for 5–10 minutes. Top with the yoghurt or
sour cream and serve with lemon wedges.

Grilled Grouper steaks
Marinade the steaks for an hour in oil, chopped garlic, rosemary,
juice of a lemon, salt and pepper; or in a chermoula or harissa
marinade (*see* page 300). Grill as on page 298, basting frequently.
Serve with a butter and lemon sauce, or *pistou*.

Grouper kebabs
Cut fish into chunks and marinade for 30 minutes in lime or lemon
juice, sprinkled with thyme and rosemary. Brush all over with olive
or peanut oil and thread on to skewers, alternating with pieces of
bacon, tomato, mushrooms and green pepper. Cook as on page 299,
basting frequently.

Mérou à la sauge – Grouper steaks fried with sage
Heat 4 tablespoons olive oil in a frying pan, add 3 whole cloves of
garlic and 2 or 3 sprigs of sage (or use rosemary if you prefer). Toss
them for one or two minutes, add the steaks and fry quickly on both
sides. Reduce the heat and cook for a further 5 minutes on each
side. Sprinkle with lemon juice and serve.

Grouper baked with herbs and spices
Heat oven to Gas Mark 6/400°F/200°C. Lay the fish on a piece of foil
large enough to make a parcel. Score it two or three times on either
side. Press crushed cumin and coriander seeds and slivers of garlic
into the slits and put some into the cavity with a sprig of rosemary
and parsley and 1 whole red chilli. Lay slices of lemon all along the
length of the fish. Season with salt and pepper, sprinkle with olive
or peanut oil. Make a parcel and bake 30 minutes.

Gudgeon

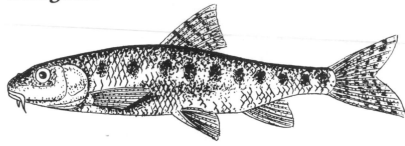

GUDGEON – *same family as:* BARBEL, BREAM, CARP, ROACH and TENCH

Habitat	Favours clean, gravelly beds of rivers, streams and lakes in UK and Continent.
Pros and Cons	A small angling fish with excellent flavour.
Size	Usually around 12 cm (5 ins).
Description	Long, spindly body coloured greenish brown or grey with yellow sides and purple or blue blotches. It has large scales, a crescent-shaped mouth with two barbels and a forked tail.
Qty per person	3 or 4 fish.
Availability	Not in shops. Caught all over British Isles except Scotland, Lake District, Cornwall and parts of Wales.
Preparation	Trim, scale and gut. Wash and rub inside and out with salt and vinegar. If caught in water with a muddy bottom, soak for half an hour in acidulated water (2 tablespoons vinegar, 1 teaspoon salt to 1 litre [1¾ pints] water). Dry well.
Cooking ideas	Fry *à la meunière* or grill.

Grilled Gudgeon
Prepare the fish, score two or three times on either side. Press herbs

such as parsley, chopped chives, tarragon into the cavities. Sprinkle over lemon juice, season with salt and pepper and leave to marinade for 30 minutes before grilling as on page 298, basting with plenty of oil mixed with lemon juice.

GUEUELE LONGUE, *see* **EMPERORS**

GULUE, *see* **KINGFISH**

Gurnards

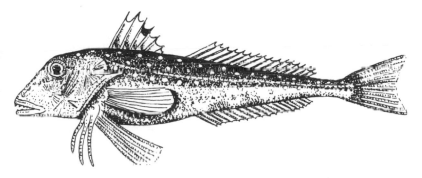

GURNARDS – three species sold: GREY GURNARD, YELLOW or TUB GURNARD and RED GURNARD

Habitat E Atlantic and Mediterranean.

Pros and Cons They have firm, tasty flesh, though a bit dry and some are rather bony; but are cheap and good value and are excellent in soups.

Size 22–40 cm (9–16 ins) depending on species.

Description All have large, armour-plated heads with long sloping foreheads; their tapering bodies are covered with small reinforced scales. Front dorsal fin is spiny and there are three separate rays attached to the pectoral fin.

GREY GURNARDS are the most common. They have a spiny gill cover and are greyish brown or red, speckled white, with a white belly, sometimes with a black smudge on dorsal fin.

YELLOW or TUB GURNARDS are yellow-brown or red, with brown or green blotches, white or pink belly.

RED GURNARDS make the best eating, they are ruby red with white belly.

How sold   Whole fish, or cut in pieces.

Qty per person   Allow 275–350 g (10–12 oz) whole, ungutted fish.

Ask fishmonger   To scale, clean and trim – and to cut off the spine attached to the grey gurnard's gill cover; or to fillet.

Availability   From the more enterprising fishmongers usually in spring through to autumn.

Notes   Some fishmongers try to pass gurnards off as red mullet, which are finer and more expensive. You can easily tell the difference by the armour-plated head of the gurnard and the lack of barbels on the chin.

Preparation   If the fishmonger hasn't done so, scale and trim the fish, taking great care not to prick yourself on the spiny fins and gill covers. Clean and wash the cavity thoroughly. Dry with kitchen paper.

Cooking ideas   Can be baked or poached whole or filleted. If grilling, try wrapping pieces of bacon round each fish and baste them frequently. Head and trimmings and small whole fish are excellent for fish stock or soup or part of a bouillabaisse.

Gurnards baked with sesame seeds
Whole gurnards weighing about 1 kilo (2 lbs) or use fillets
3 tablespoons olive oil
2 onions, chopped
1 teaspoon turmeric

1 red chilli, chopped (or 1 teaspoon chilli powder)
1 clove garlic, chopped
1 tablespoon tomato purée
1 teaspoon soya sauce
1 medium can Italian tomatoes
juice of 1 lemon
handful of breadcrumbs
1 tablespoon sesame seeds
oil

Heat oven to Gas 6/400°F/200°C. Heat the oil in a wok or frying pan and add the chopped onion, cook for a few minutes until it is soft. Stir in the turmeric. Add the chopped chilli, garlic, tomato purée, soya sauce and the tomatoes. Cook two or three minutes and add the lemon juice. If using whole fish, score it two or three times on either side and lay it (or the fillets) in a shallow oven dish, pour over the sauce. Sprinkle over the breadcrumbs, sesame seeds and moisten with oil. Bake 25–30 minutes (15–20 minutes if using fillets).

GWYNIAD, *see* POWAN

Haddock

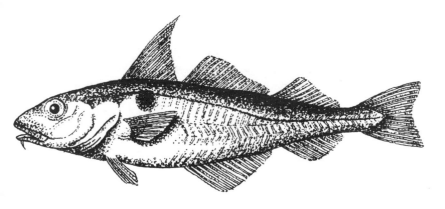

HADDOCK — *same family as:* COD, COLEY, HAKE, LING, POLLACK and WHITING

Haddock

Habitat	N Atlantic.
Pros and Cons	Has sweet, firm flesh which should be gleaming and tinged lightly pink; owing to its mass popularity tends to be somewhat expensive.
Size	Usually around 40–60 cm (16–24 ins).
Description	A thickset, long grey fish tinged with brown, green or purple; silvery sides and belly. Like the John Dory it bears the thumbprint of St Peter behind the head, and is nicknamed *faux Saint-Pierre* in northern France. It has a short barbel on its chin and no teeth.
How sold	Usually in fillets or steaks. Occasionally small, whole fish on sale weighing about 225 g (8 oz); also the ROES are sometimes on sale and SMOKED HADDOCK, page 112, is absolutely delicious.
Qty per person	Fillets: 150–175 g (5–6 oz). Steaks: 175–200 g (6–7 oz). Whole, ungutted fish: allow 225–275 g (8–10 oz).
Ask fishmonger	For small fillets which are sweeter and finer than large; or, if buying whole fish, to clean and trim.
Availability	All year, best November to February.
Notes	Haddock are mostly caught in deep water and either frozen immediately or stored on ice.
Preparation	Filleted pieces or steaks just need to be washed and dried with kitchen paper. Whole fish must be cleaned and trimmed unless the fishmonger has already done so. Make sure the cavity is clear of blood and any blackness, wash and dry.
Cooking ideas	Fillets can be baked or braised or simply poached in milk with butter. Steaks grilled (*see* page 298) or braised. Whole small fish can be baked or grilled. Cook like garfish in curry sauce, page 95; use in soups or for fish pies. Recipes for cod, hake, coley, etc. are suitable.

Baked Haddock fillets with anchovies and capers
4 fillets of haddock or steaks
salt, pepper
2 anchovy fillets, chopped
1 tablespoon capers
1 clove garlic, chopped
2 or 3 tablespoons chopped parsley
3 or 4 tablespoons fresh breadcrumbs
olive oil
lemon wedges
Heat oven to Gas 6/400°F/200°C. Put fillets in an oiled or buttered oven dish. Season with salt and pepper. Add 2 chopped anchovy fillets, 1 tablespoon capers, the chopped garlic and half the chopped parsley, top with breadcrumbs. Sprinkle liberally with olive oil. Bake 15 minutes. Serve with lemon wedges and sprinkled with remaining parsley.

Haddock with mustard
675 g (1½ lbs) haddock fillets or steaks
25 g (1 oz) butter
1 tablespoon peanut oil
4 tablespoons dry vermouth or lemon juice
salt, pepper
150 ml (5 fl oz) half or single cream
1 tablespoon Dijon mustard
few drops Worcester sauce
handful of chopped parsley
lemon wedges
Heat the butter or oil in a frying pan and cook the fish two or three minutes on either side. Add vermouth or lemon juice, salt and pepper and poach the fish gently until cooked, 5–8 minutes. Carefully lift the fish on to a hot serving dish. Pour the cream into the pan, add mustard and Worcester sauce and mix well without letting it boil. Pour over the fish. Sprinkle with parsley and serve with lemon wedges.

Haddock with mushrooms au gratin
675 g (1½ lbs) haddock fillets
thyme, bayleaf
small onion stuck with two cloves

milk to cover
50 g (2 oz) butter
150 g (6 oz) mushrooms, chopped
2 heaped tablespoons flour
salt, pepper, nutmeg
6 tablespoons grated cheese
1 teaspoon Dijon or herb-flavoured mustard
Put haddock fillets into a saucepan, add thyme, bayleaf, the onion
stuck with cloves and enough milk just to cover. Bring slowly to the
boil; as soon as it bubbles, cover the pan and set on one side. Heat
the grill. Make a sauce by melting the butter in a saucepan, add the
chopped mushrooms and cook over a medium heat until they
soften, stir in the flour. Mix and cook for a couple of minutes,
stirring constantly. Measure 300 ml (½ pint) of the cooking liquid
and gradually stir it into the mushroom mixture and cook over a
medium flame until the sauce bubbles and thickens. Lower the heat,
add salt, pepper, a pinch of nutmeg, 4 tablespoons grated cheese and
the mustard. Stir until the cheese melts. Put the fish in a shallow
heat-proof dish, pour over the sauce, top with remaining cheese and
put under the hot grill to brown.

Haddock roe baked
This is based on a Caribbean recipe for dolphinfish roe. Heat oven to
Gas 4/350°F/180°C. Mix 50 g (2 oz) butter with chopped thyme,
parsley and marjoram. Cut a piece of foil large enough to envelop
the roe. Put half the butter in the middle, then the roe. Add salt,
pepper and a sprinkling of lemon juice and the remaining butter.
Seal the parcel. Bake 20 minutes. Serve sliced with brown bread and
butter.

Haddock, Smoked

HADDOCK is smoked whole or in fillets. Whole fish
are sold as FINNAN HADDOCK or ARBROATH SMOKIES. If
you know a fishmonger who smokes his own, buy
from him, they will be far superior to those you
see laid out on supermarket counters.

FINNAN HADDOCK

This method of smoking originated in the village of Findon in Scotland but is now practised all over Britain. The fish are soaked in brine and cold smoked, which means they are still raw but cured.

Description   Heads are removed and they are split open leaving the backbone and tail intact. They should be palest gold; the darker the colour, the drier and saltier they will be.

Qty per person   Allow 175–225 g (6–8 oz) – 1 fish is often sufficient for two.

SMOKED HADDOCK FILLETS

Description   Small whole fish are split open and the backbone removed. They should be pale yellow. Avoid any that are vivid or brilliant yellow, chances are they will have been simply salted, coloured with tartrazine and finally dipped in a solution which gives them a smoky flavour. They will be tough, stringy, salty and not worth eating.

Qty per person   Fillets: 150–175 g (5–6 oz).

Cooking ideas   Poach in milk topped if you fancy with a poached egg. Or grill and cook au gratin; make a Kedgeree or add a little to an omelette. Makes good fish pie or fish cakes. Or serve in scallop shells or small pots as a starter to a dinner party. Or slice it very finely and serve it raw with buttered toast, cayenne pepper and plenty of lemon wedges.

Finnan Haddock or fillets poached in milk

Put fish into a shallow lidded pan. Add thyme, bayleaf, parsley and 6–8 whole peppercorns. Just cover with a mixture of half milk and water. Bring to the boil gently. When it bubbles, leave for 1 minute, then take off the stove. Leave covered for 3 or 4 minutes. Serve topped with a dab of butter and lemon wedges.

This method has the merit of removing some of the salt from the fish. You could offer the cooking liquid to the cat but he'll probably develop a terrible thirst.

Grilled Finnan Haddock or fillets
Pre-heat the grill and pan, brush the rack with a little oil. In a saucepan melt 50 g (2 oz) butter without letting it boil. Lay the fish on the rack and brush generously with the melted butter. Grill the fish 3–4 minutes each side, basting frequently. When the fish is cooked, to the remaining butter in the pan add some freshly milled pepper, 1 tablespoon chopped parsley and the juice of half a lemon. Pour over the fish.

Smoked Haddock au gratin
Heat oven to Gas 4/350°F/180°C. Remove the skin and bone from 450 g (1 lb) smoked haddock and flake it. Peel 3 medium potatoes and slice them finely. Put layers of fish and potato in a shallow oven dish, seasoning each layer with freshly milled pepper and dill. Beat 2 eggs into 450 ml (¾ pint) milk and pour over the fish. Dot with butter and bake for 1 hour. If you like you can sprinkle chopped onion and breadcrumbs between each layer.

Smoked Haddock in scallop shells
Poach 225 g (8 oz) haddock in milk as page 113. Heat the grill Meanwhile heat 50 g (2 oz) butter in a saucepan and cook a chopped onion until it is soft. Add 100 g (4 oz) chopped mushrooms and let them sweat and soften. Stir in 50 g (2 oz) flour. Let it cook a couple of minutes, stirring all the time and gradually add enough milk to make a thick sauce – scant 300 ml (½ pint) – add 1 or 2 tablespoons lemon juice, dry white wine or cider. Mix in 2 tablespoons grated cheese and let it melt over a very low heat while you flake the poached fish. Add this to the pan, pile the mixture into 4 scallop shells or individual dishes. Top with grated cheese and put under the grill for a couple of minutes to brown. Or make ahead of time and heat in a hot oven for 10 minutes – Gas 6/400°F/200°C.

Kedgeree is a deceptively simple dish, which actually involves four cooking processes with the accompanying battery of pots and pans. It stems from the days of the Raj and is an anglicized version of the Indian *kicheri*; the amount of work involved was obviously only of interest to the servants. Plan to make it when you happen already to have some leftover rice.

450 g (1 lb) smoked haddock fillet
75 g (3 oz) butter
1 onion, chopped
2 hard-boiled eggs
2 cups cooked rice
salt, pepper
2 beaten eggs
chopped parsley

Put the fish in a pan, cover it with boiling water, put on a lid and leave to cook and cool off the heat.

Heat the butter in a wok or large saucepan and cook the chopped onion until soft. Drain and flake the fish, removing all skin and any bones. Chop the hard-boiled eggs. Mix the fish, rice and eggs into the pan containing the butter and onion and stir over a medium heat until hot through. Season with freshly milled pepper and a little salt. Pour in the beaten eggs and stir until cooked. Garnish with chopped parsley.

ARBROATH SMOKIES

Originated in Scotland but you should be able to find them at enterprising fishmongers elsewhere. They are tied in pairs and hot smoked, so the flesh is cooked but as they contain no preservatives, they don't keep long and you should buy them when you intend to eat them.

Description   Small headless whole fish of palest gold weighing no more than 250 g (8 oz). The flesh is succulent and white.

Qty per person   1 fish.

Cooking ideas   Nice smeared with butter and heated under the grill; or baked with cheese and tomatoes. Or eat them just as they are with lemon juice and brown bread and butter.

Arbroath Smokies baked with tomatoes and cheese

2 pairs Arbroath Smokies, skinned, boned and flaked
3 or 4 tomatoes, sliced
pepper

¼ teaspoon dried oregano
4 tablespoons curd cheese
8 fl oz (½ pint) milk
50 g (2 oz) Cheddar or Cheshire cheese, grated
Heat oven to Gas 4/350°F/180°C. Butter an oven-proof dish. Put in the flaked fish, cover with sliced tomatoes. Season with pepper and oregano. Mix the curd cheese with the milk and pour over the fish, sprinkle with grated cheese. Bake 20 minutes, or until the mixture is set and the top golden brown.

Hake

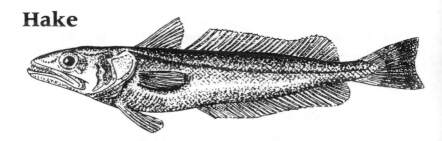

HAKE — *same family as:* COD, COLEY, HADDOCK, LING, POLLACK and WHITING

Habitat	N Atlantic and Mediterranean, also S America and southern Africa.
Pros and Cons	Soft, white flesh, with few bones and more delicate than cod or haddock.
Size	Usually around 30–45 cm (12–18 ins).
Description	Long, slim body, coloured slate grey on back with paler sides and glistening silver belly. Very prominent teeth, no barbel on chin.
How sold	Whole or in steaks or fillets.
Qty per person	Allow 225–275 g (8–10 oz) whole, ungutted fish. Steaks: 175–200 g (6–7 oz). Fillets: 150–175 g (5–6 oz).
Ask fishmonger	To clean and trim whole fish and remove the gills; or ask for steaks from the middle or upper part,

they will be moister and less bony than the tail end.

Availability Most likely during summer especially in the North-West, though much of the catch is exported to Spain and Italy and many are snapped up by the fried fish trade.

Notes Hake is a voracious and cannabalistic predator with hinged teeth which open to allow its prey entry, then snap shut to form a trap. Hake are popular in Portugal, Spain and Italy.

Preparation Wash and dry with kitchen paper. If buying whole fish, make sure the cavity is clean and free of blood.

Cooking ideas Poach, bake, fry or grill. Complement it with interesting flavours such as sorrel and spinach, leeks or mushrooms. Cook with curry sauce like garfish, page 95. Serve fried hake with a tartto sauce. Steam like rabbitfish, page 186. Use recipes for related fish, such as cod, haddock or coley. Or make couscous (*see* page 69).

Baked Hake with leeks

1 fish weighing around 900 g (2 lbs); or 4 steaks or fillets between 700 and 800 g (1½–1¾ lbs)
450 g (1 lb) leeks
50 g (2 oz) butter
1 small carton half or single cream
salt, pepper, nutmeg
4 rashers of bacon
1 lemon, sliced thinly
juice of 1 lemon
Heat oven to Gas 4/350°F/180°C. Wash the leeks well and slice them. Heat the butter in wok or frying pan and cook the leeks over a medium heat until they are soft, 5–10 minutes. Take off the heat and stir in the half or single cream, add salt, pepper and nutmeg. Butter an oven-proof dish. In the dish make a bed using half the leek mixture, lay the fish on top. If using whole fish, score it two or three times on each side and fill the cavities with the rashers of

bacon cut into pieces. Otherwise, lay the bacon slices on top of the steaks or fillets. Put slices of lemon along the top of the fish and cover with remaining leeks. Put a piece of foil over the dish and bake 20–30 minutes. Take out of the oven and squeeze over the lemon juice.

Variations: You could use spinach or sorrel instead of the leeks, and use slivers of anchovy instead of the bacon. Sorrel has a strong, quite bitter flavour, so use oranges in place of the lemons.

Grilled Hake steaks
Marinade the steaks for 30 minutes in olive oil, thyme, rosemary, lemon juice and pepper. Or use the juice of a bitter (Seville) orange instead of lemon juice. Grill as on page 298 and eat with a sauce *rémoulade* or with halved tomatoes baked in the oven with herbs and garlic.

Merlan en raïto
Make a raïto sauce (*see* page 292). Flour fillets or steaks of hake. Heat 2 or 3 tablespoons of olive oil in a wok or frying pan and fry on a high heat for two or three minutes on either side. Remove the hake from the pan, wipe it out with kitchen paper, return the fish, pour over the sauce and simmer gently, covered for 8–10 minutes, add capers and/or olives.

Halibut

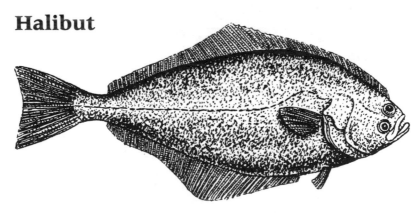

HALIBUT – *same family as:* DAB, FLOUNDER, LEMON SOLE, PLAICE and WITCH

Habitat	N Atlantic.
Pros and Cons	Highly esteemed and very tasty with firm if rather dry flesh. It is in danger of being over-fished and is therefore expensive.
Size	Usually up to 1 metre (39 ins) but can grow to more than double this size.
Description	Right facing, flat fish with a greenish or dark brown compressed oval body, large mouth, blind side is white.
How sold	Usually in steaks or fillets. GREENLAND HALIBUT or LITTLE HALIBUT are inferior in flavour but cheaper. CHICKEN HALIBUT are small halibut weighing up to 2½ kilos (5 lbs). Halibut is also sold SMOKED – treat like smoked salmon.
Qty per person	Steaks: 175–200 g (6–7 oz), Fillets: 150–175 g (5–6 oz).
Ask fishmonger	To remove dark skin from fillets and not to give you a cut from the tail which will be very dry.
Availability	All year but best in autumn and winter months. Most are snapped up by the restaurant trade, so it's fairly rare on the slab; frozen Greenland halibut is available all year.
Notes	Halibut are caught in northern waters by line and not by trawler so the catch is limited. A side product is the oil from their liver which is rich in vitamin D.
Preparation	Wash and dry. If you want to remove the skin before cooking, you'll find it easier if you pour boiling water over it.
Cooking ideas	Poach and eat hot with hollandaise or béarnaise sauce or eat cold with a green sauce (page 286) or marinade and grill basting frequently. Can be fried or baked but be generous with butter or oil. Recipes for brill, sole, turbot or cod are suitable.

Grilled Halibut steaks
4 steaks
1 clove garlic, chopped
1 teaspoon each of chilli powder, crushed cumin seeds, crushed
    coriander seeds
juice of 1 lemon
4 tablespoons olive oil
Lay the fish in a shallow china or glass dish, cover with the
marinade ingredients, and leave for 1 hour, turning once. Grill as on
page 298, basting frequently with the marinade.

Baked Halibut steaks
Heat oven to Gas 6/400°F/200°C. Oil a shallow oven dish and lay
the steaks in it. Add salt, pepper, a chopped clove of garlic, the juice
of a lemon, 1 tablespoon capers and 3 or 4 anchovy fillets. Top
with a mixture of chopped parsley and breadcrumbs. Sprinkle
liberally with olive or peanut oil. Bake 15 minutes.

HARD CLAM, *see* **CLAMS**

HEMRIMMAD LAX, *see* **SALMON, PICKLED**

Herring

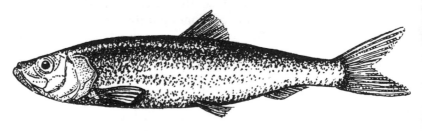

HERRING — *related to:* ANCHOVY, SARDINE (PILCHARD),
SPRAT

Habitat	Atlantic.
Pros and Cons	A most nutritious and delicious fish. Don't be put off by its reputation of being bony, the taste more than makes up for a little inconvenience. Like all oily fish it deteriorates rapidly so must be very fresh, avoid any that look dull and pallid with sunken eyes and a general limpness.
Size	Usually around 20–35 cm (8–14 ins).
Description	A slender, smooth body coloured dark green or blue, with silvery sides and belly. It has a small head with protruding jaw and no lateral line.
How sold	Whole fish, sometimes filleted. The soft, male roes are often sold separately. Herrings are also SMOKED (*see* page 124).
Qty per person	Usually 1 fish weighing about 225–275 g (8–10 oz) whole, ungutted. Filleted, allow 100–150 g (4–5 oz).
Ask fishmonger	To gut but leave in the roe which is a bonus whether hard or soft. If you want it boned or filleted, and he isn't busy, he might be cajoled into doing the job for you.
Availability	Widely available though scarce in spring.
Notes	Herrings used to be very cheap so were looked down upon as food for the impoverished; they were so overfished that for some years a ban was placed on catching them. Now the ban is lifted, herrings are recognized as fine fish, though they are no longer quite as cheap.
Preparation	Must be cleaned and washed, make sure you remove any blood remaining inside, use the point of a knife or rub the interior with salt. Dry well. The problem with herring has always been their multitude of thread-like bones. They are mostly attached to the backbone which can easily be removed at table or, if you prefer, before cooking (*see* page 315).

Cooking ideas Because they are an oily fish they are best grilled or baked although there is a traditional recipe where they are rolled in oatmeal and fried. Also good soused and eaten cold.

Grilled Herrings

If grilling whole fish try scoring them two or three times on either side and inserting slivers of garlic into the slits. Or spread whole fish or fillets with mustard either plain or flavoured with herbs or spices; or a thin spread of creamed horseradish. Grill as on page 298. Because this is an oily fish you only need a miserly amount of oil or melted butter.

Fried Herrings in oatmeal

Spread the whole fish or fillets with a little mustard and roll in coarse oatmeal (you can use breadcrumbs instead) pressing it well into the fish with your fingers. Fry as on page 295, using very little oil or perhaps some bacon fat.

Baked Herrings

Heat the oven to Gas 5/375°F/190°C.
Whole fish can be baked as they are or boned (*see* page 315) and filled with a simple stuffing. This can be the chopped roe mixed with a little chopped apple or mushrooms and a spoonful of breadcrumbs, seasoned with pepper, lemon juice and bound perhaps with a little mustard, yoghurt or beaten egg. Lay the fish on squares of foil, wrap loosely and bake for 20 minutes.
Fillets can be spread with the same stuffing mixture as above, rolled up and secured with a toothpick. Cook them in foil or in an oven dish, sprinkled with oil and baste them every 5 minutes.

Soft Herring roes on toast

Allow about 100 g (4 oz) per serving. Melt a little butter in a saucepan, stir in a teaspoon of mustard and gently cook the roes, about 4 minutes. Eat on buttered toast sprinkled with lemon juice, chopped parsley and freshly milled black pepper.

Hard Herring roes are good poached in milk, then mashed and mixed with lemon juice, cayenne pepper, a tablespoon of curd cheese and a little soya sauce. Eat on buttered toast.

There are many variations on pickling herrings in a spicy marinade either by cooking in the oven or soaking for several days. Below are three versions. Each requires that you fillet 4–6 herrings (*see* page 312) or if you have a kind fishmonger ask him to do the job for you.

Soused Herrings

Season the fillets with salt and pepper and roll them up. Put them into an oven dish in which they just fit in one layer. Add 1 tablespoon pickling spice, 1 or 2 dry chillies, 2 bayleaves and 6 tablespoons each of water and vinegar. Cover the dish and put into a cool oven Gas 1/275°F/140°C and cook 1½ hours. Leave to get cold.

Herrings marinaded in mustard

Into a saucepan put ½ litre (¾ pint) cider vinegar, 1 tablespoon pickling spice, a chopped onion, bayleaf, 1 tablespoon dark brown sugar. Bring to the boil and when it is cool, stir in 4 tablespoons mustard. Cut the fillets into pieces of about 5 cm (2 ins) and put them in a glass or china dish. Pour the cool marinade over the fish, cover and put in the fridge for 2 to 3 days. Drain and eat with potato salad.

Rollmops are made with salted herrings, you can simulate these by a preliminary pre-soaking of the herring fillets in ½ litre of water to which you add 50 g (2 oz) salt. Leave them for 3 hours. Drain them. Measure ½ litre (¾ pint) white wine vinegar into a saucepan and dip each fillet into it. Put a tablespoon of chopped onion on to each fillet, roll them up and secure with a toothpick. Pack these rolls in to jars, add to each a torn bayleaf and 2 or 3 chopped gherkins. Add 1 tablespoon pickling spices to the vinegar, bring it to the boil. Let it get cold and pour over the herrings. Store for two days before eating. They will keep in the jars for about 3 weeks.

Herrings, Smoked

HERRINGS, SMOKED The smoking of herrings is a tradition going back centuries. There are basically four different methods and you will find them sold as BLOATERS, BUCKLING, KIPPERS or RED HERRINGS. It can all seem a bit confusing when you see them shining on the slab, their colours looking like a treasure trove of newly minted coins. Lucky for you, if you know a fishmonger who smokes his own and one who really does know the difference between a bloater and a buckling, a kipper and a red herring.

BLOATER

Description   A bloater is a whole ungutted fish, complete with head. It is soaked in brine before being cold smoked, which means it is still raw so should be eaten within a day or two. It has a distinctive, gamey flavour and as its name suggests is somewhat swollen in appearance. It is coloured a gilded silver with a warm, smoky haze.

Availability   Great Yarmouth is the centre of the trade so it is in East Anglia where you will find bloaters at their best but lots of enterprising fishmongers elsewhere stock them.

Preparation   They can be simply split open or filleted if you prefer. To do this, carefully remove outer skin (you'll find this easier to do if you put it in a shallow bowl, pour over boiling water and leave it for a minute); split it down the whole length of the front from head to tail. Open it a little and stand the cut sides on a board. Press gently along the backbone to flatten the fish and at the same time ease away the bone. Turn it over, snip the bone near the tail and with a knife-point carefully ease away the backbone and the myriad of little bones with it.

Cooking ideas   Bloaters are nice split open, spread with butter and grilled for 2 or 3 minutes on either side; or grill whole fish making two or three gashes on either side and brushing with oil or butter. Fillets are lovely eaten raw. Slice the flesh and mix with sour cream or yoghurt mixed with snipped chives. Or make your own genuine bloater paste which is delicious on toast and even more so topped with scrambled eggs.

Bloater paste

Put the bloater into a bowl and pour over sufficient boiling water to cover. Leave for 5–10 minutes, then drain, skin and remove bones. Mash it with an equal weight of unsalted butter. Add the juice of half a lemon, a dash of cayenne pepper and put into a small bowl, top with a slice of lemon or a sprig of parsley. You can use half butter and half curd cheese if you prefer, but this version will keep for a shorter time, not really a problem as there is rarely any left over for a second meal. You can follow this recipe using other smoked fish such as trout, mackerel and salmon omitting the preliminary cooking. Kippers can also be used, in which case cook them first in a jug (*see* page 127).

BUCKLING

Description   A buckling is gutted and headless. It is hot smoked, which means it is cooked, but eat within a day or two as it doesn't keep very long. It should be firm and glistening like burnished copper.

Cooking ideas   Buckling, like smoked trout or mackerel, can be eaten cold just as they are with horseradish sauce or a squeeze of lemon juice. Or warm them under the grill for two or three minutes. They are nice with spinach, new potatoes or scrambled eggs. They also make a good pâté: follow the recipe for bloater paste omitting the preliminary cooking.

KIPPERS and RED HERRINGS

The heavily salted red herring was the forerunner

of all other smoked herrings. Nowadays they are hard to find but you may see them on sale in some West Indian shops. To remove the salt, either soak them for several hours changing the water three or four times, or you can put them into boiling water and stand them, off the heat, for 5 minutes. Try slicing very thinly and eating as an appetizer sprinkled with lemon juice.

Kippers cured and smoked using traditional methods are, or perhaps should be, one of our gastronomic joys, but too often the producers indulge in our national habit of trying to improve and speed things up by introducing artificial dyes and flavourings. So we find ourselves presented with the dark brown kipper sold whole and in fillets.

KIPPERS

Description A kipper is a whole fish, split down the middle and opened up. It comes complete with head and tail. It should be plump and shiny, coloured a silvery or yellow brown, shimmering gold with just a hint of red.

Notes Kippers were invented in Northumberland and the best come from there, the Isle of Man, the western coast of Scotland and East Anglia.

Cooking ideas Best grilled or simply cooked in a jug, but can also be fried or baked. Make lovely pâté: follow the recipe for bloater paste (page 125); or marinaded and eaten raw.

Grilled Kippers

Heat the grill for 5 minutes. Put them skin side up on an oiled grid 4–5 ins away from heat. Add no oil or fat, grill until the skin begins to crispen and blacken. Eat with plenty of freshly milled pepper, a squeeze of lemon juice and lots of brown bread and butter.

Kippers cooked in a jug
Put kippers in a tall jug, pour over enough boiling water to cover. Leave 5–10 minutes. Drain and eat with a knob of butter on top.

Baked in foil
Heat the oven to Gas 5/375°F/190°C. Wrap each fish in foil, putting a pat of butter on top of each and bake 10–15 minutes.

Poor man's smoked salmon
Skin the kippers (plunge into boiling water for a minute to make this easier), remove backbone. Cut into fillets and marinade them for at least 2 hours in 2 tablespoons olive oil, 2 tablespoons of lemon juice, finely chopped onion and black pepper. Slice thinly.

How to eat a kipper
Remember the fish has been split open so that the bones are close to the exposed sides, it's easier to eat if you put it skin side up on the plate and work inwards. You can eat the skin or discard it, it's up to you

---

Horse Mackerel

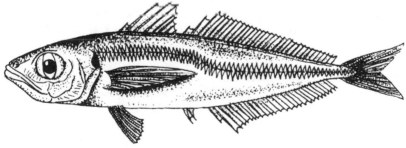

HORSE MACKEREL – *also known as:* SCAD or JACK, CARAPAU or CHINCHARD; *same family as:* CARANGIDS

Habitat   Atlantic and Mediterranean.

Pros and Cons   Not to be confused with mackerel, it's more like sardine with a stronger flavour. It's rather bony but it's a tasty buy for lean days.

Size	Between 20 and 45 cm (8–18 ins).
Description	Spindle-shaped silvery body, the back greenish blue, the belly tinged with pink and blue. The curved lateral line ending in a row of bony spurs looks like a zip or a row of neat stitching. Tail is forked, eyes big and there is a black spot behind the gill cover.
How sold	Whole fish.
Qty per person	1 fish weighing around 225–275 g (8–10 oz).
Ask fishmonger	To clean, trim and scale.
Availability	Most abundant from April to October. Look for it in shops and markets catering for ethnic minorities.
Notes	Horse mackerel have a mixed reputation. They are popular in Caribbean, Creole, Spanish and Portuguese cooking. The French are less enthusiastic; in Provence they call them *estranglo bello-mèro* – Mother-in-law's Garotte.
Preparation	Clean, trim and scale if the fishmonger hasn't done so. Cut bony spurs out with the point of a knife or scissors, or remove at table.
Cooking ideas	Grill, fry or bake *en papillote*. Follow recipes for mackerel or sardine; or prepare *en escabèche*, (*see* page 211).

Scad baked en papillote

Heat oven to Gas 4/350°F/180°C. Cut foil or buttered greaseproof paper large enough to wrap each fish. Score the fish two or three times, spread with mustard and add a squeeze of lemon juice, a quarter of an apple, chopped, pinch of cinnamon or nutmeg, salt, pepper and chopped herbs such as parsley or thyme. Top with small dabs of butter. Fold the foil or greaseproof to make loose parcels. Bake 20 minutes.

HOUTING, *see* **POWAN**

HUITRE CREUSE, *see* **OYSTERS**

HUSS, *see* **DOGFISH**

INKFISH, *see* **CUTTLEFISH**

JACKS, *see* **HORSE MACKEREL** and **CARANGIDS**

JAPANESE OYSTER, *see* **OYSTERS**

JOB GRIS and **JOB JAUNE,** *see* **SNAPPERS**

John Dory

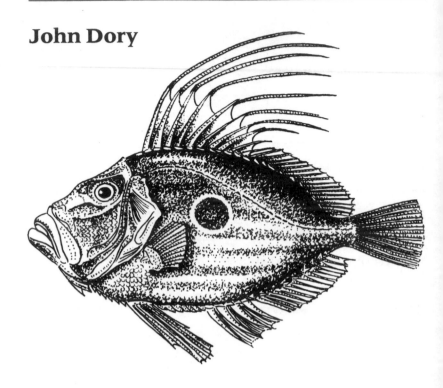

JOHN DORY – *also known as:* ST PETER'S FISH; not to be confused with the freshwater fish of the same name (*see* separate entry)

Habitat   E Atlantic and Mediterranean, and from New Zealand.

Pros and Cons   This extraordinary-looking fish has firm delicious flesh, not. cheap because the head accounts for almost half its size; but the fillets are comparable to sole and the head can be used for stock or the soup pot.

Size   Between 32 and 50 cm (13–20 ins).

Description   The John Dory looks like a fantasy fish with its huge head, protruding jaw and tall, compressed body which is encircled with fins bearing sharp barbs, quills and trailing filaments. It is coloured a dun-grey which glistens with indistinct stripes and mottlings of gold or blue. It has a large dark spot on its flank encircled with a pale halo.

How sold   Whole fish, often headless; or in fillets; sometimes frozen from New Zealand.

Qty per person   Allow 350–400 g (12–14 oz) of whole, ungutted fish. Fillets: 150–175 g (5–6 oz).

Ask fishmonger   To clean and trim the fish and remove the gills if you intend to cook it whole. Otherwise to skin and fillet but to let you have head and trimmings for stock or soup. (Or you can remove skin after cooking.)

Availability   All year either imported or our own catch during summer but generally only stocked by enterprising fishmongers. Worth snapping up if you see it.

Notes   The John Dory is known as St Peter's fish in many countries and there are conflicting versions as to why. One is that Peter complained that he couldn't pay his taxes so Jesus told him to pick out the first fish from the sea and in its mouth he would find a coin. Another says that this is rubbish, Peter happened to catch the fish in his net and it made such a fuss and looked so horrible (in France it is nicknamed *l'Horrible*) that he picked it up and threw it back in disgust. Certainly lots of other fishermen have made the same mistake, whilst others in Kent believe it was the fish that fed the 5,000 and that the print is that of Jesus himself, so they will not eat it but nail it to the door as a symbol of good luck.

Preparation   Whole fish must be cleaned, trimmed, scaled and gills removed. Wash and dry with kitchen paper.

Cooking ideas   Good poached in wine or cider and served hot or cold with a home-made aïoli or mayonnaise; fried or grilled or braised whole and served with creamy sauces; or baked. The fillets can be cooked like sole, turbot, brill or flounder. The head and trimmings make excellent soup or stock.

Poached John Dory

Poach the fish in a wine-flavoured *court bouillon* (*see* page 301). It will have more flavour if you cook it on the bone and fillet it afterwards. Simply cut along the lateral line, peel back the skin and using the flat of a knife to help you carefully lift off the top two fillets. Remove the backbone to reveal the under fillets. Turn them over and carefully skin. Serve with aïoli, mayonnaise or other sauce.

Saint Pierre à la provençale – John Dory with potatoes and tomatoes

Heat oven to Gas 6/400°F/200°C. Put a layer of very thinly sliced potatoes into the base of an oiled oven dish. Put the whole fish on top. Add salt, pepper and a generous sprinkling of olive oil, putting some inside the fish as well. Surround the fish with halves of tomatoes, putting slivers of garlic into each and a sprinkling of thyme and parsley. Pour over a glass of dry white wine. Dust with breadcrumbs, sprinkle with more oil. Cover with a piece of foil. Bake for 30 minutes, remove the foil and bake a further 10 minutes. Serve in the dish garnished with black olives.

Fillets of John Dory fried in breadcrumbs

First flour the fillets. Beat up 2 eggs, add a little salt and lemon juice. Lay the fillets in this mixture, one at a time. Take them out and dredge them with dry breadcrumbs. Fry as page 295, in a mixture of olive oil and butter. Arrange on a dish garnished with lemon wedges, parsley and frizzy endive.

Fillets of John Dory with sorrel and spinach

fillets of John Dory weighing about 550–700 g (1¼–1½ lbs)
75 g (3 oz) butter
450 g (1 lb) spinach (or use 350 g [12 oz] frozen spinach)
225 g (8 oz) sorrel (if sorrel is unobtainable, double the amount of spinach)
2 shallots or 1 small onion
salt, pepper

half dry white wine and half water to cover
2 heaped tablespoons flour
juice of half a lemon
nutmeg
2 tablespoons single or half cream
2 or 3 tablespoons grated cheese
lemon wedges to garnish
Melt 25 g (1 oz) butter, and add the cleaned spinach and sorrel from which you have removed the tough stalks. Let them soften over a low heat. (If using frozen spinach, defrost it and drain, then mix with the softened sorrel.) In the pan in which you are going to poach the fish melt 25 g (1 oz) butter and cook the chopped shallots or onion until soft but not brown, add salt, pepper and the wine and water. Heat but don't boil. Beat the fillets lightly with the flat of a spatula, so they don't curl when cooking. Add to the pan and let them poach gently without boiling for 5 minutes. Heat the grill. In a small saucepan melt the remaining 25 g (1 oz) butter and stir in the flour. Mix well and cook gently for a couple of minutes. Gradually add 300 ml (½ pint) of the poaching liquid, stirring over a medium heat until the sauce thickens. Add salt and pepper and the juice of half a lemon. Mix the spinach with the sorrel, add salt, pepper, nutmeg and 2 tablespoons cream. Spread this mixture in a shallow dish, top with the fish. Pour the sauce over, sprinkle with cheese and put under the grill for two or three minutes just to brown. Serve with lemon wedges.

JOLIE-BLEU, *see* **SNAPPERS**

KAKATOIS, *see* **PARROTFISH**

KING CARANGUE, *see* **CARANGIDS**

Kingfish

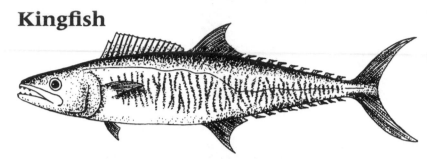

KINGFISH — *also known as:* KING MACKEREL; Creole name is GULUE; *same family as:* MACKEREL and TUNA, BONITO, WAHOO

Habitat	Warm waters such as Red Sea, Indo-Pacific Ocean, Caribbean and Atlantic.
Pros and Cons	The kingfish is a highly prized food fish related to mackerel and tuna. It is imported frozen into this country and sometimes flown in fresh.
Size	Can grow to 2 metres plus (6½ feet).
Description	Elongated body with ink-blue back marked with the typical dark, wavy stripes of the mackerels, sides and belly are silvery; the snout is pointed with sharp teeth. It has medium-sized scales and a strong, keeled tail with sickle fin.
How sold	Usually steaks or cutlets.
Qty per person	175–225 g (6–8 oz).
Ask fishmonger	For a piece away from the tail which will be bonier and drier.
Availability	Enterprising fishmongers mainly in and around London especially in shops or markets patronized by Caribbeans.
Notes	The name kingfish is given to several different fish, so check that it is the king mackerel you are buying and not the king carangue (*see* page 31),

which is not so fine. It is often wrongly called barracuda, which is a different species. In the Caribbean kingfish is salted and called *tasa salle.*

Preparation Wash and wipe dry, make sure all traces of guts are removed that might be clinging to the bone.

Cooking ideas Marinade and grill steaks, bake with stuffing or make kebabs. Use recipes for mackerel, wahoo, bonito or swordfish.

Kingfish steaks baked in parcels
4 steaks
4 tablespoons of olive or peanut oil
1 onion, finely chopped
3 cloves garlic, chopped
1 teaspoon harissa or a chopped red chilli or 1 teaspoon chilli powder
½ teaspoon oregano
cup breadcrumbs
salt, pepper
1 tablespoon capers
3 tablespoons yoghurt
glass dry white wine
1 lemon, sliced
Heat oven to Gas 6/400°F/200°C. Heat the oil in a wok or pan and fry the chopped onion until lightly brown over a medium heat, add the garlic, harissa (or chilli), oregano and mix well, remove from the heat and add breadcrumbs, salt, capers and the yoghurt. Cut squares of foil large enough to enclose each steak and put some of the mixture on each, top with the fish and cover with remaining mixture. Pour over the white wine, top each with a slice of lemon and make into loose but secure parcels. Bake 20–25 minutes according to the size of the fish.

KING PRAWN, *see* **PRAWNS**

KIPPER, *see* **HERRING, SMOKED**

LANGOUSTE, *see* LOBSTER, SPINY

LANGOUSTINE, *see* DUBLIN BAY PRAWN

LASCAR, *see* EMPERORS

LEMON DAB, *see* LEMON SOLE

Lemon Sole

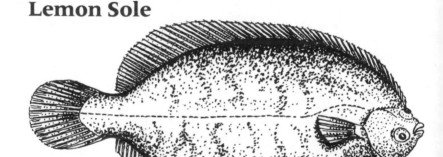

LEMON SOLE — *also known as:* LEMON DAB, MERRY SOLE, SLIPPERY DAB and SMEAR; *same family as:* DAB, FLOUNDER, HALIBUT, PLAICE and WITCH

Habitat N Atlantic, North Sea, English Channel.

Pros and Cons Lemon sole suffers from always being described as inferior to sole which immediately makes it seem no good at all. It is in fact a delicious flat fish with sweet and delicate flesh, much better than the ever-popular plaice.

Size 25–35 cm (10–14 ins).

Description	Right facing, oval flat fish coloured a drab brown or grey, mottled with green, red-brown and yellow. Its head is small, eyes are large and the skin quite slimy. Blind side is white.
How sold	Whole fish or filleted.
Qty per person	Allow 200–225 g (7–8 oz) of whole, gutted fish. Fillets: 150–175 g (5–6 oz).
Ask fishmonger	To fillet it; or if you're planning to cook it whole, you can ask him to remove dark skin.
Availability	All year but best July to February.
Preparation	Wash and dry. If the fishmonger hasn't removed the dark skin, it's easy once the fish is cooked.
Cooking ideas	Treat simply; whole fish or fillets can be grilled or fried *à la meunière*; f 'lets can be cut into goujons. Recipes for sole and other flat fish are suitable.

Grilled Lemon Sole

Use whole small lemon sole. Ask fishmonger to remove the dark skin but leave the heads, or do this yourself. Grill as on page 298, brushing and basting with melted unsalted butter. Serve with a savoury herb-flavoured butter or hollandaise sauce (*see* pages 283 and 289).

Goujons of Lemon Sole with cream and mushroom sauce

2 medium-sized lemon sole, skinned and filleted
seasoned flour
100 g (4 oz) unsalted or concentrated butter
150 g (6 oz) mushrooms, sliced
6 tablespoons half or single cream
salt, pepper
juice of half a lemon
lemon wedges and chopped parsley to garnish
Cut fillets of sole into strips using scissors, roll them in seasoned flour and fry them gently in 50 g (2 oz) butter until golden.

Make a sauce by melting the remaining butter in a small saucepan, cook the sliced mushrooms over a medium heat until they are soft, stir in half the cream. Cook until reduced, add salt, pepper and remaining cream. Put the fish on a serving dish, squeeze over the lemon juice, top with the mushroom sauce, garnish with lemon wedges and chopped parsley.

Instead of the mushroom sauce you could eat the fried goujons with aïoli, mayonnaise or tartare sauce and plenty of brown bread and butter.

LESSER SPOTTED DOGFISH, *see* **DOGFISH**

LESSER WEEVER, *see* **WEEVER**

LIMANDE, *see* **DAB**

Ling

LING — *same family as:* COD, COLEY, HADDOCK, HAKE, POLLACK and WHITING

Habitat	NE Atlantic.
Pros and Cons	Ling is a worthy member of the cod family, with quite a good flavour and texture.
Size	Up to 1 metre (39 ins).
Description	Long, slender bronze body, mottled with brown or green, belly white. The second dorsal and anal fins are very long. It has a barbel on its chin.
How sold	Usually steaks or fillets; but much of the catch is salted and dried, or smoked and then often sold as salted or smoked cod.

Qty per person	Steaks: 175–200 g (6–7 oz). Fillets: 150–175 g (5–6 oz).
Ask fishmonger	For a middle or top cut, the tail end is likely to be bonier and drier.
Availability	All year but the best arrive late winter through to spring. It's most likely to be found on the western side of the British Isles though you may find it in some fishmongers in London.
Preparation	Ling is dried and salted in some countries including Ireland, Sweden and Norway. Spillanga and Klipfisk may be either salted ling, cod or coley.
Cooking ideas	Wash and dry with kitchen paper. Prepare salted ling like salt cod, page 51.

Ling baked with tomato sauce and olives – or use cod, haddock, coley or hake

4 fillets or steaks of ling
1 tablespoon olive or peanut oil
1 onion, chopped
2 rashers unsmoked streaky bacon, chopped
1 medium can Italian tomatoes
1 tablespoon capers
pinch dried tarragon or use fresh
12 black olives
butter
salt, pepper
lemon wedges

Heat oven to Gas 5/375°F/190°C. Heat oil in a wok or frying pan, add chopped bacon and onion and cook 3 or 4 minutes over a medium flame. Add the can of Italian tomatoes, the capers, tarragon and the black olives. Season with salt and pepper. Let the sauce simmer for 5–10 minutes. Butter a shallow oven-proof dish, put half the sauce on the base, lay the fish on top, cover with remaining sauce. Cook 20–30 minutes. Serve with lemon wedges.

LITHRINI, *see* **BREAMS, SEA**

LITTLE TUNNY, *see* TUNA

Lobster

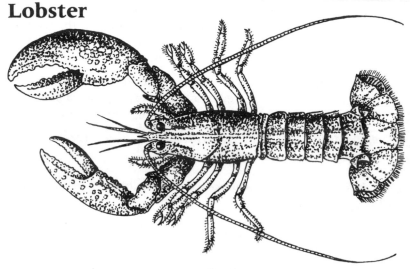

LOBSTER — *same family as:* SPINY LOBSTER (CRAWFISH) and DUBLIN BAY PRAWN

Habitat   European coastal waters.

Pros and Cons   Take a deep breath, buy a lobster and share it with someone you love. Yes, it is expensive, but it is absolutely delicious, looks spectacular and is one of the easiest feasts in the world.

Size   30–60 cm (12–24 ins).

Description   The long, armour-plated body of the live lobster with its two unequal claws is a midnight blue mottled with browns and purples. Once cooked the shell turns livid red.

How sold   Whole, either live or cooked. Buy from a good fish market or fishmonger. Live lobsters are best but if you live far from the sea, avoid those which you suspect have been slowly starved for days in a tank. They are being tormented and will be wasting away and in poor condition for the table. Frozen specimens are dull and tasteless.

Qty per person Allow 350–450 g (¾–1 lb). A lobster weighing between 700–900 g (1½-2 lbs) will feed two people. If buying for more than two, buy more than one lobster rather than one weighing over a kilo (2¼ lbs) – large lobsters are old, can be as much as 40 years, and may look impressive but are drier and less tasty.

Ask fishmonger **If buying live:** To let you feel the weight, it should feel heavy for its size; a female is more delicate and sometimes comes complete with her dark coral of eggs (she is broader in the tail than the male). Ask him to tie the claws to avoid a nasty nip and check it is very lively. Avoid those which are sleepy, they are nearly dead.

If buying cooked: It also should feel heavy for its weight, with no cracks or holes in the shell and no unpleasant smell. Check it has both claws. Make sure it was boiled when very fresh, test by pulling back the tail, it should spring back into position again. Smell it to see if it has been lying around cooked on the slab for a day or two, be wary if the smell is strong.

Availability April to November, you may have to order or go to a local fish market. Most of the catch is sent to the Continent or the restaurant trade.

Notes Most methods of killing lobster seem fairly brutal; however, the Universities Federation for Animal Welfare suggest two methods. One is to put the live lobster into a plastic bag and put it in a freezer at a temperature between $-10°$ and $-15°$ C for two hours. It will become unconscious and die and should then be immediately plunged into boiling water. Otherwise the most humane way is to plunge it directly into fiercely boiling water, allowing 4½ litres (1 gallon) per lobster, keeping the pot on a very high heat and making sure the lobster is completely submerged. The lobster will die within 15 seconds. Cold water brought slowly to the boil doesn't gently send it to sleep but slowly drowns it. Death by the knife or cleaver can be equally cruel as unless expertly done it results in slow asphyxiation as the life fluid drains away. So if you intend to give your lobster the quick chop, ask your supplier to show you exactly where the vulnerable points are and how to go about it. Trying to follow written instructions with a lobster on its back and wriggling is an unnerving experience.

Preparation   **Live lobster:** Get it home and cook it as soon as possible, see methods described above. The water should contain 3 tablespoons of salt for every litre (2 pints) used. Make sure the pan has a well fitting lid. Bring the water to the boil and plunge in the lobster head first. Cover immediately with the lid, keep the heat fierce and start timing as soon as the water returns to the boil. Boil it 12 minutes for the first 450 g (1 lb), 10 minutes for the second and then 5 minutes more for every further 450 g (1 lb). Remove from the pot with tongs and leave till it's cool enough to handle. Hold it upside down so that any water drains out, turn it and drain the other way. If eating hot prepare it right away for the table; if eating cold, leave it somewhere cool until you are ready.

Cooking ideas   Forget all those elaborate lobster dishes, eat it simply split down the middle either hot with plenty of melted butter or a mixture of half melted butter and olive oil, or a hollandaise sauce; or eat it cold with either a mayonnaise, or vinaigrette made with olive oil and lemon juice or a sauce *rémoulade*.

Lobster au naturel

Turn the cooked lobster on its back on a board and uncurl its tail. If it's a female, the dark eggs will have become a purple-orange and look like caviare, these can be left where they are or if serving cold can be removed with a teaspoon to be added to your mayonnaise. Split the lobster in half lengthwise using a sharp, pointed, heavy knife. This is easy to do in two stages, first from the middle down between the eight legs to the head, then again from the middle down the length of the tail. You'll need to exert some pressure to get through the armour-plating of the shell. Remove the small sac in the head which contains gritty bits and the long black intestine. Everything else is edible, including all the green and creamy bits.

Arrange the split lobster on a long serving dish, garnish with watercress or lemon quarters. Use small forks and perhaps skewers to dig out the stubborn bits, twisting off the claws and legs and breaking them into segments to make it easier. Have brown bread and butter, cayenne pepper, your chosen sauce, napkins and finger bowls and of course use your every last penny to buy a bottle of really nice dry white wine.

Lobster, Spiny, or Crawfish

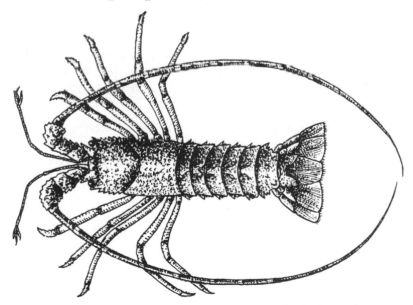

LOBSTER, SPINY, or CRAWFISH — *also known as:* CRAYFISH and in France as LANGOUSTE

Habitat	Coastal waters ranging from northern Scotland to Mediterranean and N Africa.
Pros and Cons	If you get the chance and are in funds, buy one. It has almost as much meat as a lobster despite having no large claws and is just as succulent and tasty. Frozen tails are imported, they can be good, though tend to be dry. Whole crawfish imported are often sold frozen, labelled lobster, they are not very good value.
Size	30–50 cm (12–20 ins).
Description	Lobster-shaped but with long antennae instead of claws. The reddish or violet brown mottled shell is very rough and prickly; cooked, it turns a cardinal red.
How sold	As lobster.
Qty per person	As lobster.
Ask fishmonger	As lobster.
Availability	Usually from up-market or specialist fishmongers. Sometimes where locally caught from April to October, though as with so many good things, most are exported or snapped up by the restaurant trade. Look out for them in fish markets whilst on holiday around the Mediterranean.
Notes	Spiny lobsters or crawfish are confusingly also known as crayfish but they are not the same species as the delicate freshwater crayfish.
Preparation	As for lobster.
Cooking ideas	As for lobster.

LONG-FINNED TUNA, *see* **TUNA**

LONG NOSE, *see* **GARFISH**

LOTTE, *see* **MONKFISH**

LOUP DE MER, *see* **BASS**

LYTHE, *see* **POLLACK**

Mackerel

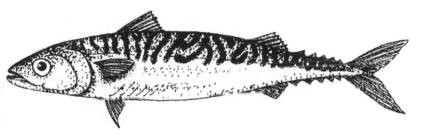

MACKEREL or ATLANTIC MACKEREL — *same family as:* TUNA, BONITO, KINGFISH and WAHOO

Habitat   Atlantic and Mediterranean.

Pros and Cons   A small mackerel makes a cheap and delicious meal with few bones. Like all oily fish they should be very fresh, so make sure they are really bright eyed and sparkling.

Size   30–35 cm (12–14 ins).

Description   The spindle-shaped body with its very small scales is a brilliant iridescent blue-green with thick, inky blue wavy stripes. Belly and sides are silver tinged with pink and blue. Dorsal fins are widely spaced and there is a row of small finlets in front of the slightly keeled tail.

How sold   Whole fish. Also SMOKED (*see* page 147).

Qty per person	Allow a whole fish weighing 225–275 g (8–10 oz) ungutted. Larger fish weighing over 450 g (1 lb) are ample for two people.
Ask fishmonger	To clean and trim and remove gills; or, if you wish, to fillet. They must be very fresh and seem to sparkle on the slab; tired, fading mackerel are useless.
Availability	All year but the best are to be found in Devon and Cornwall in spring and summer when they feed in the shallow coastal waters.
Notes	We're very fortunate that mackerel need to be eaten very fresh, otherwise we'd surely find that all of them were exported to the Continent like so many of our marvellous fish. They really are the finest of their family and very cheap. Don't buy horse mackerel expecting they are as good as plain mackerel, they are not the same family. Sometimes you might see Spanish mackerel on sale, certainly on the Continent and they are also very good.
Preparation	Wash, trim and clean if the fishmonger hasn't done so, making sure the cavity is clear of blood or any blackness. Dry with kitchen paper.
Cooking ideas	Because of its richness, mackerel is at its best when simply baked or grilled and married with a tart sauce like gooseberry or rhubarb, both of which are in season when the best mackerel is around. At other times of the year, try other flavours such as cranberry, mint or redcurrant jelly; or bake them with fennel following recipe for red mullet on page 193; or bake with mustard; or marinade them with spices; prepare *en escabèche*, page 211; or souse them like herring.

Grilled Mackerel Tunisian style

Mix 4 tablespoons olive oil, juice of 1 lemon, 2 crushed cloves of garlic, 1 teaspoon harissa (or use ½ teaspoon chilli powder), 1 teaspoon paprika, 1 teaspoon crushed cumin seeds and some black pepper. Score the fish on either side, two or three times, put into a shallow china or glass dish and pour over the marinade. Leave for 1 hour before grilling as on page 298.

Mackerel au gratin
Heat oven to Gas 4/350°F/180°C. Remove heads and tails from the fish. Put into a shallow buttered dish. Cover with finely chopped onion, a clove of garlic, chopped, handful of parsley and bread-crumbs. Add a glass of dry white wine, salt, pepper, dot with butter. Cover with a piece of buttered paper or foil and bake 25 minutes. Serve with one of the tart sauces mentioned above.

Grilled Mackerel with mushrooms
Use either whole fish or fillets. Score whole fish two or three times on each side. Grill as on page 298.

Meanwhile toss quartered mushrooms in foaming oil or butter, add a handful of chopped parsley and the juice of a lemon. Pour over the cooked fish. Eat with tomatoes grilled or baked and flavoured with herbs.

Mackerel baked with fennel
See recipe for red mullet, page 193.

Mackerel baked with mustard
Heat oven to Gas 7/425°F/220°C. Lay the mackerel in an oven dish in one layer. Mix 2 tablespoons of mustard with 6 of single cream (or yoghurt), add salt, pepper, juice of a lemon, handful of chopped parsley. Pour over the fish. Dot with butter and bake for 15–20 minutes.

MACKEREL SHARK, *see* **SHARK**

Mackerel, Smoked

Description   Cheaper than smoked trout and widely available, mackerel are either gutted and beheaded and smoked whole, or in fillets. They are first soaked

147

in brine, dried and then usually hot-smoked, which means they are cooked, although some smokers cold-smoke them. They should be pale bronze, those that are a deep red-brown all over have probably been artificially coloured.

How sold Whole fish or fillets, sometimes covered in peppercorns, although these are often on a somewhat mass-produced level.

Qty per person 1 fish or 1 or 2 fillets.

Ask fishmonger If the mackerel is hot or cold smoked; also whether he smokes his own fish, in which case you are in luck.

Availability All year.

Cooking ideas Hot-smoked mackerel is already cooked and is excellent cold with salad, or it can be heated under a hot grill. Cold-smoked is raw, so can be grilled or eaten very thinly sliced as it is, with plenty of lemon juice, freshly milled pepper and brown bread and butter.

Grilled smoked Mackerel
Skin the mackerel if you wish, though it's not necessary, and brush with melted butter. Heat grill and grill pan, oil the grid. Grill 3 or 4 minutes on each side. It's delicious with spinach.

Smoked Mackerel pâté
Follow recipe for bloater paste on page 125 (if using hot-smoked mackerel omit the preliminary cooking).

MADAME BERRIE, *see* **EMPERORS**

MAHI-MAHI, *see* **DOLPHINFISH**

MAIGRE, *see* **CROAKERS**

MAKO, *see* **SHARK**

MARLIN, *see* **BILLFISH**

Megrim

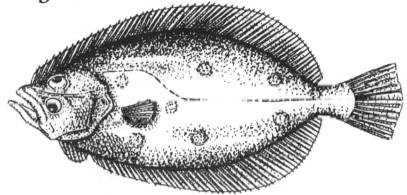

MEGRIM – *also known as:* SAIL-FLUKE and WHIFF; *same family as:* BRILL and TURBOT

Habitat   Atlantic coast of Europe.

Pros and Cons   A reasonable sort of flat fish, not on a par with brill or turbot but better than plaice. It can be dry, so needs a good sauce.

Size   25–35 cm (10–14 ins).

Description   Left-facing flat fish with an oval translucent sandy brown or duff grey body with darker blotches and rough but fragile scales. Blind side is white. Eyes are large, lower jaw protrudes.

How sold   Whole fish or fillets.

Qty per person	Allow 200–225 g (7–8 oz) of whole fish. Fillets: 150–175 g (5–6 oz).
Ask fishmonger	To fillet if you wish.
Availability	Best May to March and most easily found in coastal areas in the south-west. Sometimes labelled plaice or lemon sole, though it's easy to tell it apart as it faces left and they face right.
Notes	The megrim has a mixed reputation, in parts of France they nickname it *salope* (slut), elsewhere it's known as *mère de sole* (sole's mother) and I don't think this is meant to be a compliment. But a very fresh megrim bought near where it is caught is better than plaice or lemon sole, though don't mistake it for a true sole. People called it Sail Fluke because they believed it used its tail as a form of sail.
Preparation	Wash and wipe dry.
Cooking ideas	Bake or grill on the bone after marinading in oil, lemon juice, rubbed with herbs or spices. Serve with a sauce or flavoured butter. Bake fillets in cider, or follow recipes for plaice. Use in fish stews or soups.

Megrim baked in cider

Heat oven to Gas 4/350°F/180°C. Lay fillets of megrim in a buttered dish, add finely chopped shallots or an onion, salt, pepper, bayleaf and a good sprinkling of parsley. Pour over enough cider barely to cover. Add a handful of breadcrumbs, sprinkle generously with peanut oil and bake 20–25 minutes.

MERRY SOLE, *see* **LEMON SOLE**

Monkfish

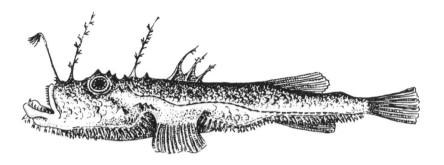

MONKFISH – *also known as:* ANGLER-FISH, FROGFISH or
SEA DEVIL

Habitat Atlantic including North Sea, Mediterranean,
English Channel.

Pros and Cons The flesh is firm and quite like lobster or scampi
but with a more delicate flavour. Not cheap but
there is little wastage as it has a central bone and
no nasty little bones to catch you unawares.

Size Tails between 15–30 cm (6–12 ins) usually.

Description Only the tapering tail end is sold, usually already
skinned and looking like a white leg of lamb
(hence the French name *gigot*). The whole fish
with its greenish or reddish brown body covered
with darker blotches, and the huge, grotesque
head which resembles a gargoyle, is judged too
off-putting for the average customer; although
one or two bolder fishmongers do occasionally
tuck a small specimen amongst their array of more
exotic fish.

How sold Whole tail or cut pieces, by weight.

Qty per person 150–225 g (5–8 oz).

Ask fishmonger	To skin it if he hasn't already done so and, depending on your choice of recipe, to bone it, or cut it into chunks or pieces.
Availability	From the more enterprising fishmongers all year round but best in summer.
Notes	Monkfish are called angler-fish because they have built in 'fishing rods' at the top of their heads with which they lure their prey, the huge mouths clanging shut like a drawbridge on the doomed fish which swim into it. This fish and the angel fish, or angel shark, which is found in the Mediterranean, are both confusingly referred to as monkfish. The angel fish is a species of dogfish and is a sort of cross between a shark and a skate. Nearly all English cookery books mean the angler-fish when specifying monkfish. Restaurant menus usually show it as LOTTE or BAUDROIE.
Preparation	If necessary, peel off any membrane and either cook whole with the bone, or fillet before cutting into slices or chunks. Wash and dry.
Cooking ideas	Whole tail is delicious roasted with tomatoes and black olives; or it can be cut into steaks and grilled, or made into kebabs; or bake like bass in foil with ginger; or use recipes for catfish or dogfish. If you can beg a head from the fishmonger, it is great for the soup pot, especially if making a bouillabaisse.

Grilled Monkfish

Marinade pieces of monkfish weighing about 200 g (7 oz) each in oil, garlic, lemon juice, salt, pepper and mixed herbs for at least 1 hour. Grill them (*see* page 298) for 3–4 minutes each side. Arrange on a dish and garnish with parsley. Serve with *beurre noisette* or an anchovy flavoured sauce (*see* Sauces).

Monkfish kebabs

750 g (1½ lbs) monkfish

For the marinade: 4 tablespoons olive oil, juice of 1 lemon, 1 teaspoon each of fennel and coriander seeds, salt and pepper

100 g (4 oz) thickly cut smoked bacon
4 tomatoes
1 green pepper
Marinade the fish, boned and cut into chunks, for at least 1 hour.
Alternate fish, bacon, halves of tomatoes and pieces of green pepper
on skewers. Grill as on page 298.

Gigot de mer
1 tail of monkfish weighing about 1 kilo (2¼ lbs)
4 tablespoons olive oil
2 cloves of garlic, cut in slivers
2 rashers of streaky bacon, cut in slivers
salt, pepper
200 g (8 oz) mushrooms, sliced
1 large can of Italian tomatoes, drained
½ teaspoon each of thyme and oregano
juice of 1 lemon
Heat oven to Gas 8/450°F/230°C. Put 2 tablespoons olive oil in a
roasting tin and put into the oven to heat for about 5 minutes. With
a pointed knife, make slits at intervals in the tail and insert pieces of
garlic and bacon, just as if you were larding a leg of lamb. Put the
fish into the tin with the hot oil and add salt and pepper. Put into the
oven for 15 minutes, basting every 5 minutes. Meanwhile in a wok
or frying pan, heat the remaining 2 tablespoons of oil and cook the
sliced mushrooms over a medium heat, add the drained tomatoes,
crushing them with a wooden spoon, season with salt and pepper
and the herbs and leave to simmer over a low heat.

When the fish has cooked for 15 minutes, lower the heat to
Gas 4/350°F/180°C and continue cooking a further 20 minutes (for
pieces of a different weight, reckon on 15 minutes to 450 g [1 lb]),
basting every 5 minutes. Put the fish on a hot dish, squeeze over the
lemon juice and pour over the sauce mixture. Serve with rice.

Baked Gigot with mussels
Heat oven to Gas 8/450°F/230°C. Make slits in a whole piece of
monkfish with the point of a knife and insert slivers of garlic. Lay it
in an oven dish and put slices of lemon along its whole length.
Sprinkle with 2 tablespoons olive oil and put in the oven for
5 minutes. Remove and throw away all the liquid which will have
come out of the fish. Add 4 more tablespoons oil and squeeze over

the juice of a lemon. Bake, allowing 15 minutes to 450 g (1 lb), basting two or three times. Five minutes before serving, add 450 g (1 lb) cleaned and scrubbed mussels. As soon as they have opened, serve the fish dusted with parsley and with lemon wedges.

Baudroie provençale
750 g (1½ lbs) monkfish boned and cut into chunks
3 tablespoons olive oil
2 onions, chopped
2 cloves garlic, chopped
1 medium can of Italian tomatoes, drained
1 glass dry white wine
thyme, parsley and bayleaf
salt, red pepper
1 teaspoon paprika
100 g (4 oz) black olives
In a wok or saucepan, heat the olive oil and when it sizzles add the chopped onions, let them cook over a medium heat until soft, 5–10 minutes. Add the chopped garlic and the drained tomatoes, crush them and when they are hot add the pieces of fish. Pour over the white wine, add herbs, salt, pepper, paprika and the black olives. Cook, covered, over a very low heat for 15 minutes.

MULLET, *see* **GREY MULLET; RED MULLET**

W E D			
T H U R S			
F R I			

Mussels

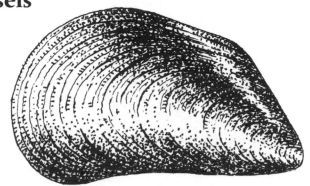

MUSSELS

Habitat	Atlantic through to Mediterranean with culturing in many places.
Pros and Cons	Mussels are lovely and not expensive. Don't be put off by fears of preparing them; it's far less of a chore than scraping stubborn new potatoes and can be done ahead of time; the actual cooking is only a matter of minutes.
Size	5–10 cm (2– 4ins) long.
Description	A double-shelled mollusc with a predominantly inky blue-black, curved shell, narrowing towards the hinged end. It often has subtle tortoiseshell variations of greens and browns.
How sold	By weight or volume. Sometimes pre-washed and packaged in bags. Also frozen in shells, or in the half shell with snail butter. Instructions on packets.
Qty per person	450 g (1 lb) or ½ litre (1 pint).
Ask fishmonger	To give you ones which are firmly closed.
Availability	Traditionally when there's an *r* in the month, though sometimes sold at other times of the year.

When it's very hot or cold, transporting is difficult and you're unlikely to find them.

Notes Wild mussels are everywhere around our coasts, clinging to rocks, seabreaks and the supports of piers; they can be the source of deadly food poisoning due to pollution, so play safe and go for those supplied by the fishmonger, which will have been cultivated under strictly controlled conditions. Or if you must gather them, listen to the locals who will know if it is safe.

Preparation For maximum freshness, eat the day you buy; although you can keep them overnight in a bucket of water, feeding them with a tablespoon or two of oatmeal or flour.

To wash: either leave them in a colander under running cold water for an hour, or wash them in several changes of water. The idea is to get rid of any sand or debris lurking in and around them. Use a short, blunt knife to scrape off the barnacles – an oyster knife comes in handy for this job. You can be quite rough, the shells are strong. Pull out, or cut off with scissors, the long, threadlike strands trailing between the shells which are not seaweed but are the mussel's means of fastening itself to objects. Finally give each a quick scrub with a brush or nylon scourer under running water. Throw away those that have a broken shell, or remain open even after being tapped sharply with the handle of your knife. They will be dead. Give them a final wash by which time the mussels should be glistening and the water be as clear as a rock pool. If you're not ready to cook them, leave them in the water, adding a teaspoon of salt.

Ready-washed mussels, sold in bags, should be rinsed two or three times and checked to see they are free of barnacles, are unbroken and unopened.

Cooking ideas Mussels are a sensational first course steamed open in a little wine with garlic, parsley and olive oil – *à la marinière*; or stuffed and heated through in a very hot oven; they make delicious soup, are great added at the last moment to an omelette or cooked with rice. A few make an interesting garnish and can be used to add flavour to other fish dishes. Any leftover cooking liquid can be used as a base for sauces or soups. Tinned mussels in brine are a good store standby.

Moules Marinière

2 kilos (4 lbs) or 2½ litres (4 pints) cleaned mussels
2 shallots or 1 onion, chopped
2 cloves garlic, finely chopped
handful of chopped parsley
freshly milled black pepper
4 glasses dry white wine or cider (or use water flavoured with the juice of 1 lemon)
4 tablespoons olive oil or 50 g (2 oz) butter

Choose a large saucepan and put in the chopped shallots or onion, the garlic, parsley, generous amount of freshly milled pepper (no salt, the mussels will be salty enough), wine, cider (or water and lemon juice) and the oil or butter. Add the drained mussels having checked that none have opened (throw them out). Put the pan on a high heat uncovered and bring to the boil. Put on a lid and cook quite fiercely for 5 minutes, no longer. Overcooked they become rubbery. Check that all the mussels have opened, discard any that remain closed. You can bring the pan straight to the table; or turn them into a large, heated tureen, strain the liquid through a sieve lined with muslin to make sure any traces of sand are removed. Serve in wide soup bowls, giving everyone a helping of mussels and some of the liquid. Everyone uses their fingers, breaking off the empty shell which can be used as a scoop to detach the mussels. Have soup spoons, napkins and finger bowls available, plenty of French bread and a big bowl for the empty shells.

Stuffed mussels

Clean 1 kilo of mussels and open them over high heat in a saucepan with 1 cup of water. As soon as they are opened remove from the heat and drain in a colander. Discard the empty shell halves. Top the mussels in their half shell with your chosen filling and put them in a hot oven Gas 8/450°F/230°C for 10 minutes. Take the dish to the table, give everyone forks, napkins and fingerbowls and have plenty of French bread to mop up the juices.

Stuffings:

A la provençale – Chop a clove of garlic, add 4 tablespoons chopped parsley, 4 tablespoons of breadcrumbs and black pepper. Top each mussel with a little of the mixture, sprinkle generously with olive oil or melted butter.

With spinach – Mix 250 g (½ lb) cooked, chopped spinach with salt, pepper and a little nutmeg. Top each mussel with a little of the mixture, sprinkle with breadcrumbs and olive oil.

With pinenuts – In a bowl mix 8 tablespoons olive oil, 1 teaspoon crushed fennel seeds, pinch of thyme and rosemary, 4 tablespoons ground pinenuts. Top the mussels with the mixture.

Soupe aux Moules à la Beaugravière
1 kilo (2 lbs) cleaned mussels
2 litres (3 pints) water
1 tablespoon olive oil
1 onion or leek, chopped
1 clove of garlic
bayleaf
1 teaspoon crushed fennel seeds
medium can Italian tomatoes
pepper
few strands of saffron, or ½ teaspoon powdered saffron or turmeric
100 g white rice or vermicelli
Put mussels and water into a large pan, bring to the boil and as soon as the mussels open, remove from the heat. Put the mussels into a colander but keep the liquid. Dry the pan, heat the olive oil and add the leek or onion. Cook several minutes, add whole clove of garlic, bayleaf, fennel seeds and after a minute or two, the tomatoes. Strain the liquid in which the mussels were cooked into the pan. Bring to the boil, season with the pepper and saffron or turmeric. Add the rice or vermicelli. Simmer, covered for 15–20 minutes. Meanwhile shell the mussels. Add them to the soup. Bring back to the boil and

remove immediately from the heat. Eat with grated cheese or rouille (*see* page 287) and lots of French bread.

Henri and Emile's pilau de riz aux moules – Rice with Mussels
This is a simple but delicious supper dish which Henri and Emile told me all about while demolishing soup bowls of mussels at La Marie-Thomas. Clean 1 kilo (2 lbs) mussels, put them in a large pot with a cup of water, 2 tablespoons olive oil, salt, pepper, finely chopped onion and some parsley. Bring them to the boil and as soon as they open, remove the mussels to a colander but keep the liquid. Heat 2 tablespoons olive oil in a saucepan and add one finely chopped onion and a leek cut small, cook them over a medium heat for two or three minutes, stir and add a finely chopped red or green pepper and two or three peeled tomatoes. Mix in 250 g (½ lb) rice. Measure 600 ml (1 pint) of the cooking liquid (it will have increased with the water from the mussels, but if necessary top up with more water). Flavour with a sprig of thyme, a bayleaf, parsley, a sprig of celery, a clove of garlic, salt and pepper. Bring to the boil. Cover, lower the heat and cook for 20 minutes. Meanwhile, discard the top shell from each mussel. When the rice and vegetables are cooked, gently stir in the mussels on their half shells and leave a further 5 minutes with the lid on but the heat turned off.

NATIVES, *see* **OYSTERS**

NEEDLEFISH, *see* **GARFISH**

NEPHROPS, *see* **DUBLIN BAY PRAWN**

NORTHERN PRAWN, *see* **PRAWNS**

NORWAY HADDOCK, *see* **REDFISH**

NORWAY LOBSTER, *see* **DUBLIN BAY PRAWN**

OCEAN PERCH, *see* **REDFISH**

Octopus

OCTOPUS or COMMON OCTOPUS – *related to:* SQUID and
CUTTLEFISH

Habitat   E Atlantic to Mediterranean, several varieties.

Pros and Cons   Though the British variety is not so good as the
ones you might taste on holiday, it nevertheless
makes a cheap and robust casserole with vegetables.
The flavour is not unlike lobster though the texture
can be a bit rubbery. Most on sale has been tenderized and it is worth buying occasionally.

Size   Usually between 20 and 60 cm (8–24ins).

Description   The strange, dome like head with its bulbous eyes
is usually removed before it goes on the slab, as is
the brown and green mottled skin. All we see is a
sort of bag of white India-rubber flesh – sometimes
covered with a purplish membrane – and the
tentacles with their double rows of suction pads.

How sold	Whole by weight, usually ready skinned, cleaned and tenderized.
Qty per person	200–225 g (7–8 oz).
Ask fishmonger	Whether it is ready prepared and tenderized, in which case your task is simplified.
Availability	Throughout the year but best May to October from the more enterprising fishmongers.
Notes	It really is true that in Greece and other countries they beat octopus against the rocks to tenderize them. You shouldn't have to do the same because those on sale here are not the same species as those from the Mediterranean and they will already have been subjected to a tenderizing process.
Preparation	If the octopus is headless and already skinned, all you need to do is to wash the tentacles and the sac inside and out before cutting it up. If you should have to deal with a whole octopus, this is how to go about it. With a sharp knife, cut off the tentacles in one piece and set aside. Turn the pouch-like head inside out and remove and discard all the innards (which includes the ink sac) and cut away the beak of the mouth and the eyes; wash the now empty pouch under running water and turn right side out. If the octopus has not been skinned, blanch it in boiling water for 5–10 minutes to loosen it, then peel off the skin and thin membrane. Using a wooden mallet or the end of a rolling pin, give the octopus and tentacles a vigorous beating to tenderize them. (You can put them in a stout plastic bag whilst doing this, to save making everything around rather messy.)
Cooking ideas	Best casseroled, although it does make a rather delicious starter with lots of garlic and parsley.

Octopus with garlic and parsley (You could use squid or cuttlefish.) Clean the octopus and cut it into thin pieces. Put them in a pan and just cover with cold water, add a little salt. Bring to the boil and simmer, uncovered, until all the liquid has evaporated. The octopus will have turned pink. Pour in two or three tablespoons of olive oil, let it sizzle over a medium flame, squeeze over the juice of a lemon, salt and pepper. Take off the heat and put into a bowl to cool. Eat it cold as a starter strewn with finely chopped garlic and parsley and if necessary adding a little more olive oil and lemon juice.

Casseroled Octopus with tomatoes and mushrooms
octopus weighing between 750 g–1 kilo (1½–2 lbs)
2 tablespoons olive oil
1 leek, sliced
4 or 5 whole cloves of garlic
thyme, bayleaf, parsley and fennel seeds
salt, pepper
glass of red wine
1 medium can of Italian tomatoes
250 g (8 oz) mushrooms, quartered
Clean the octopus and cut into bite-size pieces. Heat the oil and soften the sliced leek for several minutes, add the pieces of octopus, and turn them over and over on a high heat until brown on all sides. Add garlic, herbs, salt and pepper. Mix well. Pour in the wine and let it reduce by half before adding the can of tomatoes. Cover and simmer for about 1 hour. Check from time to time and if necessary add a little water to prevent it drying out. Add the quartered mushrooms and cook a further 30 minutes.

OLD WIFE, *see* **BREAM, BLACK SEA; GARFISH; WRASSE**

OMBRE or **OMBLE CHEVALIER,** *see* **CHARR**

OMBRINE, *see* **CROAKERS**

ORMERS otherwise called ABALONE or EAR-SHELL are available in very small quantities. They live in a gnarled ear-shaped shell, rimmed with holes and lined with mother of pearl; they were once numerous in the Channel Islands but nowadays you might come across them on holiday in Brittany or the Mediterranean or tinned and sold as abalones.

Oysters

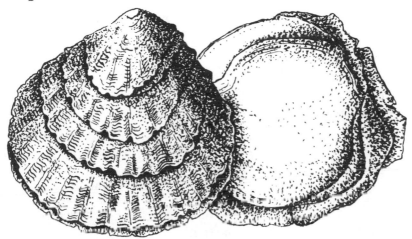

OYSTERS – three species are sold in this country, the EUROPEAN OYSTER (also known as NATIVES, BELONS or PLATES), PORTUGUESE OYSTER and PACIFIC or JAPANESE OYSTER (also known as HUITRE CREUSE and FINE DE CLAIRE)

Habitat Oyster beds cultivating European and in some cases the Pacific oysters are located in Essex, Kent, Cornwall, the Solent, Scotland and Ireland. Portuguese and Pacific oysters are imported, mainly from France.

Pros and Cons The taste of oysters is evocative of rock pools, sun, golden days of summer. Eating them is a delicious and sensual experience, though an expensive one. If you find the idea of oysters loathsome, perhaps because of a clumsy introduction, try them once more. They are ambrosia.

Size	Varies according to variety: European: up to 11 cm (4½ ins). Portuguese: up to 17 cm (7 ins). Pacific: up to 25 cm (10 ins).
Description	Like many good things, their appearance belies them, their shells are gnarled and twisted and made up of a series of concentric flounces, coloured any sort of unassuming mud shade of browns and greys.
How sold	Individually, graded and priced according to size and variety.
Qty per person	Usually 6–12.
Ask fishmonger	For those which are closed and have undamaged shells. When tapped with a knife, they should have a solid-sounding ring. Open or damaged oysters are both dead and poisonous. If you've never opened an oyster, ask for a demonstration, it's worth paying for an extra one, which you can sample on the spot.
Availability	September to April for European (it's illegal to sell them between 14 May and 4 August), though Pacific and Portuguese oysters are available throughout the year.
Notes	They will probably be named after their location i.e., Whitstable, Helford, Colchester, Pyefleet, Blackwater, etc. The European oyster is superior to the smaller Portuguese oyster; Pacific oysters, which used to be only available imported, are now being cultivated in European oyster beds and the hope is that they will be more plentiful and cheaper. Perhaps they aren't quite as fine as the European oyster but they are still deliciously succulent.
Preparation	Scrub the oysters under running water before opening them. Experienced oyster-eaters will have their own method but for those who are novices, the following is a guide. You need a knife, there's a special one sold for the purpose with a short

blunt blade, the handle protected by a sort of collar to prevent your hand from slipping. Wrap a cloth round your left hand (your right if you are left-handed). Hold the oyster firmly in this hand with the flat shell uppermost over a bowl to catch the juices. Hold the oyster knife in your other hand and feel round the edge of the oyster to find where the two shells join which is not exactly at the edge, there's a narrow lip running all round the lower shell on which the upper one sits. Press the point under the hinge, twisting it sharply upwards and the shells will part. The first few times will be a bit ham-fisted, but you'll soon get the knack. Throw away the top shell, leaving the oyster with most of its juices intact in the deeper one. Slice the oyster free leaving it in the half shell, tip back any juices from the bowl and remove any bits of broken shell. If you find holding the oyster difficult, wrap it in a cloth and hold it down on a firm work surface whilst you insert the knife under the hinge, twisting it to force the shell open.

Cooking ideas Oysters are best eaten simply, eaten raw. If you happen to have a surfeit of them they can be steamed open like mussels, grilled or baked.

To serve oysters raw
Open the oysters just before you plan to eat them. Serve them on a dish garnished with lemon wedges or to be really impressive on a bed of crushed ice. Have cayenne pepper or tabasco sauce on offer and plenty of brown bread and butter. There's a certain snobbery about eating oysters, some say they should be swallowed whole but this seems like nonsense. The only way really to savour and enjoy this divine experience is to chew them, then to sip the juices.

Grilled oysters
Heat the grill for 10 minutes. Open oysters. Put a piece of crumpled foil in the base of the grill pan and lay the oysters in their half shells on top. Sprinkle with parsley mixed with breadcrumbs. Dribble over a little olive oil and put under the grill for two minutes, no more.

Baked oysters

Heat oven to Gas 5/375°F/190°C. Lay unopened oysters flat on a baking sheet and put in the oven just until they open. Eat *at once*.

PACIFIC OYSTERS, *see* **OYSTERS**

PAGEOT ROUGE, *see* **BREAMS, SEA**

PAGRE COMMUN, *see* **BREAMS, SEA**

PALOURDE, *see* **CLAMS**

PANDORA, *see* **BREAMS, SEA**

PARGUE, *see* **SNAPPERS**

Parrotfish

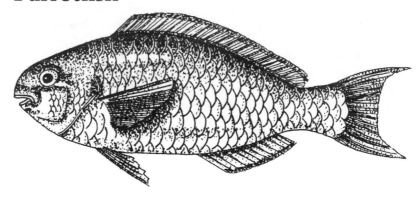

PARROTFISH – *also known as:* CACATOIS or KAKATOIS; *related distantly to:* WRASSE

Habitat Indo-Pacific, Caribbean, West Africa and Mediterranean.

Pros and Cons	You may occasionally see this exotic-looking fish on the slab, though only a few are imported and it will be expensive. It has soft, delicate flesh and should be cooked as soon as possible because it deteriorates rapidly.
Size	Usually around 30–45 cm (12–18 ins).
Description	The name is apt. Its round snout and fused teeth look like a beak and the thick-set body is a gaudy kaleidoscope of psychedelic greens, blues and violets, the large scales outlined in one colour and filled in with another.
How sold	Whole fish.
Qty per person	Allow 350–400 g (12–14 oz) whole, ungutted fish.
Ask fishmonger	To clean, remove gills, trim and scale; or, if you prefer, to fillet.
Availability	From more enterprising fishmongers though most are snapped up by the restaurant trade.
Notes	Parrotfish are much finer than wrasse so do not mistake the two. Mediterranean varieties were popular in Roman times but since then have fallen out of favour perhaps because all those colours lose their brightness after cooking.
Preparation	Whole fish must be scaled, trimmed and cleaned and the gills removed. If poaching or steaming, you need not scale, but remove the skin after cooking. They feed on coral reefs so can be chalky, so wash thoroughly and rub inside and out with salt and vinegar, one teaspoonful of each for every 450 g (1 lb) weight. Rinse and dry well.
Cooking ideas	Small fish can be fried *à la meunière*; steamed like rabbitfish (*see* page 186); or poached in a wine flavoured *court bouillon* and served with green sauce or hollandaise. Fillets can be cooked like sole or other flat fish or fry them and eat with a sweet and sour sauce. Follow recipes for sea breams

or groupers. Leftover fish is good potted, follow recipe for charr on page 41.

Parrotfish in sweet and sour sauce
1 parrotfish weighing 1–1½ kilos (2–3 lbs) filleted
salt, pepper
1½ tablespoons cornflour
½ cup pineapple juice
1 tablespoon white wine or cider vinegar
1 tablespoon soya sauce
4 tablespoons sherry
1 tablespoon sugar
2 tablespoons tomato purée
5 tablespoons olive oil
1 onion, thinly sliced
2 cloves garlic, finely chopped
thin slice of root ginger, finely chopped
1 teaspoon crushed dried red chillies
flour for coating
spring onions for garnish
Skin the fillets (page 314), and cut into chunks about 5 cm (2 ins) square, season with salt and pepper. Prepare the sweet and sour sauce by mixing the cornflour gradually with the pineapple juice to form a paste and add the vinegar, soya sauce, sherry, sugar and tomato purée. Heat 1 tablespoon of oil in a saucepan and fry the thinly sliced onion, garlic, ginger and dried chillies for a few minutes. Add the sweet and sour sauce and bring slowly to the boil, stirring until it thickens. Keep it warm on a low heat. Coat the fish in flour, heat 4 tablespoons olive oil in a wok and fry the pieces until golden on both sides. Put the fish on to a serving dish, top with the sauce and garnish with spring onions.

PEIXE ESPADA PRETA, *see* **SCABBARD FISH**

Perch

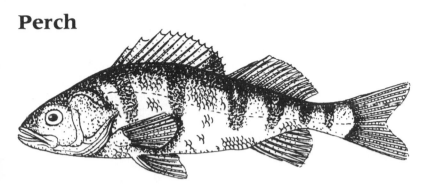

PERCH — *same family as:* ZANDER

Habitat	Mainly an angler's fish found in rivers, ponds, lakes and lowland reservoirs, though some are imported fresh, mainly from Holland.
Pros and Cons	One of the best freshwater fish, especially if caught in water with a gravelly bed, with firm, white flesh and good flavour.
Size	30–50 cm (12–20 ins).
Description	A compressed hog-backed fish, its olive green and greyish-blue body has darker bars and is covered with tough, serrated scales. The belly is pale; behind the spined and prickly first dorsal fin there is a dark smudge. The large mouth is full of teeth and the anal and pelvic fins are red.
How sold	Whole fish.
Qty per person	Allow 225–275 g (8–10 oz) whole, ungutted fish.
Ask fishmonger	To trim, clean and scale.
Availability	Mostly upmarket fishmongers in London, or where locally caught.
Notes	Perch are much appreciated on the Continent especially in areas far from the sea.

Preparation Hopefully your perch will be already trimmed, cleaned and scaled. Otherwise you'll have to do the job yourself. It's a very prickly fish with scales as tough as old Nick. Watch out for the sharp spines on the dorsal fin and at the beginning of the pelvic and anal fins, also the spikes on the gill covers and the sharp teeth. Rather than trying to remove the scales, skin the fish after it has been cooked; or plunge the raw fish into boiling water to which you've added the juice of a lemon, leave for a few seconds and you should find scales and skin will come away together.

Cooking ideas Large perch can be stuffed and baked; smaller ones can be served and marinaded in herbs, oil, lemon juice, salt and pepper before grilling or be fried *à la meunière* and served with anchovy butter. Or steam like rabbitfish (*see* page 186). All recipes for trout are suitable.

Stuffed baked Perch

Heat oven to Gas 6/400°F/200°C. Make a stuffing by heating 4 tablespoons peanut or olive oil and fry a chopped onion until beginning to brown, add 2 or 3 rashers chopped streaky bacon and after a few minutes, 50 g (3 oz) chopped mushrooms. Let them soften for several minutes, remove from the heat. Add a teaspoon soya sauce, salt, pepper, 3 or 4 tablespoons of breadcrumbs, a handful of chopped parsley, the juice of a lemon and 2 or 3 tablespoons of yoghurt. Lay the fish (skinned or not, it's up to you) on a piece of oiled foil. Fill the cavity with the stuffing, spread any over on top. Put slices of lemon down the length of the fish. Sprinkle with oil and form the foil into a loose but secure parcel. Bake 20–30 minutes according to its size.

PERIWINKLE, *see* **WINKLE**

PESCE SCIABOLO, *see* **SCABBARD FISH**

Pike

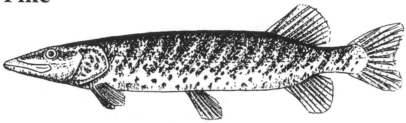

PIKE

Habitat   Shallow lakes and rivers all over Europe including UK except Spain and Portugal.

Pros and Cons   An angler's fish with a surprisingly delicate flavour considering its indiscriminate appetite which includes small waterbirds, rats, voles and frogs as well as other fish and its own species. It is a fish beloved of the restaurant trade, requiring careful treatment because it is bony and rather dry.

Size   Grows to well over 1 metre (39 ins).

Description   The long slender body with small scales is greenish grey or brownish black, with marbled sides of golden yellow. The depressed snout is long and pointed, bristling with teeth which grow even on its tongue.

Qty per person   Allow 225–275 g (8–10 oz) of whole, ungutted fish.

Notes   The pike has a mass of descriptive nicknames all testifying to its predatory nature such as Waterwolf, Freshwater Shark, Lord of the Stream and King of the Lake.

Preparation   Trim, scale and clean, discard the roe but the liver can be chopped and added to the stuffing if you are baking the fish. If the fish was caught in a muddy river, soak it in acidulated water for

30 minutes to remove any traces of mud (2 table-spoons vinegar to 1 litre [1¾ pints] of water). Large pike can be tenderized by filling the cavity with sea salt and leaving for 8 hours. Wash it well and dry before cooking.

Cooking ideas   Pike and quenelles are almost synonymous, the small, irritating bones being pounded into the mixture to give it body. However, the making of quenelles is for the experts with a host of minions to clear up after them. Best treat it simply by poaching, baking, or cutting into steaks and grilling, wrapped perhaps in rashers of bacon. Small pike can be grilled or fried *à la meunière*, follow trout recipes.

Poached Pike

Poach as on page 300 in a *court bouillon* flavoured with red wine, chopped onion, celery, thyme, parsley, bayleaf, garlic, peppercorns and salt. Eat with a strongly flavoured sauce such as *beurre blanc* or sorrel.

Baked Pike with anchovies

Heat the oven to Gas 6/400°F/200°C. Prepare the fish, score it two or three times on both sides. Fill the slits with anchovy fillets, season with salt and pepper. Lay the fish on a sheet of buttered foil, add some quartered tomatoes, lemon slices, dollop of yoghurt and dabs of butter. Wrap over the foil to form a parcel and bake 25–40 minutes depending on size. Serve with anchovy sauce, new potatoes and a green salad.

Baked Pike with cream and almonds

Heat the oven to Gas 4/350°F/180°C. Put the fish on a baking sheet, score it two or three times on each side, season with salt and pepper and dot with butter. Pour over a glass of dry white wine. Bake allowing 15 minutes per 450 g (1 lb). Ten minutes before end of cooking time, pour over 1 small carton single or half cream and a cupful of chopped almonds or other nuts such as walnuts or hazelnuts.

Baked stuffed Pike
Follow the recipe for perch on page 170, adding the chopped liver to the stuffing.

PIKEPERCH, *see* **ZANDER**

PILCHARD, *see* **SARDINE**

Plaice

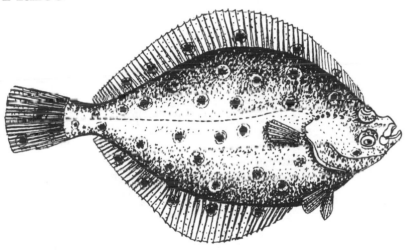

PLAICE — *family of:* DAB, FLOUNDER, HALIBUT, LEMON SOLE and WITCH

Habitat   N Atlantic and W Mediterranean.

Pros and Cons   Plaice is very abundant and very popular though you won't come across it on many haute cuisine menus or featured with any prominence in the great cookery books. Maybe one of the tests of a good fishmonger should be that he sells you a really fresh, top quality plaice, and doesn't palm you off with watery fillets that have appeared on the slab on more than several occasions.

Size 25–40 cm (10–16 ins).

Description A right facing, round flat fish, with smooth skin of a warm brown with distinctive orange-red spots. It has 4–7 bony nodules running from the back of its head to the eyes. Blind side is white, sometimes with dark blotches.

How sold Whole fish or fillets.

Qty per person Allow 200–225 g (7–8 oz) whole fish. Fillets: 150–175 g (5–6 oz).

Ask fishmonger If buying whole fish, you can ask him to remove dark skin; if buying fillets make sure he gives you a fair amount with dark skin, as these have the best flavour.

Availability All year but best May to February.

Preparation If the fishmonger hasn't removed the dark skin, you can do this before or after cooking but leave the white skin, it helps to hold the fish in shape, but if frying or grilling, score it lightly in a criss-cross pattern to prevent the fish curling in the heat. Wash the fish and dry with kitchen paper.

Cooking ideas For the best flavour plaice are best cooked on the bone fried in butter or marinaded with spices before grilling. Fillets and large whole plaice are also good baked in a well-seasoned sauce, or in foil. Use straightforward recipes for other flat fish in the same family as well as those for brill and sole.

Fried Plaice
Allow 1 small plaice or 2 fillets per head, rub the fish with salt and wipe them dry. In a frying pan melt 50 g (2 oz) unsalted butter and gently fry a chopped onion until soft, add 1 or 2 tablespoons chopped parsley and ½ teaspoon dried thyme (or use fresh lemon thyme in season), let them cook very gently for a few minutes. Raise

the heat and when the butter begins to sizzle, add the fish and let it cook a moment or two. Turn it over and let the other side have a couple of minutes on this high heat. Lower the heat and let the fish cook gently for five minutes more. Add a squeeze of lemon juice or 2 tablespoons white wine. Serve dusted with fresh chopped parsley and lemon wedges.

Grilled marinaded Plaice

4 small plaice
1 teaspoon of each of the following: coriander seeds, fennel seeds, sea salt, chilli powder and chopped fresh ginger root
4 tablespoons yoghurt
1 clove garlic, chopped
Crush the coriander and fennel seeds and the sea salt and mix with the chilli powder, ginger, yoghurt and garlic. Wash and trim the fish and score two or three times on either side. Rub each fish well with the marinade mixture and put them in a shallow glass or china dish for an hour. Grill (*see* page 298), basting the fish with the marinade, allow 5 minutes each side.

Plaice baked in cider

750 g (1½ lbs) fillets or whole fish weighing in total around 900 g (2 lbs)
1 tablespoon mustard
1 onion, chopped
4 tomatoes, chopped
salt, pepper
parsley
cider to cover
2 tablespoons grated cheese
2 tablespoons fresh breadcrumbs
butter or olive oil
Heat oven to Gas 5/375°F/190°C. Spread the fish with the mustard and lay it in a buttered gratin dish. If using whole fish score them two or three times on either side (it's up to you whether you cook them with their heads or not). On top put the onion, tomatoes, season with salt and pepper and dust with parsley.

Pour over enough cider barely to cover. Add the cheese and breadcrumbs and dot with butter or sprinkle over a little olive oil. Bake 30 minutes.

PLATES, *see* **OYSTERS**

POISSON BECUNE, *see* **WAHOO**

POLE DAB, *see* **WITCH**

Pollack

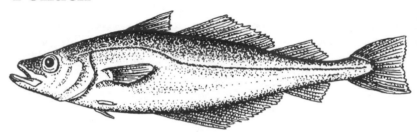

POLLACK — *same family as:* COD, COLEY, HADDOCK, HAKE, WHITING and LING

Habitat European Atlantic.

Pros and Cons Much cheaper than cod, a bit drier, a bit coarser but a good standby for lean days.

Size Usually around 40–50 cm (16–20 ins) but can grow to twice this size.

Description Long slender deep olive green or brown body, with paler sides, often spotted or striped with yellow or orange. The lower jaw protrudes and there is no barbel.

How sold Fillets, steaks or cutlets.

Qty per person Fillets: 150–175 g (5–6 oz). Steaks or cutlets: 175–200 g (6–7 oz).

Availability	All year but not as common as cod, coley or haddock.
Notes	Pollack is very closely related to coley and may even be labelled such at the fishmonger's.
Preparation	Wash and dry and before using in any recipe marinade in lemon juice, salt and pepper; perhaps a little chopped garlic and a sprinkling of herbs such as thyme or oregano. Leave it in the marinade for 2–3 hours.
Cooking ideas	This is a fish which benefits from robust flavours such as peppers, tomato and garlic, perhaps bacon or anchovies. It's a useful addition to soups or stews. Use it as a cheaper substitute in recipes for cod or haddock, or follow coley recipes.

Pollack with peppers, aubergines, tomatoes and anchovies (or use coley, haddock or cod)

700 g (1½ lbs) fillets of pollack
4 tablespoons olive oil
1 onion, chopped
1 clove garlic, chopped
2 anchovy fillets
1 small aubergine, cubed
1 green or red pepper, roughly chopped
1 teaspoon crushed coriander seeds
thyme and oregano
1 small can Italian tomatoes
salt, pepper
juice of half a lemon

Heat the oil in a wok or saucepan, cook the onion until golden over a moderate heat, add the garlic and anchovy fillets, crush them with a wooden spoon and add the chopped pepper and cubed aubergine. Cook over a brisk heat for several minutes, add the herbs, coriander and the can of tomatoes. Bring to the boil, season with salt and pepper and the juice of the lemon. Lower the heat and cook for 15 minutes. Meanwhile heat the oven to Gas 5/375°F/190°C.

Lay the fish in an oiled gratin dish, pour over the sauce, cover with a piece of buttered paper or foil and bake for 20 minutes. Squeeze over some more lemon juice just before serving.

POLLAN, *see* POWAN

Pomfret

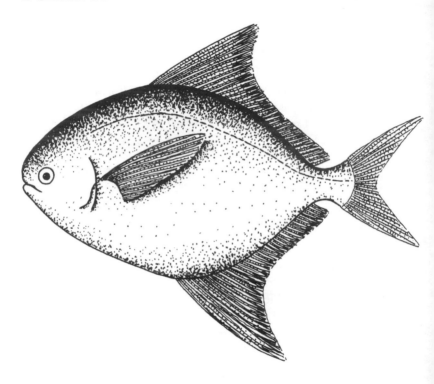

POMFRET

Habitat Indian Ocean.

Pros and Cons Occasionally on sale, sometimes fresh, more often frozen. Buy them if you can afford to, they have delicious flesh, tender yet firm.

Size Around 20–30 cm (8–12 ins).

Description A moon-shaped, compressed fish, its small head and mouth giving it a rather sheepish expression.

The general colour is grey, shading from dark to silver to white, stippled with black dots. Scales are delicate.

How sold Whole fish.

Qty per person Allow 225–275 g (8–10 oz) whole fish.

Ask fishmonger To clean, scale and trim (though the lower fin and tail are said to be delicious). Or ask him to fillet. Check whether they are fresh or frozen.

Availability Specialist fishmongers or those patronized by Indians, Chinese or other Far Eastern peoples.

Notes Pomfrets are one of the most prized fish in Indian and Chinese cooking and you may come across recipes for them in cookbooks of those countries. There are several varieties distributed throughout the oceans of the world, those imported here are flown in from India. Delicious though they are, local fishermen regard them as rather stupid fish which can be simply tricked to follow one another like sheep into the nets. Their expression certainly suggests that possibility.

Preparation Must be cleaned and scaled with care (if poaching, no need to scale as the skin can be removed after cooking). Wash and dry with kitchen paper.

Cooking ideas Can be grilled, fried, baked or steamed, flavoured with spices and used in Chinese or Indian recipes like the rabbitfish (*see* page 186) or cook fillets like garfish in curry sauce on page 95.

Grilled Pomfret

Score the fish two or three times on either side, insert slivers of garlic, rub with 1 teaspoon chilli powder, 1 tablespoon of dark brown sugar and sprinkle over 2 tablespoons of good quality soya sauce, such as Tamari or Shoyu and 2 tablespoons olive or peanut oil. Marinade for 1 hour before grilling as on page 298, basting frequently with the marinade. Serve garnished with lemon or lime wedges.

POMPANO, *see* CARANGIDS

PORBEAGLE, *see* SHARK

PORGIES, *see* BREAMS, SEA

PORTUGUESE OYSTER, *see* OYSTERS

Powan

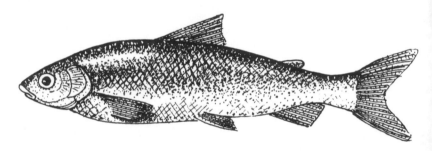

POWAN, related species known as HOUTING, SKELLY or SCHELLY in Lake District, GWYNIAD in Wales, POLLAN in Ireland (these are the lake whitefishes) — *same family as:* SALMON and TROUT

Habitat Lakes.

Pros and Cons Angler's fish which make dainty eating and are locally highly regarded.

Size 22–45 cm (9–18 ins).

Description Herring-shaped body which is blue tinged with green or grey with a white belly and grey fins; like other members of the salmon family it has a lateral line and a small adipose fin near the tail.

Qty per person	Generally one fish.
Availability	Only locally available in some Scottish lochs, occasionally in the Lake District, in Lake Bala in Wales and in some loughs of Ireland.
Preparation	Trim and clean. Wash and dry well.
Cooking ideas	Grill or fry, or bake *en papillote* flavoured with herbs and lemon juice. Follow trout recipes, or bake on a bed of spinach as for garfish, page 95.

Prawns

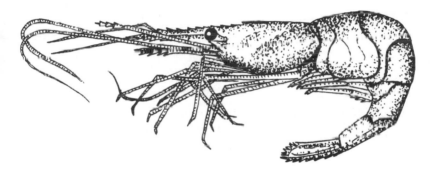

PRAWNS – several species are on sale in this country, these include DEEP-WATER or NORTHERN PRAWN, the COMMON PRAWN, the PACIFIC or KING PRAWN, occasionally the MEDITERRANEAN PRAWN – *see also* SHRIMPS

Habitat	Atlantic waters and Mediterranean.
Pros and Cons	Prawns bought in their shells are infinitely more exciting than the pre-shelled frozen variety, which look pretty in a dish but don't have much flavour. Most prawns on sale will have been pre-cooked so are ready to eat cold, but they can be made into

hot dishes needing only sufficient cooking time to make them piping hot.

Size   Vary in size from around 5–15 cm (2–6 ins) depending on variety.

Description   Cooked prawns curl in on themselves, the shells vary in colour from a rosy pink to pale coral striped with white, that of the Pacific variety being a grey-green tinted with pink; the flesh is white or pinkish.

How sold   Usually by weight or volume.

Qty per person   Allow 225 g (8 oz) in shells, half this amount if already shelled. If sold by volume allow 300 ml (½ pint).

Ask fishmonger   If they are fresh or frozen, and if frozen make sure they have not been thawed and re-frozen; this will be indicated by their limp and pallid state; their colour should look bright and lively and the bodies feel firm and be undamaged.

Availability   February to October but available frozen all year.

Notes   Prawns and shrimps are often confusedly labelled and referred to in recipes. A simple solution is to count prawns as the bigger of the two and shrimps as those which are too fiddly to be peeled before eating. So if a recipe says shrimps and tells you to peel them, buy prawns, the only exception being potted shrimps.

Preparation   Rinse in a colander under running cold water. To shell: hold them by the head, uncurl the tail, pull off the legs and peel away the shell. The tail is then easily slipped out of the head with a gentle tug. Remove the thin, black thread of the intestines.

　　If they are frozen it is vital you allow them to defrost slowly in a shallow china or glass dish, and then drain off the liquid. Don't be tempted to thaw them in a microwave, say, or eat them still half frozen – they will taste of nothing.

Cooking ideas Delicious eaten just as they are with a home-made mayonnaise or other cold sauce, letting everyone peel their own. They are marvellous fried whole with lots of garlic and parsley; or peeled and eaten on brown bread. Or make a delicious curry, using the recipe for garfish on page 95, simply add the peeled prawns right at the end of the cooking time. Remember to give prawns the absolute minimum of cooking time. Mediterranean or king prawns can be cooked using recipes for Dublin Bay prawns or scallops. Use the discarded shells as part of a fish stock, or make prawn butter (follow recipe for crayfish butter on page 67).

James's fried Prawns

This is a lovely starter to a meal. The prawns glisten with their buttery cooking juices and are deliciously flavoured with the garlic and herbs which must be fresh, not dried.
450–675 g (1–1½ lb) or 1–1½ pints prawns in their shells
juice of 1 lemon
1–2 cloves of garlic, finely chopped
2 or 3 tablespoons finely chopped parsley
1 tablespoon finely chopped thyme
cayenne pepper, a generous pinch or more depending on your taste
50 g (2 oz) butter
4 tablespoons olive oil
lemon wedges
Thirty minutes before cooking the prawns put them in a single layer in a shallow glass or china dish, squeeze over the juice of a lemon, sprinkle with the garlic, herbs and cayenne pepper.

To cook the prawns, a wok is ideal, otherwise use a frying pan. Heat the butter and oil together and when it is very hot add the prawns and cook 3–5 minutes, tossing them over high heat. Turn them on to a hot dish with all their cooking juices and surround with the lemon wedges. Eat with your fingers with lots of French bread for mopping up. Have more cayenne and soya sauce on offer, as well as napkins and finger bowls.

Prawns on cracked ice

Arrange whole, unpeeled prawns on a bed of cracked ice, surrounded by lemon wedges. Make a mayonnaise or aïoli, cut plenty of brown bread and butter, give everyone a finger bowl and a napkin and have a bowl handy for the discarded shells.

Prawns on bread
Slice brown bread quite thickly and spread with butter. Top with shelled prawns, add a little salt, freshly milled black pepper and a squeeze of lemon juice. Eat with a knife and fork.

Prawn cocktail
This must be quite the most popular starter in most restaurants and it's often the most disappointing. Try it this way. For four people allow 1 litre (2 pints) prawns in their shells. Set aside two or three per person to use as a garnish. Shell the rest, discarding heads, tails etc. (use to make prawn butter or add to a soup pot if you wish). Put them to marinade sprinkled with pepper and a teaspoon or two of brandy. Make a mayonnaise (*see* page 285), using 1 egg yolk, a teaspoon mustard, 8 tablespoons olive oil, cayenne pepper, 1 teaspoon tomato ketchup, a little salt and the juice of half a lemon. Mix in the prawns. Line glasses, small bowls or plates with salad leaves. Put the prawns on top and garnish each with whole prawns with their heads left on but legs and shells removed.

QUAHOG, *see* **CLAMS**

QUEENS, *see* **SCALLOPS**

Rabbitfish

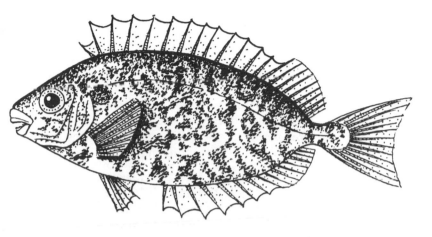

RABBITFISH or Creole CORDONNIER BRISANT

Habitat	W Indian Ocean and E Mediterranean and SE Asia.
Pros and Cons	Once in a while you just might come across this fish with its very apt name. A few are flown in fresh from the Seychelles and some come frozen from Thailand, Singapore and Malaysia. They enjoy a good local reputation, and are worth trying if you get the chance.
Size	Usually around 25 cm (10 ins.)
Description	An oval dull-olive grey or brown body, marbled with pale gold. The spines on the fins are venomous. It has a rounded snout and small scales.
How sold	Whole fish.
Qty per person	One fish.
Ask fishmonger	To clean and make sure all the venomous spines are removed.

Availability	Most likely to be found in fishmongers in London and the SE patronized by Chinese, West Indians or Greeks.
Notes	These fish feed on seaweeds and sea grasses which in conjunction with their rabbity appearance accounts for their name. They are enjoyed in the Far East, Greece and Cyprus as well as in countries of the Indo-Pacific. Attempts are being made to culture them, so they could become more widely available in the future. In Australia these fish are nicknamed Happy Moments, a typically laid-back way perhaps of describing the agony which can be caused by the venomous spines.
Preparation	If the fishmonger hasn't removed these venomous spines, handle the fish with gloves and cut them away carefully using kitchen shears. If you prick yourself, immerse immediately in hot water, it can be very painful for up to 30 minutes.
Cooking ideas	Fry, grill, steam or use in soups. Use recipes for black sea bream or flyingfish.

Rabbitfish steamed in Chinese fashion
4 rabbitfish
salt
slice of root ginger cut in slivers
1 teaspoon sugar
1 teaspoon soya sauce
1 teaspoon wine vinegar
2 or 3 spring onions, chopped
1 green pepper, cut in strips
1 lemon, sliced
Rub the cleaned fish inside and out with salt, score it lightly and insert slivers of fresh ginger. Put it on a plate. Mix sugar, soya sauce and vinegar and pour over the fish. Add two or three chopped spring onions, a green pepper cut in strips, and put slices of lemon on top. Set aside for an hour. Steam as on page 303.

RAINBOW RUNNER, *see* CARANGIDS

RAINBOW TROUT, *see* TROUT

Rascasse

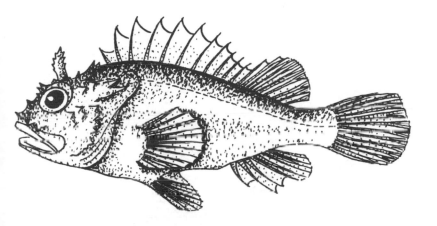

RASCASSE or SCORPIONFISH – *same family as:* REDFISH

Habitat	Mediterranean and Atlantic to Biscay.
Pros and Cons	An extremely spiny fish which is mainly used to give flavour to Mediterranean fish soups and bouillabaisse.
Size	Around 20–45 cm (8–18 ins.)
Description	A spectacular if bad-tempered looking fish with an armour-plated reddish body frilled with spiny fins.
How sold	Whole fish.
Ask fishmonger	To clean, but leave the spiny fins and head. Its fierce appearance is all part of its appeal in the bouillabaisse.

Availability	A few are imported and you might just find one at Billingsgate or other large fishmarkets; if you do snap it up and make an authentic Marseille bouillabaisse.
Preparation	Handle the rascasse with care, those spines can inflict a nasty wound.
Cooking ideas	Use rascasse in bouillabaisse or soups.

RAY, *see* **SKATES and RAYS**

RAZOR-SHELL, *see* **CLAMS**

RED ADMIRAL, *see* **SNAPPERS**

Redfish

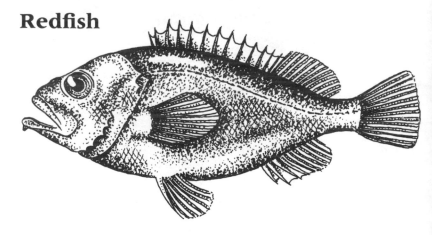

REDFISH — *also known as:* OCEAN PERCH or NORWAY HADDOCK; *same family as:* RASCASSE

Habitat	N Atlantic.
Pros and Cons	This is a fish with good flavour, viewed with suspicion because of its unfamiliarity and therefore

not expensive. Sold by some fishmongers as bream. Make sure it is sparkling and fresh, it doesn't have good keeping qualities and can be limp and vapid. A relation of the rascasse, or scorpionfish, so watch out for spiky fins and bones.

Size Usually around 25–50 cm (10–20 ins.)

Description The oval, compressed, scaly body is a bright orange-red. The gill covers are spiny and so are the rays of the first dorsal fin. It has large eyes, a protruding lower jaw and a broad tail fin.

How sold Whole fish or filleted.

Qty per person Allow 225–275 g (8–10 oz) whole, ungutted fish. Fillets: 150–175 g (5–6 oz).

Ask fishmonger If buying whole fish: to scale, trim fins, gut and remove gills and gill covers. Or ask him to fillet or cut into steaks, if you prefer, and to give you the head and trimmings for stock.

Availability Scarce January and February, most abundant in summer. Becoming increasingly available.

Notes The redfish has become commercially very important, large quantities of it are sold in disguise as fish fingers and suchlike, not because it is inferior but because of our inbuilt prejudice to anything unfamiliar.

Preparation The fish must be scaled, cleaned and trimmed. Take care not to prick yourself on the sharp spines on fins and gill covers. If cooking whole make sure the gills are removed.

Cooking ideas Good stuffed, baked or braised; or poach and eat with aïoli; the fillets can be fried and the steaks grilled; or make kebabs. Use recipes for sea breams, groupers, snappers or cod. Or make couscous, page 69.

Stuffed Redfish
1 redfish weighing around 900 g (2 lbs)

Redfish

25 g (1 oz) butter
100 g (4 oz) unsmoked streaky bacon
1 onion, finely chopped
1 clove of garlic, chopped
handful of chopped parsley
1 cup breadcrumbs
juice of 1 lemon
salt, pepper
1 egg
1 teaspoon fennel seeds
sprigs of fresh thyme (or use 1 teaspoon dried)
1 glass dry white wine
olive oil

Heat the oven to Gas 5/375°F/190°C. Make a stuffing by melting the butter and adding the chopped bacon. Let it cook several minutes over a medium heat, add the onion and cook a few moments more. Stir in garlic, parsley and breadcrumbs. Mix well, remove from the heat and add lemon juice, salt, pepper and the beaten egg. Lay the cleaned fish on a sheet of oiled foil, fill the cavity with the stuffing. Season the outside of the fish with salt and pepper, sprinkle over the fennel seeds, add the thyme. Pour over the glass of wine and sprinkle with olive oil. Make the foil into a loose but secure parcel and bake 45 minutes.

RED GURNARD, *see* **GURNARDS**

RED HERRING, *see* **HERRINGS, SMOKED**

Red Mullet

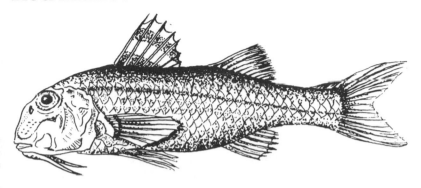

RED MULLET — more than one variety sold including GOLDEN MULLET or ROUGET BARBES. Not the same family as the Grey Mullet.

Habitat   E Atlantic and Mediterranean, as well as tropical and sub-tropical waters elsewhere.

Pros and Cons   Red mullet are delicious despite being a bit bony, though fresh are often expensive. If you eat them ungutted, as in Mediterranean cooking, they have a rich, gamy flavour. Watch out you are not sold red gurnard instead, which is not so fine, but is easily recognized by its armour-plated face and lack of barbels.

Size   20–35 cm (8–14 ins.)

Description   A rosy fish glowing with sunset colours from pale pink, to deep red with blue and orange tints and a silver belly. It has a steep forehead with two spiny barbels on the chin and large scales.

How sold   Whole fish; sometimes fillets.

Qty per person   Usually 1 or 2 fish depending on size; allow 225–275 g (8–10 oz) of whole, ungutted fish, 150–175 g (5–6 oz) fillets.

Ask fishmonger	To scale, trim and remove gills but leave ungutted; if you don't fancy this, at least ask him to leave in the liver, which will give it a gamy flavour.
Availability	Fresh from SW England in summer months; or imported fresh and frozen throughout the year.
Notes	In France red mullet are nicknamed after two highly prized birds which they also eat ungutted – *bécasses* or *grives de mer* (sea woodcock or sea thrush). Related species the golden mullets are imported and may be cooked exactly in the same way.
Preparation	Fish must be washed and scaled and gills removed. The skin is fragile so scale with care. Eat ungutted, it really is extremely tasty.
Cooking ideas	Grill, barbecue, bake or fry or cook *en papillote*, with flavourings like thyme, rosemary and fennel, tomatoes and olives. Grill, fry or bake fillets with flavours such as garlic, fennel, rosemary and thyme.

Grilled Red Mullet
Score the fish diagonally on both sides. Crush 1 tablespoon of fennel seeds and mix with a chopped clove of garlic, a sprig of rosemary and one of thyme. Press into the slits and brush with olive oil. Marinade for 30 minutes. Grill as on page 298. Serve with lemon wedges. Eat with a vinaigrette sauce made from olive oil and lemon juice.

Fried Red Mullet – Rougets à la niçarde
In Nice, they might roll the fish in breadcrumbs, fry in hot olive oil for about 5 minutes each side and serve with stuffed tomatoes, lemon slices and a garnish of green or black olives. Fillets can be cooked in the same way.

Baked Red Mullet – Rougets à la marseillaise
Heat oven to Gas 6/400°F/200°C. Heat 2 or 3 tablespoons olive oil in a pan and fry the mullet over high heat to sear the skin. Transfer to an oiled oven dish. Soften a chopped onion in remaining oil, add a chopped clove of garlic, two or three chopped tomatoes, a handful

of chopped parsley, salt, pepper and pour over a glass of dry white wine. Bring to the boil. Pour over the fish and bake in the oven for 15 minutes. (Cook fillets in the same way, omitting preliminary frying.)

Baked Red Mullet with fennel – Rouget au fenouil
Heat oven to Gas 6/400°F/200°C. Heat 2 tablespoons olive oil in a pan and cook a chopped onion and sliced bulb of fennel until soft. Cut two slashes on both sides of each fish. Make a bed of the onions and fennel in a shallow dish, add the fish, season with pepper. Cover with a layer of breadcrumbs and sprinkle with oil. Bake 15–20 minutes. Serve sprinkled with lemon juice and dusted with parsley.

En papillote
Heat oven to Gas 4/350°F/180°C. Cut squares of foil and put one fish (or a fillet) on each. Season with salt and pepper, a sprig of thyme and rosemary, some crushed fennel and a thread of saffron or a pinch of saffron powder. Squeeze over lemon juice and add a sprinkling of olive oil. Make into parcels and bake 25–30 minutes.

RED PORGY, *see* **BREAMS, SEA**

RED SNAPPER, *see* **SNAPPERS**

RIGG, *see* **DOGFISH**

Roach

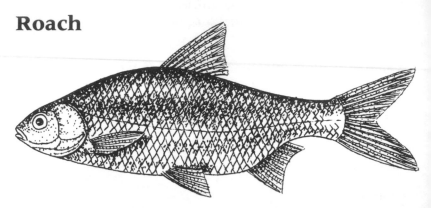

ROACH – *same family as:* BARBEL, BREAM, CARP, GUDGEON and TENCH

Habitat Well-weeded lowland lakes and rivers as well as reservoirs and ponds in Britain and Europe; some imported from Holland and France.

Pros and Cons A popular angling fish; if it's caught from a river with a gravelly bed, the flesh is quite fine but beware of masses of small forked bones.

Size Up to 40 cm (16 ins.)

Description A rounded, rather humped dark-green or blue body with slivery sides; pelvic and anal fins are tinged with red and the scales are large. The mouth is small with a projecting upper lip; iris is red and it has no barbels.

Qty per person Whole fish ungutted: 250–300 g (8–10 oz).

Preparation Scale as soon after catching as possible, or use a wire brush, or dip the fish in boiling water for a few seconds to loosen them. Or cook the fish and skin it afterwards. Trim fins, remove gills, clean and rub out well with salt and vinegar. If there is a chance of muddiness, soak for 30 minutes in acidulated water (2 tablespoons vinegar, 1 teaspoon salt to 1 litre [1¾ pints] water).

Cooking ideas Fry small roach *à la meunière*, or follow recipes for trout; cook large fish like carp, or cook in curry sauce like garfish, page 95.

Fried Roach

Roll the fish in flour seasoned with salt and cayenne. Fry *à la meunière* as on page 296. Serve with a dusting of parsley and lemon wedges.

ROCK COD, *see* **GROUPERS**

ROCK EEL, *see* **DOGFISH**

ROCK FISH, *see* **CATFISH, SEA; DOGFISH**

ROCK SALMON, *see* **CATFISH, SEA; DOGFISH; COLEY**

ROCK TURBOT, *see* **CATFISH, SEA**

ROUGET BARBES, *see* **RED MULLET**

ROUGH HOUND, *see* **DOGFISH**

ROUND ROBIN, *see* **CARANGIDS**

SABRE FISH, *see* **SCABBARD FISH**

SAILFISH, *see* **BILLFISH**

SAIL-FLUKE, *see* **MEGRIM**

St Peter's Fish

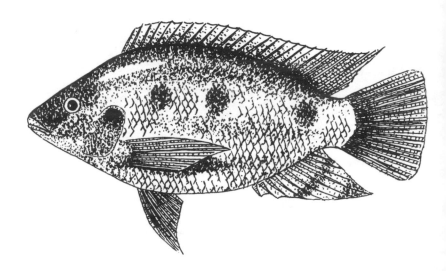

ST PETER'S FISH or TILAPIA

Habitat   Freshwater fish living in warm rivers, lakes and brackish waters such as estuaries in Africa, Middle East and elsewhere by introduction; those sold here are imported from Belgium and Israel.

Pros and Cons   Flesh is firm and full of flavour, comparable to perch or sea breams.

Size   Around 20–25 cm (8–10 ins).

Description   A rather compressed, oval body coloured a deep charcoal grey-blue, with paler sides and silvery belly; some have 3 or more distinct dark blotches along each side; the large scales give the fish a chequered appearance; the first rays of the long dorsal fin are sharply pointed.

How sold   Whole fish.

Qty per person   Allow 1 fish weighing around 300 g (12 oz).

Ask fishmonger   To clean, scale, remove gills and trim; or, if you prefer, to fillet but ask for trimmings for stock.

Availability   All year from enterprising fishmongers especially in shops or markets used by Chinese, Filipinos or Malaysians.

Notes   These fish, of which there are several varieties, have been valued since the days of the ancient Egyptians. Their name derives from the same stories that surround the John Dory, the dark blotches on the sides are supposed to be the fingermarks of St Peter; this fish has perhaps the higher claim as it is much more likely to have been found in the Sea of Galilee than the John Dory. More recently they were hailed as one answer to the world's protein problems. After several false starts and near disasters, farming methods have been developed making them increasingly available They thrive in warm water, feeding on plankton and small insects, reproducing 4–8 times a year; they are mouth brooders, the female retaining the eggs in her mouth during the 4–6 days of incubation.

Preparation   Must be cleaned, trimmed and scaled, if cooking whole. Wash and dry with kitchen paper.

Cooking ideas   Whole fish can be fried or grilled and served with a herb or anchovy butter; or poach and eat with hollandaise sauce lightened with a tablespoon or two of cream (*sauce mousseline*); or bake *en papillote*; or steam like rabbitfish as on page 186. Fillets can be fried *à la meunière* or poached and served with a hollandaise or other sauce such as sorrel or a cream sauce flavoured perhaps with mustard or chives (*see* page 290); prepare whole fish or fillets *en escabèche;* or follow recipes for Black Sea Bream.

St Peter's Fish en papillote

Heat oven to Gas 7/425°F/220°C. Cut rectangles of foil large enough to wrap the fish. Lay each fish on one and fold up the sides to make a boat shape, leaving sufficient foil eventually to close over the top. On each fish put a generous mixture of chopped herbs such as parsley, chives, thyme and rosemary, or you could use dill, tarragon and fennel. Season with salt and pepper. Carefully pour 1 tablespoon of water and 1 of white wine into each boat. Top each fish with a slice of lemon or lime. Fold over the foil to form a sealed parcel. Bake 20–25 minutes.

Fillets of St Peter's Fish with tomatoes provençale

Heat oven to Gas 7/425°F/220°C. Allow 1 large tomato per head, cut each in half and cut two crosswise slits in each. Insert slivers of garlic. Top each with a tablespoon of breadcrumbs mixed with chopped parsley, thyme and oregano. Sprinkle with olive oil and bake in the top of the oven for about 10 minutes. Meanwhile fry the fillets of fish *à la meunière,* page 296. Serve dusted with chopped parsley, lemon wedges and the tomatoes.

SAINT-PIERRE, *see* **ST PETER'S FISH; JOHN DORY**

SAITHE, *see* **COLEY**

Salmon

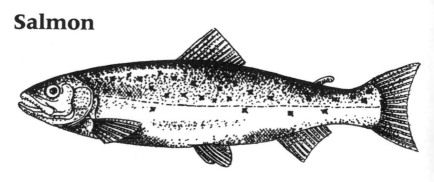

SALMON — *same family as:* TROUT, CHARR, POWAN and SMELT

Habitat   This is an Atlantic seafish which migrates to the upper regions of rivers to spawn. It is caught in rivers, lakes and estuaries as well as at sea by drift netting and trawling the winter grounds. There is also a very large industry producing farmed salmon which accounts for over 90 per cent of the catch.

Pros and Cons   Salmon are magnificent. The pink flesh is rich and delicious and though it may seem expensive, you don't need a lot and it is absolutely simple to prepare. The good news is that with farming now being so developed, this fish is becoming increasingly available.

Size   Usually between 50–100 cm (20–39 ins). The smaller specimens are known as GRILSE and are young salmon returning to rivers after their first winter at sea. (Very large salmon are usually smoked.)

Description   The streamlined slender body with its narrow tail stalk, bearing a small adipose fin, is silvery with a steel-blue back, paler sides and belly; the head and back has many criss-cross or round black dots. Scales are small. Small salmon can be confused with sea trout; to tell the difference look at the bone of the upper jaw, in salmon it does not extend beyond the eye, whereas it does in sea trout; the tail stalk of the salmon is much narrower than that of the trout.

How sold   Whole fish, or by weight in cut pieces, steaks or cutlets. Also SMOKED SALMON (*see* page 204) and PICKLED SALMON (*see* page 203). Salmon heads are sometimes offered by the fishmonger and can be used for stock or soups (some people say the cheeks are the best part). The tail end may be cheaper; it's a good buy being juicy though a bit bony. Sometimes small salmon (smolts) which are under the legal limit of 30 cm (12 ins) are sold as SALMON TROUT.

Qty per person Allow 225 g (8 oz) of complete fish with head. Cut pieces: 100–175 g (4–6 oz).

Ask fishmonger If buying whole fish to clean, scale, trim and remove the gills and ask for one with a small head. Ask for steaks about 2½ cm (1 in) thick.

Availability Farmed and imported salmon is available all year. Wild salmon is available from 1 February to 31 August.

Notes Very few people blindfolded can tell the difference between a wild or a farmed salmon, so don't be intimidated by food snobs who insist that only wild salmon will do. This attitude can only cause harm to an industry which needs a pat on the head for courage and enterprise.

Pacific salmon is a slightly different story. There are in fact several species, some of which are used for canning, others sold as Canadian frozen salmon. This last in no way compares to our Atlantic salmon, being really quite humdrum, but it is very cheap and is useful perhaps for mousses or made-up dishes.

Preparation Wash whole salmon and trim, remove gills and gut if the fishmonger hasn't already done so; make sure all traces of blood or any blackness has been removed. Dry well with kitchen paper before cooking.

Cooking ideas Whole salmon or a large piece can be poached or baked in foil and eaten hot with melted butter or a hollandaise or sorrel sauce. Or eat it cold with mayonnaise or a walnut horseradish sauce. Cutlets and steaks can be poached, grilled, fried *à la meunière*, baked *en papillote* or made into kebabs. Eat it with simple accompaniments such as new potatoes, creamed spinach or green salads, nothing jarring like beetroot or tomato. You're unlikely ever to have a surfeit of leftover salmon but if you do, pot it like charr (*see* page 41), flavour a quiche or make a mousse, or a koulibiac or even a kedgeree.

Poached Salmon
Poach as described on page 300, skin and serve on a long dish garnished if hot with lemon wedges. If serving cold you could surround it with thinly sliced cucumber and whole unpeeled prawns, with a row of lemon slices down the centre of the dish.

Salmon baked in foil
A whole salmon needs a large fish kettle which you may not have. Cooking it in foil is a very good method. Heat oven to Gas 2/300°F/150°C. Cut a piece of foil large enough to envelop the salmon. Oil it if eating cold, or butter it if eating hot. Lay the salmon on top, season it inside and out with salt and pepper and squeeze over the juice of a lemon. Cook the fish allowing 12 minutes per 475 g (1 lb). If eating hot, let it rest in the foil for 15 minutes before opening; if eating cold, let it cool in the parcel. Serve on a long dish garnished as above.

Grilled Salmon steaks or cutlets
Grill cutlets as on page 298, brushing them with plenty of melted butter. Serve with melted butter or hollandaise sauce, garnished with parsley and lemon wedges.

Salmon kebabs
Cut the salmon into chunks and marinade in salt, pepper, dill and tarragon, sliced onion and lemon juice for 30–60 minutes. Alternate with mushrooms, pieces of courgette and green pepper. Cook as on page 299.

Salmon en papillote
Heat oven to Gas 6/400°F/200°C. Cut squares of foil and lay a steak on each. Add salt, pepper, lemon juice, a sprinkling of herbs such as dill, tarragon or parsley, dot with butter, put a slice of lemon on top and fold into secure but loose parcels. Cook 10–15 minutes.

Salmon mousse or use other cooked leftover fish
225 g (8 oz) cooked salmon
25 g (1 oz) butter
1 bunch spring onions, chopped
300 ml (½ pint) of the *court bouillon* or juice left in the foil when
   cooking the salmon
3 level teaspoons powdered gelatine
300 ml (½ pint) whipping cream (or use a mixture of half double
   and half single)
1 tablespoon tomato purée
few drops tabasco sauce
juice of 1 lemon
salt, pepper
Heat the butter in a small saucepan and cook the chopped spring
onions until they are soft over a low heat. Heat the stock and
sprinkle in the gelatine and let it dissolve. Set aside to cool. Flake the
fish, remove all skin and bones and either put into a food processor
or pound using a mortar and pestle. Whip the cream until it is thick
but not too stiff. Add to the fish the tomato purée, tabasco, onions,
lemon juice, stock, salt and pepper. When the mixture beings to
thicken as the gelatine sets, carefully fold it into the cream. Taste
and if necessary add more seasoning. Put into an oiled mould or
individual pots and leave in the fridge to set. Turn out and garnish
with watercress or cucumber.

Salmon kedgeree
Follow the recipe on page 114, adding the juice of a lemon and
tasting before adding extra salt and pepper.

Koulibiac
Like kedgeree this Russian dish is easy to make if you happen to
have some leftover rice and you buy ready-made puff pastry. It will
make a meal for 6 people and can be eaten hot or cold.
450 g (1 lb) cooked salmon
2 eggs
75 g (3 oz) butter
1 onion, chopped finely
225 g (8 oz) mushrooms, chopped
1–2 cups cooked rice or cook 175 g (6 oz) rice
salt, pepper

juice of 1 lemon
350 g (12 oz) puff pastry
1 egg, beaten with a few drops of water
Flake the salmon and remove all skin and bones. Hard-boil the eggs, cooking them for eight minutes, then set aside in a bowl of cold water. Heat half the butter in a wok or frying pan and cook the chopped onion for a few minutes, add the mushrooms and cook them until they have softened – about 5 minutes. Stir in the cooked rice, season with plenty of salt and pepper and the lemon juice. Divide the pastry in two, one piece about two-thirds of the other and roll out thinly into two rectangles. Set the largest piece on a baking tray and put half the mushroom and rice mixture down the centre, leaving a margin of pastry all around, lay fish on top. Slice the eggs and lay them on the fish. Cover with the rest of the mushrooms and rice, and dot with the remaining butter. Fold up the edges of the pastry, lay the second piece on top and crimp the edges together to form a parcel, use a little of the beaten egg to seal if necessary. You can use any bits of leftover pastry to form leaves, flowers or what you will. Brush the pastry all over with egg wash and add your decorations if any. Put in a cool place while you heat the oven to Gas 6/400°F/200°C. Bake for 25–30 minutes until the pastry is golden. Serve with a cream sauce (*see* page 290).

SALMON BASS, *see* **BASS**

Salmon, Pickled

SALMON, PICKLED – **Gravlax** is the Swedish method of pickling salmon and like smoked salmon is expensive to buy. It is simple to make and quite a lot cheaper. You don't need a whole salmon, a piece will do.

1 piece of salmon weighing about 450 g (1 lb)
2 teaspoons salt
2 teaspoons caster sugar
2 teaspoons crushed white peppercorns
handful of fresh dill

Cut the salmon in half along the back, ease open and remove the backbone. Put half the dill in a shallow china or glass dish, top with one of the pieces of salmon, skin side down. Mix the salt, sugar and pepper and rub each cut side of salmon with the mixture. Put the remaining dill on the salmon in the dish and lay the second piece on top to form a sandwich. Cover with greaseproof or waxed paper and put a board or plate on top, weighing it down with something heavy. Keep in the fridge for 2 or 3 days, turning and basting the sandwiched pieces each morning and night. To serve: remove the seasonings and dill and slice very thinly, cutting diagonally using a very sharp knife. Eat with a sauce made by mixing in a mortar with a pestle 1 tablespoon of mild mustard with 1 tablespoon of sugar and 2 of vinegar. Mix well and gradually work in about 5 fl oz (¼ pint) of oil, use olive or peanut. Or you can put all the ingredients in a screw-top jar and shake it vigorously, although it won't be so thick or so good.

Hemrimmad Lax is a variation using twice as much salt as sugar.

Salmon, Smoked

Description   Should be a fresh, shiny pink with intense, moist flesh, avoid any that looks dry and very orange.

How sold   Whole sides or by weight. It's best to buy it freshly sliced but some pre-packaged is good, more especially whole sides interleaved with waxed paper. The scrapings and off-cuts are sometimes sold quite cheaply and can be used to make mousse or pâtés or to fill avocado pears.

Qty per person   50–75 g (2–3 oz).

Ask fishmonger   For freshly sliced rather than any that has been left standing on the slab which will be dry and just as expensive.

Availability   From upmarket fishmongers as well as delicatessens, stores and supermarkets. Frozen is in no way comparable but is useful for made up dishes.

Notes Large salmon which are very oily and rich are smoked rather than sold fresh. They are boned, rubbed with salt and spices and after several hours washed and dried before being cold smoked over oak sawdust, or in Scotland perhaps birch and juniper and in Ireland peat. The wood and length of time salting and smoking affects the flavour. So try salmon from different smokers to find the one you like the best.

Preparation If you have to slice your own, remove any small bones at the sides. Use a very sharp knife or an old-fashioned cut-throat razor can be effective. Begin in the middle and work towards the tail, cutting as thinly as possible, so that the slices are almost transparent and the pieces are as big as possible. Spread the salmon in one slightly overlapping layer on a large flat dish. Keep the trimmings and bits for made up dishes.

Cooking Ideas Top quality smoked salmon is far too good to fuss about with. Eat it just as it is, garnished with lemon wedges, with freshly milled or cayenne pepper and lots of thinly sliced brown bread and butter. Use off-cuts or bits mixed with mayonnaise to fill avocado pears or add at the very last minute to scrambled eggs or an omelette, or make into pâté or combine with salmon to make tartare.

Smoked Salmon pâté – or use other smoked fish such as mackerel, trout, buckling

225 g (8 oz) smoked salmon bits
50 g (2 oz) butter
1 tablespoon olive oil
juice of 1 lemon
4 tablespoons curd cheese
black pepper and cayenne pepper
Chop the smoked salmon, making sure it is free of skin and bones, and mash it with the softened butter. Beat in the olive oil a little at a time as if making mayonnaise, add the lemon juice and stir in the

curd cheese. Season with black pepper and a pinch of cayenne. Put into a bowl and garnish with a sprig of parsley or dill.

Smoked Salmon and Salmon tartare

This makes a light and unusual starter.
150 g (6 oz) smoked salmon pieces
1 salmon steak weighing around 225 g (8 oz)
1 tablespoon finely chopped spring onions
1 tablespoon finely chopped green pepper
juice of 1 lemon
cayenne pepper
½ teaspoon paprika
2 teaspoons capers
3 or 4 gherkins, chopped
handful of chopped parsley
watercress and lemon wedges to garnish

Skin the salmon, remove bones and mince. Mix with the smoked salmon cut in bits, add spring onions, green pepper, lemon juice, cayenne, paprika, capers, gherkins and the parsley. Mix lightly together. Put on to individual plates and garnish with watercress and lemon wedges. Eat with thin slices of buttered toast.

SALMON TROUT, *see* **TROUT**

SAND SOLE, *see* **SOLE**

Sardine

SARDINE (PILCHARD) — *related to:* ANCHOVY, HERRING, and SPRAT

Habitat English Channel and French coast, Atlantic coast of southern Europe and Mediterranean.

Pros and Cons Delicious tasty small fish which are inexpensive and make excellent eating despite being bony. Like all oily fish, they deteriorate quickly so make sure they are spanking fresh with sparkling eyes.

Size Usually around 15–20 cm (6–8 ins).

Description Slender rounded body coloured green or blueish black, with golden sides and silver belly. It has large scales and raised ridges on gill covers.

How sold Whole fish fresh and frozen.

Qty per person 175–225 g (6–8 oz) of whole, ungutted fish.

Ask fishmonger For small ones (tastier than large).

Availability Mostly all year except in bad weather.

Notes Sardines and pilchards are the same fish; in this country we call the young ones sardines and the mature fish pilchards, but this distinction is not made in France, from where most of our supplies are sent, the name *sardine* being used for young and mature fish.

In the summer you may be lucky to find local sardines (sold as pilchards) in Devon, Cornwall and S Wales. All sorts of small fish, including sardines, are sold as canned sardines or pilchards. They are a useful store standby, nice eaten cold sprinkled with lemon juice, or eaten on toast and put under a hot grill for a few moments or with a salad of tomatoes and black olives dressed with lemon juice and olive oil.

Preparation   Scale, remove fins and gut, either through the belly or the gills (*see* page 310). Rinse and remove all traces of black and blood. Dry with kitchen paper.

Cooking ideas   Sardines are delicious grilled, baked or fried or you can make a traditional stargazy pie; or prepare them *en escabèche* (page 211) or use instead of anchovies baked as in Naples (page 4).

Grilled Sardines

Clean the sardines but leave their heads on. Brush with plenty of oil and lemon juice and grill as page 298. Nice served with a bowl of aïoli or a flavoured butter such as garlic or lemon.

Greek baked Sardines with lemon

Heat oven to Gas 4/350°F/180°C. Arranged gutted sardines in an oven dish. Mix 4 tablespoons of olive oil with 4 of lemon juice and pour over the fish, add pepper and sprinkle with fresh marjoram or thyme. Bake for about 15 minutes.

Fried Sardines

Roll the washed and dried fish in flour. Heat 3 or 4 tablespoons olive or peanut oil and add a few sprigs of thyme and a chopped clove of garlic, let them sizzle then throw them out. Fry the fish three or four minutes on each side. Remove and put on a hot dish. Wipe out the pan with kitchen paper, add a tablespoon or two of fresh oil and three or four chopped tomatoes, cook over fierce heat; add another chopped clove of garlic and a few more sprigs of thyme. Stir well, and put on top of the fish. Sprinkle with lemon juice and garnish with parsley.

Sardino au gratin ei poumo d'amour – Sardines baked with tomatoes

Heat oven to Gas 6/400°F/200°C. Chop 900 g (2 lbs) tomatoes. Put half in the base of an oven dish. Arrange a layer of cleaned sardines on top, season with salt and pepper. Cover with remaining tomatoes. Add two chopped cloves of garlic and a handful of chopped parsley, sprinkle generously with olive oil. Cook 20 minutes.

Sardines baked with spinach

12 sardines
salt, pepper
6 tablespoons breadcrumbs
2 or 3 chopped anchovy fillets
parsley, thyme, oregano
450 g (1 lb) spinach (or use a packet of frozen spinach)
2 tablespoons olive oil
1 or 2 cloves garlic, chopped
nutmeg
juice of 1 lemon
2 eggs, beaten
Heat oven to Gas 4/350°F/180°C. Remove heads, split the fish down the front and bone, see page 315. Season with salt and pepper. Mix the breadcrumbs with the chopped anchovy fillets and the herbs and stuff the fish with half this mixture. Cook the spinach in a pan with half the olive oil and the chopped garlic. Let it soften, drain, season well with salt, pepper, nutmeg and lemon juice. Add the beaten eggs. Lay spinach in a buttered oven dish, put sardines in close ranks, heads to tails. Sprinkle with remaining breadcrumb mixture and oil. Bake 20–25 minutes.

Stargazy pie

It's definitely the name which makes this pie seem so very appealing, it derives from the fact that the sardines were arranged with their heads protruding, gazing at the heavens. The reason for this was not romantic: sardine heads are inedible but they contain rich oil, so this way none of the oil was lost and no pastry or space in the pie was wasted. If you want to try it, heat the oven to Gas 6/400°F/200°C. Clean and bone (page 315) 8 sardines, leave on their heads, and fill their cavities with a smear of mustard, some finely chopped onion, chopped thyme and parsley. Line a pie plate with short pastry and brush the outside edge with beaten egg. Arrange the fish like the spokes of a wheel, their heads overlapping the rim. Cover with another circle of pastry, letting the heads hang out, but sealing the pastry between each fish. Cut a slit in the centre, brush all over with beaten egg and bake 30–35 minutes.

SAR, *see* **BREAMS, SEA**

SAUPE, *see* **BREAMS, SEA**

SAURY PIKE, *see* **GARFISH**

Scabbard Fish

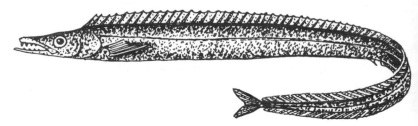

SCABBARD FISH, SILVER and BLACK – *also known as:* SABRE FISH

Habitat N Atlantic and Mediterranean; many species found elsewhere.

Pros and Cons Watch out for these unusual fish which provide good eating providing you avoid the thin and bony tail end.

Size Can grow up to 1½ metres (5 feet) but usually much smaller.

Description Long scabbard shape, coloured silver or a dull black with a long dorsal fin, small forked tail fin and ferocious teeth.

How sold	Whole or in pieces by weight.
Qty per person	175–200 g (6–7 oz).
Ask fishmonger	To give you a piece away from the tail and to cut into pieces about 6–8 cm (2½–3 ins) long.
Availability	Enterprising fishmongers most probably in London and SE and in areas frequented by Chinese.
Notes	You may not see this fish very often although it is imported. Most of the catch is caught off Portugal, where it is much appreciated and its name is *peixe espada preta*. It is also popular in Italy, where it is called *pesce sciabolo*; another species of the fish features in Chinese cooking.
Preparation	If the fishmonger hasn't already done so, cut it into pieces about 6–8 cm (2½–3 ins) long. Wash and dry well with kitchen paper.
Cooking ideas	May be fried in oil, dusted with parsley and served with lemon wedges and home-made tomato sauce, or with a sweet and sour sauce (*see* the recipe for parrotfish on page 168); or marinade pieces in lemon juice, olive oil, chopped garlic and herbs before grilling and basting with the marinade; or bake; or prepare *en escabèche*, which is a method of preserving fish.

Peixe espada preta de Escabeche (en escabèche)

Instead of scabbard fish you can use small, whole gutted fish such as anchovies, horse mackerel, mackerel, sardines, smelts or sprats (herbs and spices can be varied according to taste). Coat the fish in flour and fry the pieces in 2 tablespoons olive oil in a wok or frying pan, then transfer them to the dish in which you plan to serve them. In the same pan heat 6 tablespoons fresh olive oil and fry a chopped onion, a sliced carrot and two or three chopped cloves of garlic; when they are soft add salt, bayleaf, thyme, a dried red chilli, pinch of saffron (optional) and mix in 1 cup of wine vinegar and ½ cup of water. Bring to the boil, lower the heat and simmer uncovered for 15 minutes. Let it cool then strain over the fish, garnish with bayleaves, slices of lemon. Refrigerate. Eat within 2 weeks.

SCAD, *see* **HORSE MACKEREL**

Scallops and Queens

SCALLOPS and QUEENS

Habitat   Atlantic, Channel, North Sea, Mediterranean.

Pros and Cons   Scallops and the smaller queens are delectable, they make an attractive though not very cheap starter to a meal.

Size   Scallops: up to 15 cm (6 ins).
Queens: up to 8 cm (3 ins).

Description   Both have fan-shaped, ribbed shells coloured a dirty brown or pink with variations of creams and yellows; scallops have one round and one flat shell, both shells of queens are rounded. They should have a bright orange coral and translucent greyish flesh, if it is pristine white you can be fairly certain it has been frozen.

How sold   Scallops: either live in whole shells, or cleaned and displayed on the half shell; also just the meat

either fresh or frozen in bags by weight.
Queens: live in their shells.

Qty per person   Scallops: 1 large or 2 small. Queens: 4–6. Fresh or frozen in bags: 150–175 g (5–6 oz).

Ask fishmonger   If you are buying scallops which you intend eating fairly soon, ask him to open the shells and clean them. The scallops will be attached to their flat shells, so ask for the rounded ones as well, these are perfect vessels in which to serve them.

Availability   Mainly upmarket fishmongers from autumn to early summer. Most are exported to Europe or the States, or frozen and breaded; so if you want them fresh, ask for them.

Notes   They must be very fresh with a distinct smell of the sea, so buy them live and be wary about those displayed on the slab, they could have been there for hours. Avoid any that are damaged, watery or pallid. The roe should be sparkling orange.

Preparation   If the fishmonger hasn't opened them, steam them in a pan or heat them gently on top of the stove, just until they begin to open. It is then easy to separate the two shells. Save the juices that you find inside and release the mollusc with a thin, sharp knife. Wash under running water and pull away membrane, grey-brown frill and the black thread of the intestines, leaving just the nut of white flesh and the orange coral.

Cooking ideas   You don't need to do anything very elaborate with these shellfish, the simpler the better, and don't overcook or you'll spoil their delicate texture and flavour. They are lovely simply poached before being served on the half shell after a brief glazing on the grill; or make kebabs with bacon and mushrooms (*see* page 299); or stir fry briefly with ginger and garlic. Queens are delicious grilled in their half shells and eaten with lemon juice and plenty of garlic bread.

Scallops in the half shell
4–8 scallops
300 ml (½ pint) milk
salt, pepper
50 g (2 oz) butter
50 g (2 oz) mushrooms, chopped
2 tablespoons flour
½ teaspoon Dijon mustard
1 tablespoon dry vermouth or dry sherry or use lemon juice
4 tablespoons breadcrumbs
4 tablespoons grated cheese
lemon wedges and parsley
Clean scallops and slice them in half. Put them into a small saucepan with their liquid, the milk, salt and pepper. Bring slowly to the boil. Remove immediately from the heat and leave 3–4 minutes. Heat the grill. Drain the scallops but keep the milk. Melt the butter, add the chopped mushrooms and cook a few minutes, stirring. Over a low heat, stir in the flour and let it cook for a couple of minutes, stirring all the time. Add mustard, vermouth and the milk, using only sufficient to make a thick, creamy sauce. Put the scallops on to 4 half shells, pour over the sauce. Sprinkle with breadcrumbs and cheese and put under the hot grill for a couple of minutes to bubble and brown. Garnish with chopped parsley and serve with lemon wedges.

Coquilles St Jacques à la bretonne
8 scallops
50 g (2 oz) butter
1 small onion, chopped
2 shallots, chopped
4 tablespoons dry white wine
parsley
4 tablespoons breadcrumbs
salt, cayenne pepper
Heat the grill. Melt half the butter in a small pan and fry the onion and shallots. Cut the scallops into small pieces and add to the pan. Pour over the wine, add chopped parsley and 1 tablespoon breadcrumbs. Stir and remove from the heat. Stir in remaining butter cut in pieces. Add salt and cayenne. Put into 4 half shells, sprinkle with breadcrumbs and put under a hot grill to brown.

Stir-fried Scallops

Remove from the shells and clean. Allow 2 scallops per head, cutting them into two or three pieces. Put 2 tablespoons of oil and 25 g (1 oz) butter in a wok and when it is foaming add 1 finely chopped onion or 4 spring onions, two cloves of garlic chopped, 1 piece of ginger cut thinly from the end of a root and chopped. Stir fry over a high heat for 3 or 4 minutes, add the scallops or queens and toss until they become opaque. Turn them on to a hot dish, sprinkle with lemon juice and parsley and serve with French bread to mop up the juices.

Grilled Queens

Wash and clean the queens and put each in a half shell. Heat the grill. Stand them in the grill pan (put crumpled foil in the base to stop them falling over). Sprinkle them generously with freshly milled pepper, dot them with butter and put them under a very hot grill for the butter to melt. Eat immediately with plenty of garlic bread.

SCAMPI, *see* **DUBLIN BAY PRAWNS**

SCHELLY, *see* **POWAN**

SCORPIONFISH, *see* **RASCASSE**

SEA BASS, *see* **BASS**

SEA BREAM, *see* **BREAMS, SEA**

SEA DEVIL, *see* **MONKFISH**

SEA TROUT, *see* **TROUT, BROWN, SEA, AND RAINBOW**

SEA URCHINS — there are several kinds of these shellfish with their hedgehog bristles. In south-west Ireland there is a small fishery, most of the catch being sent to France and ending up in the restaurants of Paris. You might come across others in Brittany or in the Mediterranean. The French name is *oursins*. A special knife is used to open them thus revealing the only edible part, the ovaries grouped like an orange star.

SEA WOLF, *see* **CATFISH, SEA**

Shad

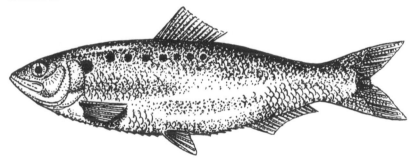

SHAD includes TWAITE SHAD and ALLIS SHAD — *same family as:* HERRING

Habitat European coastline including Mediterranean, comes into the rivers in spring to spawn.

Pros and Cons At their best caught in rivers before spawning when the flesh is sweet and succulent and the roe of the female like a cluster of seed pearls tastes like crunchy caviare; that of the male is also delicious. They have myriads of small bones like herrings and if caught in the sea or after spawning, the flesh is thin and dry.

Size	Twaite shad: 20–50 cm (8–20 ins). The rarer Allis can grow up to 60 cm (24 ins).
Description	A silvery fish coloured with the blue-green of the herring family but distinctly more rotund. It has no lateral line, a forked tail and small, weak teeth. There are many lines on the gill covers.
Qty per person	Allow 1 fish weighing around 225–275 g (8–10 oz).
Availability	Once common but due to pollution hardly ever for sale here though you may find them on the Continent between April and June, especially in restaurants close to estuaries and rivers. They are at their best before spawning begins; in many countries their name means May Fish, so doubtless they are better avoided in June.
Notes	Shad used to be abundant in rivers on western coasts of England and Ireland, like the Severn and Shannon. They eat nothing from leaving the sea until returning after spawning, although some live permanently in alpine lakes such as Como, Maggiore and Garda, as well as in the Killarney lakes. They are nicknamed King of the Herrings.
Preparation	Must be cleaned and trimmed. Like herring, the central bone with its myriad of smaller bones can be removed before cooking (*see* page 315).
Cooking ideas	Most recipes for shad suggest cooking it with sorrel for several hours to reduce the bones to a manageable pulp though you could bone it first and reduce the cooking time to something more normal. It can also be grilled, baked, steamed or poached in a wine-flavoured stock and eaten with *beurre blanc*.

Alose d'Ardèche – Shad as cooked in the Ardèche

Cut the shad into slices. Wash 450 g sorrel and line the base of a casserole with it. Put the fish on top, season with salt, pepper and pour over 300 ml (½ pint) dry white wine. Cook covered for 3 hours at Gas 2/300°F/150°C. Check occasionally that liquid has not evaporated; if necessary top up with a few spoonfuls of water.

Shark

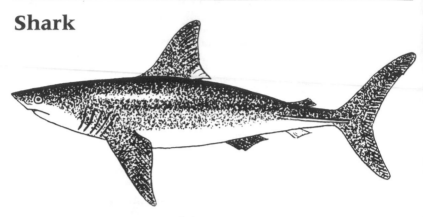

SHARK – of the 500 or so species of shark, only a few dozen are caught and marketed, the best being the PORBEAGLE, TOPE and MAKO

Habitat   N and W Atlantic and Mediterranean.

Pros and Cons   Don't be alarmed, sharks make really excellent eating and being cartilaginous have no irritating bones, but pink tinged flesh which turns white when cooked.

Size   Up to 2–3 m (10 feet).

Description   The muscular, streamlined body is blue-grey with a white belly, large mouth with ferocious teeth.

How sold   Steaks, fresh and frozen.

Qty per person   175–200 g (6–7 oz).

Availability   Quite widely available especially in summer and in markets and shops patronized by the ethnic minorities.

Notes   Sharks are valued all over the Mediterranean as well as other parts of the world including the Caribbean, though they're reviled in Jamaica, whilst being loved in Trinidad. It takes the British to give a nervous laugh at the very idea of eating them. Of course the film *Jaws* did nothing to make the shark endearing but forget any feelings of unease that you might be eating a creature that might have eaten a person; the sharks on sale are not the same sort.

Preparation   If frozen, allow to defrost. Wash and dry steaks before cooking.

Cooking ideas   There's a tendency for shark to be a bit dry, so marinade before grilling it, barbecueing over charcoal or making kebabs. Don't overcook or it will have the texture of flannel. You could use swordfish, barracuda or dogfish recipes.

Grilled Shark steaks

Marinade the steaks for an hour in 4 tablespoons olive oil, the juice of a lemon, chopped garlic and onion, 1 tablespoon chopped parsley, salt, chilli powder and 1 tablespoon of brandy. Heat the grill and cook as page 298, brushing with the marinade at frequent intervals. Serve with chopped parsley sprinkled over them, plenty of lemon wedges and perhaps a sauce such as caper cream sauce (*see* page 291).

Libyan braised Shark steaks – or use firm steaks from other fish

4 shark steaks
olive or peanut oil
2 cloves garlic, chopped
1 teaspoon cumin seeds, crushed
handful chopped fresh coriander or use parsley
sprig of celery
salt, pepper
1 onion, thinly sliced
2 or 3 potatoes, peeled and very thinly sliced
1 medium can tomatoes
juice of 1 lemon
Heat oven to Gas 5/375°F/190°C. Heat 1 tablespoon oil in a wok or frying pan and add the garlic and cumin seeds, let them sizzle for a minute then turn the contents into a shallow oven dish. Put the steaks on top, add the coriander or parsley, celery, salt and pepper. Cover with the slices of onion and potatoes. Empty the tin of tomatoes into the wok, crushing them, add the lemon juice and

4 tablespoons oil, bring to the boil and pour over the fish. Bake 30–40 minutes until the potatoes are soft.

Shrimps

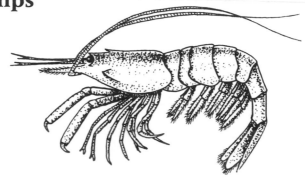

SHRIMPS or BROWN SHRIMPS — *see also* PRAWNS

Habitat	Atlantic, Channel, North Sea and Mediterranean.
Pros and Cons	A cheap feast for lunch or high tea or a great and easy starter. Forget ideas of pre-peeling, this is a desperate task – everyone can deal with their own at table.
Size	Usually around 3–5 cm (1½–2 ins).
Description	Living they are almost transparent, when cooked they turn brown and curl in on themselves.
How sold	Ready-cooked and by volume or weight.
Qty per person	300 ml (½ pint) or 225 g (½ lb).
Ask fishmonger	Check that they are freshly boiled and haven't been frozen, thawed and refrozen, although admittedly this is a tricky question to ask any fishmonger.
Availability	February to October.
Notes	Shrimps and prawns are often confused, especially in recipes. It's simplest to think of shrimps as being smaller and needing no peeling before eating. As

well as the true brown shrimp, you will sometimes see the so-called pink shrimps with their pink and white candy-stripe antennae. Buy them, they are delicious but are in fact a species of small prawn. You see how difficult it is to classify them.

Preparation   Simply rinse the cooked shrimps in a colander under cold running water.

Cooking ideas   Shrimps are sold ready cooked and simply need to be rinsed before eating them whole. If a recipe tells you to buy a lot of shrimps and peel them, buy prawns – that is what is intended. The only time it is worth the fiddly chore of shelling them is if you intend to make potted shrimps.

If you do a bit of shrimping and shramping on holiday, boil your catch in sea water or highly salted ordinary water for 3–5 minutes, but better be sure you are in an unpolluted area.

Shrimps au naturel

Put a bowl of shrimps on a dish surrounded, if you feel fancy, by crushed ice. Serve with lots of brown bread and butter, lemon wedges and a freshly made mayonnaise, aïoli, pistou or rouille. Eat legs, body, heads and all; or if this makes you feel squeamish, pull off the legs and antennae, put the bodies in your mouth tail first, and bite them off at the neck saving the heads etc. for the soup pot; or make shrimp butter following the recipe for crayfish butter on page 67.

Potted Shrimps

½ litre (1 pint), 450 g (1 lb) shrimps (you can pot crab meat in the same way)
50 g (2 oz) butter
pinch each of mace, cayenne and nutmeg
Pull off legs and heads, carefully peel away the shell from each shrimp. Melt the butter and add the spices. Add shrimps and mix gently until they are hot but not actually boiling. Put into individual pots and chill. To serve: stand the pots for a few moments in a bowl of very hot water, as soon as the butter softens you can turn them out on to individual plates garnished with lettuce leaves. Put lemon

wedges and sprigs of parsley on each plate. (If you want to keep them for a week or two, cover with a layer of clarified butter [*see* page 296].)

SILVER SCABBARD FISH, *see* **SCABBARD FISH**

Skates and Rays

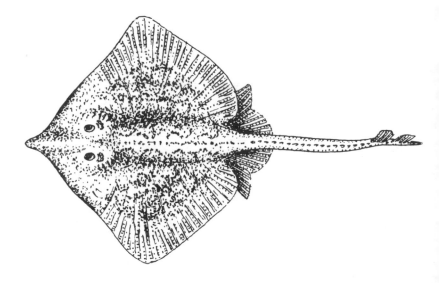

SKATES and RAYS – several species are caught and marketed – *related to:* DOGFISH and SHARKS

Habitat   Temperate, cold and tropical seas.

Pros and Cons   Simple to cook, sweet tasting with no small bones to contend with. The *wings* are laced with a cartilaginous mesh from which the fibrous flesh lifts easily.

Size   Up to 90 cm (36 ins).

Description   Only the fins and tail end are sold so you're unlikely to see a whole skate or ray. They're extraordinary-looking fish like water-logged kites with their wing-like fins and dragon tails.

How sold Fins called WINGS, usually ready-skinned. Sometimes small pieces from the tail, called SKATE NOBS.

Qty per person Allow 175–200 g (6–7 oz).

Ask fishmonger Buy by weight and if necessary ask him to divide the wings into the number of portions you need. Ask for thick, firm pieces which should be tinged with pink. Don't worry about the slight smell of ammonia, it disappears on cooking.

Availability Widely available, best May to February.

Notes The name skate covers both skates and rays, there are several species sold. These fish are incredibly tough when caught, and are usually hung for two or three days before skinning.

Preparation Wash and dry and if necessary cut into portions.

Cooking ideas Wings are best poached or shallow fried and served with *beurre noir* (which isn't black butter at all, but brown butter) or a caper sauce. The nobs can be rolled in flour and fried in butter, served with parsley and lemon wedges. Don't overcook because as the skeleton softens it turns to gelatine and you will have a fish tasting of glue.

Skate with black butter

4 pieces of skate weighing about 225 g (7 oz) each
1 onion, sliced
2 tablespoons white wine vinegar or lemon juice
bayleaf
6 peppercorns
1 teaspoon salt
water to cover
100 g (4 oz) butter
2 tablespoons wine vinegar
handful of chopped parsley
2 tablespoons capers
lemon wedges

Put skate, onion, wine vinegar or lemon juice, bayleaf, peppercorns and salt into a large pan or fish kettle. Just cover with water. Bring slowly to the boil over a medium flame. As soon as the surface of the water begins to shudder, cover the pan and lower the heat. The cooking time will be about 10 minutes, but it's a good idea to check after 5. The fish will begin to turn white and come away from the bones.

Meanwhile have the butter waiting in a small frying pan, and put the vinegar, parsley and capers into a small jug. Make sure the serving dish and plates are hot. Have everyone to the table. Drain the cooked fish, put it on the serving dish and keep it warm.

Melt the butter until it turns from straw to the colour of hazelnuts, immediately pour the mixture in the jug into the side of the pan, as soon as it bubbles and sizzles pour it over the fish. Garnish with the lemon wedges and rush the dish to the table. It must be eaten piping hot.

Fried Skate wings or nobs with cream and caper sauce

Coat the wings or nobs in seasoned flour and fry 3 or 4 minutes on either side in butter. Make the sauce by melting 50 g (2 oz) butter, stir in 3 tablespoons cream. Keep stirring over a medium heat to let the sauce thicken and reduce, add 3 more tablespoons of cream, salt, pepper and 2 tablespoons capers.

SKELLY, *see* **POWAN**

SLIP SOLE, *see* **SOLE**

SLIPPERY DAB, *see* **LEMON SOLE**

SMEAR, *see* **LEMON SOLE**

Smelt

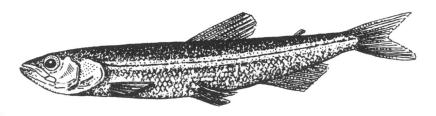

SMELT or SPARLING – *related to:* SALMON and TROUT

Habitat Estuaries and coastal European waters, spawns in rivers.

Pros and Cons Freshly caught smelt are fragrant with the perfume of cucumber, violets or rushes and make delicious eating. They are a rare treat, snap them up if you are able.

Size 10–20 cm (4–8 ins).

Description The spindle-shaped, slightly compressed body with its fine scales has an olive grey back separated from the creamy belly with a wide band of silver. The eyes and jaw are large, and it has teeth both on the tongue and the roof of its mouth.

How sold Whole, usually already gutted.

Qty per person Allow 175–200 g (6–7 oz) of whole, gutted fish.

Availability The catch is limited but perhaps in summer months from local fish markets or fishmongers.

Notes These small fish are cousins of salmon and trout, spending parts of their lives in fresh water as well as in the sea. We crudely use most of the catch for cattle fodder or pike bait but naturally they are more appreciated elsewhere; the French name means pearly fish and they treat them as a delicacy.

Preparation	Wash under running water and wipe dry with kitchen paper. If they need gutting, do so through the gills (*see* page 310). They may be cooked with their heads on or not, as your please.
Cooking ideas	Small smelt are best fried, larger ones can be baked or cooked like whiting.

Fried Smelts
Roll the fish in flour and fry in a mixture of oil and butter until crisp and golden. Sprinkle with lemon juice and eat them with sauce *rémoulade*.

Baked Smelts
Butter an ovenproof dish. Chop an onion very finely and put it and the fish into the dish. Score them on each side. Add a handful of chopped parsley, a few sprigs of thyme, pepper, salt and a glass of white wine. Cover loosely with foil and bake 15–20 minutes.

Eperlan en brochette
In France they fry small smelts *en brochette* – threading 5 or 6 together on small skewers through the eyes. They are then dipped into a jug of milk, then into flour and deep fried until crisp and golden.

SMOKED FISH, *see under fish names*

SMOOTH HOUND, *see* **DOGFISH**

Snappers

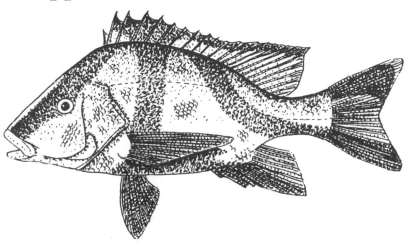

SNAPPERS OR RED SNAPPERS – often sold using the Creole names BOURGEOIS, JOB GRIS, JOB JAUNE, THERESE and VARA VARA

Habitat	Tropical or semi-tropical seas.
Pros and Cons	The flesh of snappers is firm and white, a little coarse and dry but combined with robust sauces, they make good eating and are not madly expensive.
Size	According to species from 15 cm to over a metre (6–39 ins).
Description	Most have a long, triangular-shaped head with canine teeth, a compressed body with a high back, a spiny front dorsal fin and large, tough scales. They come in the colours of a lurid sunset from red, to grey or sunset pink, orange brown or red, often with a sheen of pearl, violet or silver.
How sold	Whole fish, both fresh and frozen.
Qty per person	Allow 225–275 g (8–10 oz) of whole, ungutted fish.

Ask fishmonger	To scale, trim and clean and remove the gills if you plan to cook it whole. Or ask him to fillet larger fish or cut into steaks, if you prefer. If they're frozen, let them defrost before doing the job yourself.
Availability	All year, from enterprising fishmongers. Snappers are popular in the Caribbean, so look out for them in shops and markets patronized by West Indian communities.
Notes	There are a great many varieties of snappers with all sorts of weird and wonderful local names. In the Caribbean they call them Red Snapper, Red fish, Pargue, Vivenot, Jolie-Bleu. Those imported from the Seychelles are usually sold under their Creole titles. The following may help to sort these out a little:

BOURGEOIS or Emperor Snapper also sold as Red Admiral – up to 80 cm (32 ins) coloured a pinkish red. (The THERESE is similar but smaller than BOURGEOIS.)

JOB GRIS or Green Jobfish can grow up to 75 cm (30 ins), a grey, blue-green.

JOB JAUNE or Rosy Jobfish up to 90 cm (36 ins).

VARA VARA – Twinspot Snapper, up to 80 cm (32 ins).

Preparation   Must be cleaned, trimmed and the strong scales removed (be careful of the spines in the dorsal fin), remove gills if you're cooking it whole. Wash inside and out making sure you get rid of all the blood and black in the cavity. Dry well with kitchen paper.

Cooking ideas   Snappers are delicious with strong flavourings, be generous with herbs and spices, cook them with green peppers, aubergines and courgettes, lots of onion and garlic. Large ones can be stuffed and baked and served hot or cold. Or baked with ginger, *see* recipe for bass, page 13. Or poach and serve cold with aïoli or sauce *rémoulade*. Smaller ones or steaks are also good baked or marinaded and grilled; they are excellent barbecued with lemon juice, olive oil and herbs or use Moroccan chermoula or a harissa marinade. Fillets can be braised or baked. In the Caribbean and S America, they often prepare small snappers *en escabèche*, follow the recipe on page 211, but add ½ teaspoon of nutmeg, ginger and cumin to the sauce. Leftover snappers make an excellent poupeton (page 281). Use recipes for groupers or sea bream, or make a couscous, page 69.

Snapper(s) baked with green peppers and ginger

Use 4 small snappers, steaks or a large fish
4 tablespoons olive or vegetable oil
1 large onion, chopped
1 aubergine, cut in cubes
1 green pepper, roughly chopped
2 courgettes, sliced
2 cloves garlic, chopped
1 thin slice of fresh ginger root, chopped (or 1 teaspoon ground ginger)
½ teaspoon each of chilli powder, nutmeg, cumin seeds, oregano
1 tablespoon tomato purée
4 large tomatoes, roughly chopped (or 1 medium can Italian tomatoes)
3 lemons or limes
salt, pepper
1 cup fresh breadcrumbs plus a little oil to moisten

Heat the oil in a wok or saucepan, add chopped onion, let it soften for a few minutes, add the aubergine, a few minutes later the green pepper and cook over a medium heat for about 5 minutes, stirring from time to time. Add the courgettes, cook a few minutes more before putting in the garlic, ginger, chilli powder, nutmeg, cumin and oregano. Cook for a couple of minutes stirring and add and mix in the tomato purée. Add tomatoes, cover the pan and lower the heat. Simmer for about 10 minutes during which time you can prepare the fish and heat oven to Gas 5/375°F/190°C. If using a large whole fish, score it two or three times on each side. Add the juice of 1 lemon, or lime, and salt and pepper to the vegetables. Lay half of them in a shallow ovenproof dish and put the whole fish or steaks on top. Slice the second lemon, or lime, and lay the pieces on the fish. Cover with remaining vegetables, sprinkle over the bread-crumbs and moisten with oil. Bake for 20–35 minutes, testing to see fish is done with the point of a skewer, the flesh should be opaque and lift easily from the bone. Serve sprinkled with the juice from the remaining lemon, or lime. This is good with rice or other grain such as bulgar wheat.

Grilled Snapper

Use small whole fish or steaks. Whole fish should be scored two or three times on each side. Marinade for 30 minutes in oil, lemon juice, chopped garlic, teaspoon each of cumin, marjoram and thyme and a little chopped ginger. Grill as page 298.

Mexican baked Snappers

Heat oven to Gas 4/350°F/180°C. Use a whole fish weighing about 1½ kilos (3 lbs). Score it two or three times on both sides and rub with salt, pepper and lemon juice. Put a peeled banana in the cavity. Lay it in a buttered or oiled oven dish. Make a sauce by heating 1 tablespoon peanut oil and frying 3 or 4 chopped spring onions (or a small onion), a green or red pepper for a few minutes over a medium heat. Add the grated peel and juice of a lemon or a lime, 4 tablespoons dry white wine, 2 tablespoons chopped parsley, salt, pepper. Simmer gently for 5 minutes. Add 12 stoned black or green olives. Pour over the fish, cover with a piece of buttered paper or foil and bake for 40 minutes, basting once or twice. Eat with rice and garlic bread.

Sole

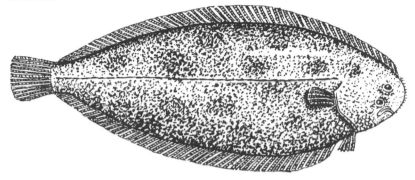

SOLE or DOVER SOLE

Habitat From southern North Sea, Channel to Mediterranean.

Pros and Cons This is the flat fish beloved of chefs, the one and only true sole. It is expensive but is most delicious when simply treated.

Size Usually around 30–40 cm (12–16 ins).

Description A very timid-looking right-facing flat fish, coloured a mousy grey-brown with darker blotches. It is scaly along the lateral line, has a black mark on the tip of the pectoral fin and the long dorsal and anal fins are attached to the square cut tail.

How sold Whole fish.

Qty per person 1 sole weighing around 375 g (13 oz) will feed two people, but if you can afford it buy individual soles weighing about 225–250 g (8–9 oz) each.

Ask fishmonger To trim and remove dark skin and, if you wish, get him to cut off head; alternatively ask him to fillet it.

Availability All year but scarce in spring and early summer.

Notes Soles came to be known as Dover soles because it was from there that London obtained its supply. Sometimes you may see SLIP SOLES for sale, these are small sole around 15 cm (6 ins), or the less common members of the same family such as BLACK, THICKBACK or SAND SOLES – treat them as you would a Dover sole.

Preparation Remove the tough dark skin (page 314) and trim if the fishmonger hasn't already done so, and if you wish, cut off the head. Leave the white skin but score it lightly to prevent the fish curling. Wash and dry.

Cooking ideas Sole is delicious cooked very simply and unless you happen to be very rich, you are unlikely to eat it so often that you need to dress it up in complicated ways, so leave those elaborate recipes to the professionals.

Grilled Sole
Grill as on page 298, brushing with melted butter. Serve garnished with parsley and lemon wedges.

Sole à la meunière
Use whole fish or fillets, with the black skin removed. Fry as described on page 295.

Poached Sole à la bonne femme
2 sole weighing in total about 800 g (1¾ lbs)
1 onion, very finely chopped
100 g (4 oz) mushrooms, chopped
handful chopped parsley
3 tablespoons white wine
3 tablespoons hot water
juice of half a lemon
1 tablespoon butter mixed with 1 tablespoon flour
25 g (1 oz) butter
florets of parsley
Heat oven to Gas 5/375°F/190°C. Butter a shallow oven dish and make a bed of finely chopped onion, mushrooms and parsley. Put

the whole fish on top, add 3 tablespoons white wine and 3 of hot water and the juice of half a lemon. Put into the pre-heated oven for 5 minutes, then add the butter and flour mixture in small pieces. Return to the oven for 10–12 minutes. Have the grill heated. Put the fish on a serving dish, add the butter in small pieces to the liquid in the oven dish; pour this over the fish and put under the grill to brown. Garnish with florets of parsley.

SPARLING, *see* **SMELT**

SPINY LOBSTER, *see* **LOBSTER, SPINY**

Sprat

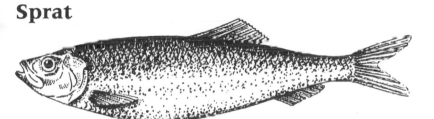

SPRAT — *related to:* ANCHOVY, HERRING and SARDINE (PILCHARD)

Habitat	European inshore waters.
Pros and Cons	These are great little fish for a simple lunch or high tea, eaten just as they are without being gutted.
Size	10–15 cm (4–6 ins).
Description	The long oval body with its thin, fragile scales is a deep blue or green divided by a band of pale gold or violet from the silvery sides. Beneath the belly the scales form a flattened sharp keel.
How sold	Whole fish also sometimes SMOKED.
Qty per person	Allow 175–200 g (6–7 oz).

Sprat

Availability	Best during winter.
Notes	Sprats are also sold canned often under the names Brisling or Swedish Anchovies.
Preparation	Wash under running water and pat dry. No need to gut, although if you want you can gut large sprats preferably through the gills (page 310) so as not to break them up.
Cooking ideas	Cook whole, ungutted. May be coated in flour and fried, grilled for 2–3 minutes each side, basted in oil and lemon juice or simply baked. Sprats are nice soused, follow the recipe for herrings on page 123, baking for 30 minutes only, or prepare *en escabèche* (*see* page 211). Use recipes for other small fish such as anchovies or sardines.

Baked Sprats

Heat oven to Gas 7/425°F/220°C. Follow recipe for baked sardines on page 208, adding a teaspoon of crushed fennel seeds. Make sure you have really hot plates to hand, plenty of lemon wedges and brown bread and butter.

SPRAT, SMOKED

Description	Should be pale gold with moist, firm flesh.
Notes	Sprats are soaked in brine for quarter of an hour, before being drip dried and hot smoked for about 4 hours, which means they are cooked.
Cooking ideas	Eat hot or cold with lemon juice, pepper and brown bread. To heat, put under a hot grill for a minute or two on either side.

SPUR DOG, *see* **DOGFISH**

Squid

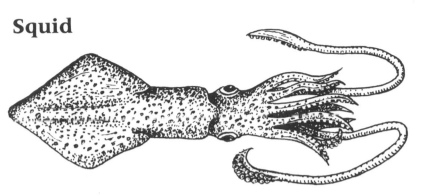

SQUID – *also known as:* CALAMARI; several species are caught; they are related to: OCTOPUS and CUTTLEFISH, forming a group known as the cephalopods

Habitat	NE Atlantic and Mediterranean.
Pros and Cons	Squid make excellent eating so don't be put off by their somewhat repulsive appearance; once cleaned, they are simple to prepare and the body can make a perfect pocket for a stuffing.
Size	Usually 15–40 cm (6–16 ins) in length.
Description	Squid have a pouch-like body with arms and tentacles growing from the head. Sold ready-skinned, but sometimes covered in a thin, purple speckled membrane.
How sold	Whole squid by weight.
Qty per person	1 each for stuffing. Allow 150–175 g (5–6 oz) for other recipes.
Ask fishmonger	If he's not busy to clean and prepare but you will most likely have to do it yourself.
Notes	Squid, like other cephalopods, contain an ink sac from which they squirt a dark liquid to cloud the water and shield their escape from their enemies. There are several varieties caught worldwide and

they are very popular in France, Italy, Greece and other Mediterranean countries, where they have many delicious ways of preparing them.

Preparation Cut off the tentacles and set aside. Gently pull the head from the body, discarding head, eyes and all the innards which includes the ink sac. If you want to use the ink to colour the dish, slit open the head and cut out the sac – first time you'll probably end up splitting it and find your hands covered in ink, but persevere. Remove the quill, which looks like a piece of transparent plastic, from inside the body-pouch and wash out all the white fluid. You can turn it inside out like a sock. If you want remove the membrane under running water, but it's not necessary. You're left with body-pouch with two attached triangular fins and the tentacles. At the base of the tentacles is the beak-like mouth, squeeze it out and discard.

Cooking ideas The body can be stuffed, the tentacles being used in the stuffing, and cooked in a sauce; or it can be cut in rings and fried like whitebait; or poached or battered and deep fried and it is delicious served cold with olive oil, garlic and lemon juice. Cuttlefish recipes can be used.

Squid stuffed with spinach
4 squid cleaned and prepared
2 tablespoons olive oil
2 cloves of garlic, chopped
3 fillets of anchovy
2 tablespoons cream
225 g (8 oz) frozen spinach or (450 g [1 lb] fresh spinach, blanched, drained and chopped fine)
½ teaspoon nutmeg
½ cup breadcrumbs
pepper
For the sauce:
  2 tablespoons olive oil
  1 onion chopped

1 medium can Italian tomatoes
1 tablespoon tomato purée
1 tablespoon flour
1 glass dry white wine or cider
salt, pepper
thyme, parsley and bayleaf

Heat 2 tablespoons oil in a flame-proof casserole, add half the garlic and the anchovy fillets. Stir well and cook 2 or 3 minutes. Add the chopped tentacles, cream, spinach, nutmeg, breadcrumbs and pepper. Stir well and remove from the heat. Three-quarters fill the body-pouches and, using a needle and thread, over-sew the openings.

Heat the remaining two tablespoons of oil in the casserole and fry the onion, when it is soft add the second chopped clove of garlic and the tomatoe purée. Stir and add the flour, cook two or three minutes before mixing in the wine or cider and adding the can of tomatoes, crushing them with the spoon. Season with salt, pepper and the herbs. Add the squid, cover the pot and simmer gently for 30–45 minutes. Serve the squid on a bed of rice.

Calmars farcis à la marseillaise – Stuffed Squid with tomatoes
As in the above recipe the squid is cooked in a tomato sauce for the same length of time but the stuffing uses only tomatoes.

Soften a chopped onion in 2 tablespoons olive oil, add the chopped tentacles, plus 4 large, ripe tomatoes, chopped, peeled and deseeded. (To peel put tomatoes in a bowl, cover with boiling water and leave for a couple of minutes when the skin will come off paper thin. Cut in half horizontally and squeeze out the seeds.) Add 1 cup of breadcrumbs, 2 finely chopped cloves of garlic, salt, pepper, 2 or 3 basil leaves (or use oregano or marjoram) and a sprig of thyme. Mix well and add a glass of white wine and 3 beaten eggs. Fill the squid, prepare the tomato sauce as in the above recipe, add the squid, cover and simmer gently for 30–45 minutes.

Squid salad
Cut the squid into rings. Heat 2 tablespoons olive oil in a wok or frying pan and cook a chopped onion until it is soft. Raise the heat, add the squid and toss it over a high heat for 4–5 minutes. Add crushed garlic, 2 tablespoons water and poach gently for 5 minutes. Cool. Mix with the juice of a lemon, 3 tablespoons olive oil, black pepper, chopped clove of garlic and chopped parsley.

STRIPED BONITO, *see* **BONITO**

SWEETLIPS, *see* **WRASSE**

Swordfish

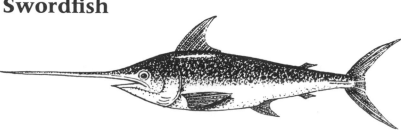

SWORDFISH

Habitat Temperate to tropical seas and oceans.

Pros and Cons Not widely available but you may come across swordfish which has pink, meaty, though somewhat dry flesh, which turns white after cooking. It is similar to the billfish and is best grilled or barbecued.

Size Usually around 1–1½ metres (3–5 feet).

Description The spindle-shaped body is ink blue, bronze or dark green with lighter sides and belly. The skin is rough. The long snout is flattened like a sword and accounts for a third of its length.

How sold Steaks or cutlets, usually frozen.

Qty per person 175–200 g (6–7 oz).

Ask fishmonger For a middle or top cut, tail end will be drier.

Notes You'll come across swordfish all over the Mediterranean. It is especially abundant around Sicily and you'll be offered it on many of the Greek islands. All sorts of wild and wonderful fishermen's tales relate to the swordfish with its powerful beak which is said to be capable of piercing the hull of a boat.

Preparation Like tuna, swordfish benefits from being soaked for 30 minutes in acidulated water (2 tablespoons vinegar, 1 teaspoon salt to 1 litre [1¾ pints] water). Drain and dry very well. If it has been frozen make sure you get rid of any black pieces lurking around the bone, or it will be bitter.

Cooking ideas Marinade and either grill or fry or make into kebabs. Excellent barbecued over charcoal. Raw swordfish has a slightly pink tinge, it turns white on cooking. Don't overcook or you'll end up with a texture like damp flannel. You can use recipes for sailfish or billfish or even tuna.

Grilled Swordfish

Marinade the fish in olive oil, 1 or 2 chopped anchovy fillets, oregano, bayleaf, chopped garlic, basil, lemon juice and a generous amount of freshly milled black pepper. Leave for 1 or 2 hours. Grill as on page 298, basting frequently with the marinade and cooking just until the flesh turns white and opaque. Squeeze over the juice of a lemon or sprinkle over a little wine vinegar as you serve them.

Kebabs

Cut into bite-size pieces and marinade as above. Alternate on skewers with pieces of anchovy or bacon, red or green peppers, mushrooms and tomatoes. Cook as page 299.

Fried Tunisian Swordfish

Rub steaks with salt, 1 teaspoon chilli powder and the juice of a lemon. Marinade half an hour. Melt 50 g (2 oz) unsalted butter and when it is sizzling fry 50 g (2 oz) slivered almonds. Remove and set aside. Fry the steaks 3 or 4 minutes each side. Sprinkle over the juice of a lemon and return the almonds. Cover and cook very gently for 10–12 minutes.

Tench

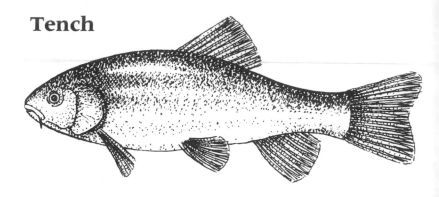

TENCH – *same family as:* BARBEL, BREAM, CARP, GUDGEON, ROACH

Habitat   In British and European slow rivers, backwaters and oxbow lakes overgrown with vegetation; also reared in carp ponds.

Pros and Cons   A few tench are imported but you'll probably only get the chance to eat this fish via an angler friend. It is a slow and sluggish fish which wallows in the mud, feeding on weeds, worms and snails, though it can be quite good eating. In non-maritime parts of France and in Germany it is treated as a delicacy.

Size   From around 20–60 cm (10–24 ins).

Description   The sturdy, thickset body with its rounded fins and small firmly embedded scales is a muddy green colour with a creamy belly which shimmers with a golden sheen. It has small red eyes, two barbels and is covered with thick slime which used to be thought medicinal.

Qty per person   Allow 225–275 g (8–10 oz) whole, ungutted fish.

Preparation   If possible scale as soon as caught, or if this is not possible dip in boiling water for a few seconds to loosen the firmly embedded scales. Trim and gut, and rub with salt and vinegar. To remove all traces of mud, soak in acidulated water for 30 minutes (2 tablespoons vinegar and one teaspoon of salt to every litre [1¾ pint] of water).

Cooking ideas   Can be baked, stuffed or braised; smaller ones grilled or cooked *en matelote*. Use receipes for carp and other members of its family.

Stuffed Tench

Heat oven to Gas 3/325°F/160°C. Make a stuffing using ½ cup breadcrumbs, ½ cup grated cheese mixed with a handful of chopped parsley, 2 chopped sage leaves, 2 chopped cloves of garlic, a bayleaf, salt and pepper. Bind with two beaten eggs. Fill the cavity of the fish, lay it on a large piece of oiled foil. Season with salt and pepper, sprinkle over two or three tablespoons dry white wine, or the juice of a lemon and dribble over some olive oil. Fold the parcel loosely but firmly and bake 1 hour.

THERESE, *see* **SNAPPERS**

THICKBACK SOLE, *see* **SOLE**

TILAPIA, *see* **ST PETER'S FISH**

TOPE, *see* **SHARK**

TORBAY SOLE, *see* **WITCH**

TREVALLY, *see* **CARANGIDS**

Trout, Brown, Sea and Rainbow

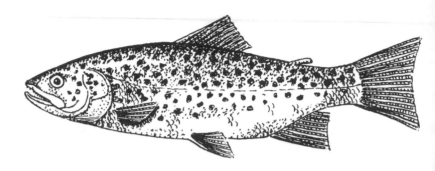

TROUT – this includes two different species: our native BROWN TROUT (of which the SEA TROUT otherwise called SALMON TROUT is a migratory form) and the RAINBOW TROUT which originated from America; *same family as:* SALMON

Habitat BROWN TROUT: usually wild in streams, brooks, rivers, lakes and reservoirs.
SEA TROUT: are wild spending part of their lives in the sea, migrating to rivers to spawn and breed.
RAINBOW TROUT: live in fresh water, but those on sale are cultivated.

Pros and Cons BROWN TROUT and the SEA TROUT are the same species, both are delicious. Brown trout is likely to be a rare and expensive treat; sea trout is similar to salmon but not so oily and with paler flesh.
RAINBOW TROUT are a different species, mostly farmed. They may not be in quite the luxury class as the other two but they are extremely tasty and inexpensive. Good farming produces good fish, so if the trout you buy is disappointing, search out another supplier or complain to your fishmonger; fresh trout is superior to frozen.

Size 20–40 cm (8–16 ins).

Description   The shape of the trout is similar to but more thickset than that of the salmon. It has a broader tail stalk, and the tail is slightly concave rather than forked. The bone of the upper jaw extends beyond the back of the eye.

BROWN TROUT are slimy, with river colours of greenish browns mottled with darker and lighter marks, and with creamy sides and belly.

RAINBOW TROUT – also slimy – are so called because of their iridescent, shimmering colours which vary from olive or blue green, striped with pink or red with silvery sides and darker speckles.

SEA TROUT reflect the sea with their silvery grey backs, lighter sides and belly scattered with a few criss-cross dark spots especially on the gill covers.

How sold   Whole fish; but large sea trout are sometimes sold in cutlets; also SMOKED.

Qty per person   Allow 225–275 g (8–10 oz) whole, ungutted fish. Cutlets: 175–200 g (6–7 oz).

Ask fishmonger   To trim, scale and clean and remove gills.

Availability   Brown trout are rarely on sale.
Rainbow trout are available all year being best in summer.
Sea trout are in season between 1 March and 31 August.

Notes   Brown trout and sea trout are twins who have adapted and changed according to their life style and environment. One spends all its life in fresh water and the other lives in the sea and only enters rivers to spawn.

Rainbow trout were introduced to Europe from America in the late nineteenth century and are still to be found wild in small numbers. Sea trout usually have pink flesh due to their diet which includes shrimps and other crustaceans. Fresh-water trout have creamy flesh though that of the farmed trout is often pink, due to colouring being added to their food.

Sea trout is often sold under the name of salmon trout and to confuse matters further, small salmon (smolt) under the legal limit of 30 cm (12 ins) are sometimes sold as salmon trout. Whatever the name, you may be fairly sure you are in for a treat.

Preparation Must be trimmed and cleaned and scales removed if the fishmonger hasn't already done so. Make sure you remove any traces of blood or blackness left inside. Wash and dry.

Cooking ideas Brown, rainbow and small sea trout are lovely grilled, fried or baked *en papillote* or steamed; or cook with sorrel following recipe for grayling on page 98. Large sea trout or large lake trout are best simply poached or baked in foil and eaten hot or cold with a sauce such as hollandaise or mayonnaise. Both freshwater and sea trout can be potted like charr (*see* page 41).

Grilled Trout

Score the fish two or three times on each side, sprinkle with salt and paprika, fill the cavity with herbs such as sprigs of rosemary and dill, or thyme and oregano; fennel and parsley; brush all over with melted butter or olive oil and grill as on page 298.

Fried Trout

Roll trout in flour. Heat 3 or 4 tablespoons oil in a frying pan and when it is hot fry the trout until they are golden on both sides (*see* page 295). Drain away the oil, add 50 g (2 oz) butter, let it melt and then put the fish on to a hot serving dish. Add slices of lemon to the butter, toss over high heat for a minute or two, pour in a glass of white wine, let it bubble and evaporate a little, pour over the fish. Dust with parsley and add salt and pepper.

Trout with almonds

Follow the above recipes but add 2 tablespoons of slivered almonds instead of the lemon slices and toss over high heat till golden; omit the wine.

Trout baked with bacon
Heat oven to Gas 6/400°F/200°C. Wrap pieces of bacon in a spiralling fashion round each trout. Alternate them head to tail, pack closely together in an oiled baking dish. Bake 15–20 minutes.

Trout baked in wine
Score the trout two or three times on either side and marinade for 1 hour in the juice of a lemon, 3 or 4 tablespoons olive oil, pepper, rosemary, bayleaf and thyme. Heat oven to Gas 6/400°F/200°C. Lay the trout in a shallow dish, put slices of lemon along each, pour over 2 or 3 tablespoons of dry white or rosé wine. Bake 15–20 minutes, basting two or three times.

Trout en papillote with dill and lemon
Heat oven to Gas 8/450°F/230°C. Put each trout on a sheet of foil, add finely chopped shallot or put a piece of dill or fennel into each cavity. Sprinkle with dry vermouth and olive oil, put two slices of lemon on each fish. Wrap them loosely but firmly into a parcel and bake 10 minutes.

Sea Trout poached or baked in foil
A sea trout served hot or cold makes the most perfect dinner party dish on a summer's day. The pale, moist flesh is more beautiful than that of salmon. It needs the simplest of accompaniments, a lemon sauce, or hollandaise if hot and a home-made mayonnaise or green sauce if serving cold. Follow instructions for salmon (page 201).

Trout, Smoked

Description	Fish are left whole but gutted and should be golden brown. If they are red brown, they have probably been artifically coloured.
Qty per person	1 fish.
Ask fishmonger	If he smokes his own, if so you are in luck.

Availability	The more enterprising fishmongers, supermarkets and delicatessens.
Notes	The fish are soaked in brine before being hot smoked, which means they are cooked.
Preparation	Skin them before serving if you wish but they look so beautiful as they are, that it seems a pity.
Cooking ideas	Simply eat cold sprinkled with lemon juice and horseradish sauce mixed with a spoonful or two of yoghurt or cream. Or make into pâté (*see* recipe for bloater paste on page 125) but omit the preliminary cooking.

TUB GURNARD, *see* **GURNARDS**

Tuna

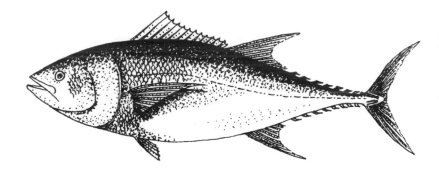

TUNA or TUNNY – there are several different varieties on sale, which may be labelled simply tuna or tunny or be called by specific names such as: BLUE-FIN, YELLOW-FIN, ALLISON, ALBACORE or LONG-FINNED, or BIG-EYE TUNA; *same family as:* BONITO, MACKEREL, WAHOO

Habitat   Atlantic, Mediterranean and Indo-Pacific waters.

Pros and Cons	Tuna is very meaty, it varies from pale to dark red according to species. It is rich and densely packed and a little goes a long way. Frozen tuna is not as good as fresh but provided it is properly treated provides a deliciously robust meal.
Size	Varies from 50 cm (20 ins) to more than double depending on species.
Description	Tunas have long spindle-shaped bodies with dark blue backs and silvery sides and belly. Fins can be blue, reddish or bright yellow. There is a row of small keels on each side of the tail stalk which has a crescent-shaped fin.
How sold	Usually in steaks or cutlets. SMOKED TUNA is also sold, treat like smoked salmon.
Qty per person	Allow 150–175 g (5–6 oz). If steaks are very large, you can cut them in half.
Ask fishmonger	For the best cut which is from the belly. Find out if it is fresh or frozen, it will make a difference to how you cook it.
Availability	Supplies are limited but several species of tuna are imported fresh and frozen, some from Europe and others flown in from the Seychelles.
Notes	Tuna is unlike other fish in that it is warm-blooded, it looks more like steak than fish. It is a favourite in many countries including the Mediterranean and the Caribbean.
Preparation	It's very imporant when cleaning your piece or steaks to make sure you get rid of every trace of dark innards, blackness or blood clinging to the bone, otherwise the result will be bitter. This is particularly important with tuna that has been frozen, when the fish will not have been gutted. Tuna meat is rich, oily and quite bloody so to make it sweeter tasting it should be *dégorgé* which is the French term meaning to soak in water with salt and lemon juice or vinegar. The water will

turn red and the meat whiten. Use 1½ teaspoons salt, 1 tablespoon lemon juice or vinegar to 1 litre (1¾ pints) water. Leave it from 5–30 minutes depending on the redness of the flesh. Finally rinse it under running water. Let it drain then dry well before cooking.

Cooking ideas Fresh tuna can be grilled, fried, cooked *en papillote*, made into kebabs, roasted or braised. Remember it is very like meat so it can stand longer cooking times than most other fish. Frozen tuna is probably best braised. Leftover tuna can be used in salads, made into pilaff or kedgeree, or used instead of salmon in koulibiac. You can use recipes for bonito, or kingfish.

Roast Tuna
Marinade a whole piece of tuna weighing from 1–1½ kilos (2–3 lbs) in oil, lemon juice, chopped onion, salt, pepper for at least 2 hours. Heat oven to Gas 4/350°F/180°C. Put tuna on roasting rack with the marinade and dot with butter. Roast for 30–45 minutes.

Grilled Tuna steaks
Marinade steaks in chopped onion, salt, bayleaf, olive oil for 1 hour. Mix 5 tablespoons olive oil with two chopped cloves of garlic, some chopped parsley and 1 tablespoon capers. Grill the steaks as on page 298, brushing liberally with the oil mixture. Serve with a tomato sauce or sauce *rémoulade*.

Fried Tuna steaks
Marinade steaks as above recipe. Fry them as on page 295, serving them sprinkled with lemon juice, salt, pepper and parsley and serve with a lemon sauce, sauce *rémoulade* or aïoli.

Thon catalane
2 slices of tuna weighing about 350 g (12 oz) each
1–2 tablespoons flour
4 tablespoons olive oil
2 onions, chopped
1 tablespoon tomato purée

450 g (1 lb) ripe tomatoes (or 1 medium can Italian tomatoes)
2 cloves garlic, chopped
thyme, bayleaf, oregano or parsley
salt, pepper
1 lump sugar
Heat 2 tablespoons olive oil in a wok or saucepan, add the chopped onion and let it soften. Add tomato purée, chopped tomatoes or the can of tomatoes, garlic, thyme, bayleaf, oregano or parsley, a very little salt, some pepper and the sugar. Let it simmer for about 10 minutes. Coat the prepared fish in the flour, shake off any excess. Heat the remaining oil in a frying pan, when it is hot, fry the slices of tuna on both sides to seal the surface. Pour over the sauce, put on a lid and simmer very gently for about 25 minutes. Serve with rice.

Thon à la chartreuse
For this you need a slice or two of tuna weighing around 700 g (1½ lbs) in total. Oil a wide ovenproof dish, line it with a layer of lettuce leaves, followed by a layer of finely sliced onion, a layer of tomatoes and several slices of lemon, add salt and pepper and lay the tuna on top, cover with another layer reversing the order, so you have lemon, tomatoes, onions and a topping of lettuce leaves. This last should be quite thick because the top ones are going to get quite burnt. Add salt and pepper. Pour over a glass of water and another of white wine and if you wish a tablespoon or two of brandy. Heat the oven to Gas 4/350°F/180°C and cook the tuna for 1–1½ hours. Remove the charred lettuce leaves before serving.

Thon basquaise
In this recipe the tuna is cooked on a bed of onions. Buy a piece or pieces weighing around 800 g (1¾ lbs). Heat 2 tablespoons oil and add 675 g (1½ lbs) of sliced onions and 2 teaspoons sugar. Cover with a lid and let them cook gently until soft, about 30 minutes. Make slits in the prepared tuna and insert slivers of garlic and pieces of anchovy. Heat 2 tablespoons oil in a frying pan and when it is hot, brown the tuna for a few minutes on each side. Lay the fish on the bed of onions, add the juice of a lemon, salt and pepper. Cover and cook very gently for 1 hour.

Turbot

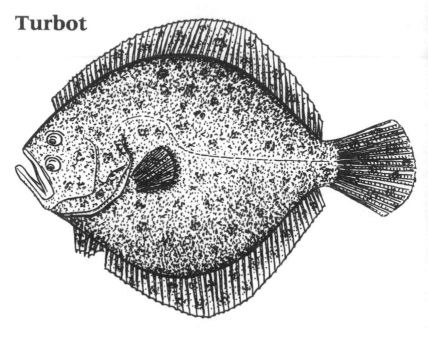

TURBOT – *same family as:* BRILL and MEGRIM

Habitat E Atlantic, W Baltic and Mediterranean (turbot is now being farmed but so far not in commercial quantities).

Pros and Cons This is a most excellent fish with firm, white flesh; one of the biggest and the best of all flat fish though it's not often seen on the slab, the catch is limited and most find their way to restaurants so the price is high. If you're in funds, it's a must.

Description A left-facing flat fish, its almost diamond-shaped body studded with bony tubercles; colour varies from light to dark brown, spotted with green or black; blind side is white.

How sold Whole, filleted or in steaks. Small turbot weighing around 1 kilo (2 lbs) are known as CHICKEN TURBOT.

Qty per person	Allow 200–225 g (7–8 oz) whole fish complete. 150–175 g (5–6 oz) fillets. 175–200 g (6–7 oz) steaks.
Ask fishmonger	If you don't want to cook whole fish, to fillet or cut into steaks but ask for the bones and head for a delicious fish stock or soup.
Availability	The more up-market or specialist fishmongers; all year but best March to September.
Notes	Some specialist kitchen shops sell turbotières – diamond-shaped fish kettles. A prize to give yourself if you often poach flat fish; never mind if you can't afford one, a large flat pan or a roasting tin and foil will serve your purpose.
Preparation	Wash and dry. Can be cooked in its skin which can be removed afterwards or eaten, it's up to you.
Cooking ideas	Unless you are very rich you are unlikely ever to eat so much turbot that you need to tart it up with fancy recipes. It is so delicious, so beautiful that it needs only simple cooking. Best of all poached on the bone or baked in foil, follow recipe for bass with ginger; or you can grill steaks; fillets can be prepared like sole, brill or other flat fish.

Poached Turbot

If you haven't a turbotière, use a large flat pan or a roasting tin. Poach in a mixture of milk and water following the method described on page 300 for poaching fish. Allow 6–7 minutes for every 450 g (1 lb). Transfer the cooked fish to a hot serving dish, garnish with lemon slices and serve with a hollandaise sauce.

Turbot can be served cold in which case poach it but use a wine-based *court bouillon*. Use half wine and half water, flavoured with a finely chopped onion, thyme, parsley, bayleaf, 12 peppercorns and a tablespoon of rock salt. Serve with a sauce *rémoulade*. A small amount of turbot (75–100 g, 3–4 oz per head) cooked in this way makes a delicious starter to a meal. Divide it into portions and arrange it on individual plates with a simple garnish such as lettuce, cucumber, lemon wedges or watercress and spring onions. Nothing too strong in flavour or colour to detract from the fish.

TWAITE SHAD, *see* **SHAD**

VARA VARA, *see* **SNAPPERS**

VENUS SHELL, *see* **CLAMS**

VIELLE MACONDE
VIELLE PLATTE } *see* **GROUPERS**
VIELLE ROUGE

VIVENOT, *see* **SNAPPERS**

Wahoo

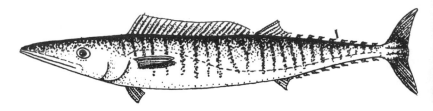

WAHOO – Creole name: POISSON BECUNE – *same family as:* MACKEREL, KINGFISH, TUNA, BONITO

Habitat   Tropical seas worldwide.

Pros and Cons   You may occasionally see this delicious fish which lives mainly on squid and cuttlefish and is reputed to be one of the tastiest fish in the seas; the name surely echoing the excitement of the fishermen when they catch it. It is flown in from the Seychelles and mostly snapped up by restaurant owners. Buy if you see it.

Size	Can grow to 2 metres (6½ feet).
Description	The narrow, tubular body is deep blue divided from the silvery sides and belly by a green band. It has wavy, vertical stripes, a beak-like snout, spiny first dorsal fin and a crescent tail.
How sold	Cutlets, steaks and joints.
Qty per person	150–175 g (5–6 oz).
Ask fishmonger	For a middle or top cut, rather than the bonier tail end.
Availability	Occasionally at enterprising fishmongers probably in London and surrounding areas. Look for it in markets and shops patronized by West Indian communities.
Notes	The wahoo is a member of the mackerel family, note the characteristic wavy stripes. It is on a par with kingfish or the Spanish mackerel.
Preparation	Wash and wipe dry, making sure all traces of guts are removed that might be clinging to the bone.
Cooking ideas	Grill steaks, or make into kebabs, or bake *en papillote*. Follow recipes for kingfish, mackerel, swordfish or bonito.

Grilled Wahoo steaks
Marinade steaks for 1–2 hours in the juice of a lime (or use lemon), thyme, chopped garlic, a thin sliver of root ginger chopped, 1 red chilli and 2 tablespoons olive oil. Grill as on page 298, basting frequently.

Wahoo steaks en papillote
Heat oven to Gas 6/400°F/200°C. Lay steaks on pieces of foil large enough to make a parcel. Top them with chopped garlic, a sprig of rosemary, a chopped anchovy fillet, pepper, and a slice of lemon. Sprinkle with olive oil. Fold the foil to make secure but loose parcels, put in the oven and cook 20 minutes.

WARTY VENUS, *see* CLAMS

Weever

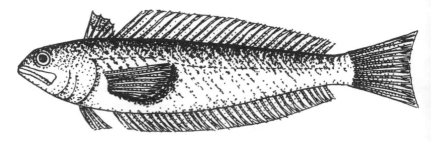

WEEVER — GREATER and LESSER

Habitat	Sandy coasts around Europe and Mediterranean.
Pros and Cons	The catch is very small but you might come across weever. The GREATER provides tasty fillets; or whole fish can be used in soups or bouillabaisse.
Size	GREATER: up to 30 cm (12 ins). LESSER: around 15 cm (6 ins).
Description	Deep compressed head, scaly body coloured sandy grey or brown, brushed with darker diagonal stripes; frilled with long dorsal and anal fins; first part of the dorsal having venomous spikes.
How sold	Whole fish or fillets.
Qty per person	Fillets: 150–175 g (5–6 oz).
Ask fishmonger	For fillets of the GREATER; or if buying whole fish or the LESSER for soup or bouillabaisse make sure he has removed the gill covers and first dorsal fin with its venomous spikes.
Availability	Perhaps where locally caught, or in large fish markets or on holiday on the Continent.
Notes	Weevers bury themselves in the sand waiting for

shrimps and small fish and at low tide if stepped on by the unwary, the venom in the dorsal fin and spine covers can cause an agonizing wound, the effects of which can last for half an hour or days. If you are unlucky enough to be pricked, wash the wound immediately in very hot water and get medical advice. Weevers are highly esteemed on the Continent, in France they are called *vive* or *vipère de mer*.

Preparation   If the fishmonger hasn't done his job, you'll have to trim those venomous fins and gill covers (or cut off the head), wear gloves and be careful. Clean the fish and wash and dry well; or cut it into fillets (page 312).

Cooking ideas   The flesh is firm and the flavour good but can be rather dry. Cook like gurnards, or the fillets like whiting. Add to bouillabaisse or soups.

Braised fillets of Weever

Heat oven to Gas 5/375°F/190°F. Butter a shallow oven dish. Make a bed of finely chopped vegetables, including 1 small onion, 1 clove of garlic and 100 g (4 oz) mushrooms. Put the fillets on top and cover with 3 or 4 roughly chopped tomatoes, salt, pepper, the juice of a lemon and glass of dry white wine. Put into the oven covered with a piece of foil. After 15 minutes, pour in a small carton of cream, and return to the oven for a few minutes. Serve with a garnish of chopped parsley and lemon wedges.

Whelks

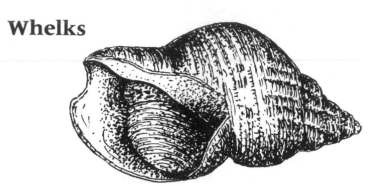

WHELKS

Habitat	N Atlantic.
Pros and Cons	Whelks are cheap with a strong flavour not unlike squid and should be juicy though they can be rubbery.
Size	Can be as big as 10 or 15 cm (4–5 ins).
Description	The ribbed shells spiral like that of a snail though usually all you can see on the slab are the cooked naked molluscs.
How sold	Usually ready-cooked and shell-less.
Qty per person	Shell-less: 75–175 g (3–6 oz). In shells: 300 ml (½ pint).
Ask fishmonger	If they are in their shells, if they have been cooked.
Availability	Usually from stalls and fishmongers at the seaside or outside pubs especially around southern and eastern coasts. Sometimes further inland.
Notes	It might be tempting to gather your own whelks but they can absorb and retain toxins from the molluscs on which they live; so be wary and buy only from the professionals.
Preparation	You're unlikely to deal with fresh whelks but if you do, wash them in plenty of changes of water

and soak them for several hours in salted water to purge them. To cook, steam for about 5 minutes in a covered pan with very little water.

Cooking ideas   Eat them as they are. If they are in their shells, extract them with a pin, discarding the hard disc which forms a sort of door, sprinkle with lemon juice or vinegar, salt and pepper and eat with unsalted butter or aioli. Or for a starter chop them up with garlic and mushrooms.

Whelks with garlic and mushrooms

225 g (8 oz) cooked whelks
100 g (4 oz) button mushrooms, sliced
1 clove of garlic, finely chopped
2 teaspoons Dijon or herb mustard
juice of 1 lemon
3 tablespoons olive oil
salt, pepper
chopped parsley

Into a bowl put the whelks cut into three or four pieces, the mushrooms and the garlic. Combine the mustard, lemon juice, olive oil, salt and pepper and pour into the bowl. Mix well and pile into small individual dishes or scallop shells. Garnish with chopped parsley.

WHIFF, *see* **MEGRIM**

Whitebait

WHITEBAIT is not a single species but is the fry of other species, most notably HERRINGS and SPRATS

Habitat Estuaries and shallow coastal waters especially North Sea and E Atlantic.

Pros and Cons Fresh whitebait is delicious though expensive as there are very strict limits to our own catch. Most on sale is imported frozen.

Size 4–5 cm (2 ins).

Description Slender, silvery-grey fry of the herring and the sprat.

How sold By weight; frozen in free-flow packs which are easier to deal with than those frozen in blocks.

Qty per person 100 g (4 oz).

Availability Fresh may be found from February to July; otherwise all year frozen.

Notes Whitebait have caused an awful lot of trouble between naturalists. It all seems to have been started by a plausible rogue in the eighteenth century. Alan Davidson in *North Atlantic Seafood* tells how a certain Richard Cannon of Blackwall was given permission to sell whitebait by convincing the Lord Mayor that it was not the fry of other fish but a separate species; he was so convincing that there are still some people who believe his story.

Preparation If they are frozen, let them thaw gently.

Cooking ideas Best dipped in flour and deep fried until golden and crisp.

Fried Whitebait
450 g (1 lb) whitebait
6–8 tablespoons flour for coating, seasoned with salt and pepper
oil for frying
Begin to heat the oil in a deep fryer with a basket or use a wok. Put the flour into a paper or plastic bag. Put the fish into a sieve and dip it into a bowl filled with salted water; this will ensure the fish are all evenly damp so that the flour will cling all over. Shake the sieve to get rid of excess water and put all the fish into the bag of flour, shake well to coat all sides. Make sure you have a dish warming on which to serve the fish. As soon as the oil begins to smoke, empty a handful of the fish directly into the frying basket, shake out any excess flour and plunge fish into the hot oil. In one minute they will be golden and cooked, drain them on crinkled greaseproof paper, put them on the warm dish and fry the remaining fish a handful at a time.

Serve immediately with a sprinkling of parsley, lemon wedges and cayenne pepper to hand as well as brown bread and butter.

Whiting

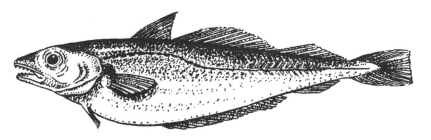

WHITING — *same family as:* COD, COLEY, HADDOCK, LING and POLLACK

Habitat E Atlantic and small numbers in Mediterranean.

Whiting

Pros and Cons	Whiting's association with invalids makes them seem genteel and mustily old-fashioned. This is a pity. They are cheap, light and delicate.
Size	Around 30 cm (12 ins).
Description	A tapering silvery-grey body tinged with sandy brown or blue green with silvery mottled sides and rounded belly. It has soft scales, long upper jaw, small teeth and a dark spot behind the pectoral fin.
How sold	Whole fish or fillets.
Qty per person	Allow 225–275 g (8–10 oz) of whole, ungutted fish. Fillets: 150–175 g (5–6 oz).
Ask fishmonger	Check that it is quite fresh, stale whiting are abysmal. Have whole fish scaled, trimmed and cleaned, or filleted if you prefer.
Availability	Widely available all year but best during winter.
Notes	The poor whiting deserves better than being relegated to invalid food and being cooked with its tail in its mouth. The French, who prize this fish quite highly, call it *merlan* though in southern France this is the name for hake, a more robust and tasty fish.
Preparation	Scale, trim and gut if fishmonger hasn't already done so. Wash the cavity well and dry with kitchen paper.
Cooking ideas	Poach whole fish in a court bouillon flavoured with wine or cider and eat with lemon sauce; fry, steam or bake, or cook *en papillote*. Fillets can be treated like sole or used in recipes for cod, hake or haddock. Avoid grilling as it can be rather dry.

Filets de merlan à la crème – Fillets of Whiting with cream
675 g (1½ lbs) whiting fillets
75 g (3 oz) butter
250 g (8 oz) mushrooms

juice of 1 lemon
2 shallots or an onion
1 glass dry vermouth
4 tablespoons single or half cream
salt, pepper
handful of chopped parsley
Heat oven to Gas 6/400°F/200°C. Put the butter into an ovenproof dish and put in the oven to melt, 3 or 4 minutes. Chop mushrooms coarsely, sprinkle with half the lemon juice. Peel and chop shallots or onion finely. Take the dish from the oven, add mushrooms and onions and mix well with the melted butter, return to the oven for 5 to 10 minutes. Add whiting, pour over the vermouth, cover with a piece of buttered paper or foil and put in the oven, test after 10 minutes to see if the fish is cooked, if not give it a few extra minutes. Transfer fish to a hot dish. Pour the cooking juices into a saucepan, put over high heat and reduce by a third. Lower the heat, stir in the cream, don't let it boil, add remaining lemon juice and season to taste with salt and pepper. Pour this sauce over the fish and sprinkle with chopped parsley.

Winkles

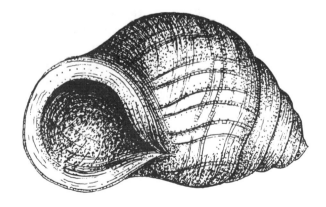

WINKLES or PERIWINKLES

Habitat	Atlantic coasts.
Pros and Cons	These tiny shellfish make a tasty starter or a light lunch.
Size	1–2½ cm (½–1 in).
Description	A pointed snail-like shell, varying in colour from dark to reddish brown, grimy greens or greys.
How sold	Usually ready-cooked in their shells.
Qty per person	300 ml (½ pint).
Ask fishmonger	If they're cooked or raw.
Availability	Seaside stalls and some fishmongers.
Notes	Mostly we seem to limit ourselves to collecting empty winkle shells on our beaches whereas in France these *amuse-gueules* (appetizers) are *très snob*, featuring on menus in expensive restaurants.
Preparation	If they are raw, wash them well in plenty of changes of salted water and soak for several hours in salted water to remove any impurities. Then steam them for about 5 minutes in a covered pan with a little salted water, lemon juice, pepper and herbs such as thyme or rosemary.
Cooking ideas	Eat cooked winkles straight from the shells, using a pin to extract them and discarding the small hard disc that acts as a front door. Have lemon wedges, butter and black pepper on the table. In Provence they eat *bigorneau* or *gros biéu*, a similar shell-like mollusc, with aïoli, try it.

Witch

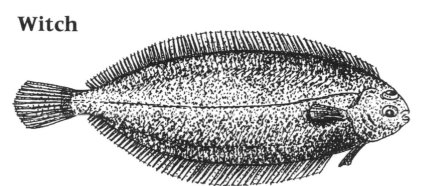

WITCH – *also known as:* WITCH FLOUNDER, TORBAY SOLE or POLE DAB; *same family as:* DAB, FLOUNDER, HALIBUT, LEMON SOLE and PLAICE

Habitat	N Atlantic.
Pros and Cons	Not very big with a thin body, nevertheless the flesh is good, so buy if you see it.
Size	Usually around 25 cm (10 ins).
Description	Right-facing flat fish, with a narrow oval body coloured sandy brown with faint blotches and freckles, sometimes scattered with orange. It has a small mouth, large eyes, an almost straight lateral line and finely serrated scales.
How sold	Whole fish or fillets.
Qty per person	Allow 200–225 g (7–8 oz) of whole fish. Fillets: 150–175 g (5–6 oz).
Ask fishmonger	To trim and remove dark skin and if you wish to fillet.
Availability	May to March. From coastal fishmongers or the more enterprising elsewhere.
Notes	The witch is very like the sole in appearance and is sometimes passed off as such. The sole faces the

same way but can be distinguished by its smaller eyes, the black mark on the pectoral fin and by the thin membrane which joins the dorsal and anal fins through the tail.

Preparation   Trim and remove skin on dark side if fishmonger hasn't done so. Wash and dry well.

Cooking ideas   Best grilled or fried on the bone, or poach and steam. Cook fillets like plaice or other flat fish.

Fillets of Witch with tomatoes

Heat oven to Gas 5/375°F/190°C. Heat 2 tablespoons of oil and cook a chopped onion until brown, add 3 or 4 roughly chopped tomatoes, salt, pepper, a clove of crushed garlic and some chopped parsley. Cook 10 minutes. Oil a fireproof dish, lay fillets of witch in it, add salt, pepper, a glass of dry white wine and the tomato mixture. Put it in the oven for 10–15 minutes. Serve sprinkled with lemon juice and parsley.

WITCH FLOUNDER, *see* **WITCH**

WOLF-FISH, *see* **CATFISH**

WOOF, *see* **CATFISH**

Wrasse

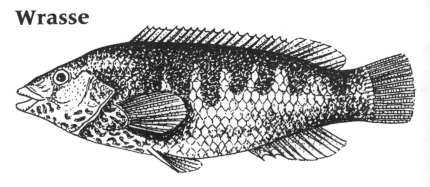

WRASSE – species sold: BALLAN or GREEN WRASSE and CUCKOO WRASSE sometimes called OLD WIFE or SWEET-LIPS – *related distantly to:* PARROTFISH

Habitat	Mediterranean, E Atlantic and Channel.
Pros and Cons	A fish with coarse, sweet flesh which is most suitable for adding to fish soups or stews.
Size	Around 30 cm (12 ins) but can be up to 50 cm (20 ins).
Description	Various bright colours from a child's paintbox from greens, to brownish reds, to orange and blue mottled and speckled with lighter and darker hues; the tough, hard scales filled in with one colour, outlined in another; lips are thick, dorsal fins are spiny.
How sold	Whole fish.
Qty per person	Allow 275–350 g (10–12 oz) of whole, ungutted fish.
Ask fishmonger	To clean and remove gills.
Availability	Enterprising fishmongers especially in summer.
Notes	Wrasse and parrotfish are sometimes confused. The fishmonger may tell you his wrasse are parrot-fish. They are not. The parrotfish is superior and being imported from the Seychelles is more expensive.
Preparation	If the fishmonger hasn't done so clean fish, scale and remove gills; wash and dry it with kichen paper.
Cooking ideas	Best used in fish soups or stews such as bouillabaisse.

YELLOW CROAKER, *see* CROAKERS

YELLOW-FIN TUNA, *see* **TUNA**

YELLOW GURNARD, *see* **GURNARDS**

YELLOWTAIL, *see* **CARANGIDS**

Zander

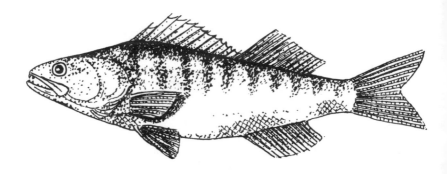

ZANDER or PIKEPERCH – *same family as:* PERCH

Habitat Lakes, rivers, canals in southern England and the Continent.

Pros and Cons This powerful angler's fish, rarely on sale, is an appropriate last fish. Whilst some enthusiasts compare its soft, flaky white flesh to that of Dover sole, others predict that because of its rapacious nature it will eventually destroy all other fresh-water fish!

Size Grows to over 1 metre (39 ins).

Description The long, cylindrical body with its small rough-edged scales is a dark olive-green with vertical stripes, paler sides and a white or silver belly. The head is pointed, slightly depressed with a large mouth full of voracious teeth. The front dorsal fin is fan-shaped and spiny.

How sold   Mainly an angler's fish. Some are imported from the Continent, so it might sometimes be on sale at specialist fishmongers.

Qty per person   225–275 g (8–10 oz) whole, ungutted fish.

Notes   Zanders were first brought to England by the ninth Duke of Bedford, who kept them in a lake in Woburn Park. Then someone had the idea of introducing them into other waterways. Since then zander-panic hits the press at intervals and everyone is urged to catch as many as they can before they accomplish the massacre of all the other fish. Zanders, it is explained, are programmed to destroy and are as voracious and bloodthirsty as sharks, preying for pleasure as much as for food. Maybe this is so, but despite these fears and the efforts of some to gain a livelihood by marketing zanders, they just don't seem to multiply and if you ever do eat zander, the chances are it will have been imported from Belgium, France or Holland.

Preparation   Should be scaled, cleaned and trimmed as soon as it is caught if possible. Otherwise follow instructions for preparing perch.

Cooking ideas   Large fish may be poached or baked; the recipe for stuffed perch on page 170 would be suitable; or cook like garfish with spinach on page 95, but increase the cooking time to 30–40 minutes. Or bake in foil. Small zander may be grilled or follow trout recipes.

Zander baked in foil

Score the fish two or three times on either side and spread 2 tablespoons Dijon mustard all over it. Lay it in a china or glass dish and sprinkle with 4 tablespoons olive oil, 1 teaspoon coriander seeds (crushed), 1 clove of garlic chopped, bayleaf, thyme, the juice of a lemon and pepper and leave to marinade for 30–60 minutes. Heat oven to Gas 5/375°F/190°C. Take a sheet of foil large enough in which to wrap the fish. Put fish and marinade in the centre. Lay slices of lemon all along the fish and sprinkle over 2 tablespoons dry white wine. Fold the foil into a secure but loose parcel and bake 30–40 minutes.

Fish Medley

This section is devoted to fish dishes which use more than one sort of fish, such as soups, sea fish stews like bouillabaisse and *cotriade* as well as those for freshwater fish – the matelote of France and the Flemish waterzooi. There's a recipe for fish pie and fish cakes, ideas for a seafood platter and a *fritto misto di mare*; as well as a fish pilaff and *le poupeton*, a sort of fish loaf that comes from Provence.

Avgolemono – egg and lemon soup
This Greek soup is made from a fish stock thickened with eggs and flavoured with lemon.
900 g (2 lbs) white fish trimmings including heads, bones, etc.
1 onion, sliced
2 carrots, sliced
thyme, bayleaf, parsley
whole clove garlic
8 black peppercorns
wine and water to cover
salt
3 eggs
2 lemons
Put the fish pieces into a saucepan, add onion, carrot, herbs, garlic, peppercorns, salt and sufficient wine and water to cover, ideally the ratio should be half and half, but you can use less wine and more water. Bring to the boil and simmer uncovered for 30–40 minutes. Remove from the heat and strain. In a roomy bowl, beat the eggs until they are light and frothy, add the juice of 2 lemons. Into this mixture, add a ladleful of the soup, mixing well before adding another, then away from the heat gradually stir this egg mixture into the soup. Return the pan to a low heat and stir until the soup thickens, it must not boil or it will curdle.

Provençale fish soup
This wonderful, robust soup takes time and energy so make it ahead
of time and reheat when you are ready to eat. In Provence the
fishmonger will sell you a selection of fish for your soup pot, he
understands exactly that you want a well flavoured soup that won't
break the bank. His selection will include different kinds of wrasse,
small rascasses or scorpion fish, nonats which are tiny, young fish as
well as young crabs and pieces of conger eel. If your fishmonger isn't
quite such a dream, it is still possible to beg from him the sort of fish
pieces which you need so it shouldn't be expensive. Tell him you are
making a soup and persuade him to let you have some of the bones,
heads and trimmings he would otherwise throw away such as the
head of a John Dory or a monkfish.

1 kilo (2 lbs) selection of whole and pieces of white fish, heads, tails,
    bones, skin, prawn shells, tail end of conger, what you will
2 tablespoons olive oil
1 onion, sliced
1 leek, sliced
1 tablespoon tomato purée
2 cloves garlic
bayleaf
sprig of fennel or 1 teaspoon fennel seeds
450 g (1 lb) tomatoes, chopped, or 1 can Italian tomatoes
2 or 3 medium potatoes, sliced
2 litres (3½ pints) water (or use the remains of a *court bouillon* or
    fish stock)
pepper, salt
1 handful of vermicelli (optional)
few strands of saffron or use ½ teaspoon powdered*
100 g grated hard cheese (optional)

Wash the fish, discard the gills. Heat a large pot and add the oil.
When it is hot add the onion and leek and cook over a medium heat
until soft but not brown. Stir in the tomato purée, crushed garlic,
herbs and tomatoes. Put in the potatoes and pieces of fish, pour in
the water, add a generous amount of pepper and cook over a high
heat uncovered for 15 minutes. Remove the pieces of fish a few at a
time, put them into a sieve over a bowl and use a pestle or wooden
spoon to crush the pieces, pushing through as much as you can.

---

* Saffron gives a special taste and colour to this soup, but it is expensive. You could
use turmeric instead, it has a different flavour but will add gold to the soup.

Discard the crushed fish and either sieve once more the contents of the bowl with the stock and vegetables from the saucepan, or liquidize them. Add salt and pepper to taste. Pour back into the pan, bring to the boil and add the saffron. If the soup is to be a complete meal add the vermicelli and cook a further 5–10 minutes until it is soft. Eat the soup with grated cheese, rouille or aïoli and garlic bread; or rub slices of French bread with a cut clove of garlic and put one in each bowl before adding the soup.

Bouillabaisse

You'll often be told we can't make bouillabaisse because we don't have the right fish. This is really not true because in the south of France they make bouillabaisse with any and every sort of fish. The name is used to describe a simple method of cooking for the days when the cook is in too much of a hurry to do much more than throw vegetables, fish, olive oil, seasonings and water all into a pot, which is then boiled rapidly until everything is cooked. In Marseille they perfected the dish and it is their version which has become elevated to an almost mystical level, though the only fish likely to prove elusive is the rascasse and even that is being imported. So if you feel like making a bouillabaisse, have a go and if it doesn't taste quite the same blame the weather, not the fish. You should have at least seven different fishes in your pot, so make it when you have at least 6 people to feed; it really isn't worthwhile for less. It is essential that everything boils rapidly uncovered, not only so that the soup can reduce and thicken but also so that the olive oil mixes with the water, it must not separate and float on top.

For 6 people buy seven or eight different fish, making sure you have a mixture of bony, firm and soft fleshed and cartilaginous, you'll need about 2 kilos (4 lbs) plus 1 or 2 extra fish heads. Choose from the following, those in bold type are the ones you're likely to find in a Marseille bouillabaisse:

bass; conger eel; grey mullet; gurnard; John Dory; monkfish; rascasse; sea bream; sole; turbot; weever; whiting; wrasse
brill; cod; coley; dab; flounder; haddock; hake; halibut; lemon sole; ling; megrim; plaice; pollack; redfish; skate; snappers; witch.
2 litres (3½ pints) boiling water
6 tablespoons olive oil
1 large onion, finely sliced
1 leek, finely sliced
4 tomatoes, chopped

2 cloves garlic, chopped
few strands of saffron or ½ teaspoon powdered saffron
a piece of orange peel
herbs – sprigs of thyme, fennel (or 1 teaspoon fennel seeds), parsley
    and a bayleaf
salt and pepper
First boil the water. In a large pan heat the olive oil and when it is hot add the onion, leek, tomatoes and garlic. Cook over a medium heat until they turn golden but not brown. Add the bony and firm fish. Pour over 2 litres (3½ pints) boiling water and boil hard for five or six minutes with the pan uncovered. Then put in the more tender fish, the saffron, the herbs and the orange peel. Continue to boil a further 5 minutes. Remove from the heat. Taste and add salt and pepper. Arrange the fish on a serving platter, discarding the extra fish heads. Strain the broth into a tureen. Serve with rouille (page 287) and slices of French bread sprinkled with olive oil and baked for 5–10 minutes at the top of a hot oven.

There are no hard and fast rules as to how you eat bouillabaisse except the fish and broth are served as part of the same course. Some people like to have fish and broth from the same soup plate, others like to have the soup in a bowl and fish on a plate. Some people add the rouille to their broth, others spread it on to their bread. Some people rub their bread with raw garlic. It's all a question of taste.

L'Aigo-sau is another Provençale fish stew, similar to bouillabaisse except it uses none of the bony fish like rascasse, wrasse or gurnards but white fish and potatoes and no saffron.

For 6 people select five or six different white fish such as cod, haddock, coley, hake, whiting, sea bream, John Dory, monkfish, or any of the flat fish, allowing about 1½ kilos (3 lbs) plus 1 or 2 fish heads
2 tablespoons olive oil
2 cloves of garlic, crushed
4 or 5 potatoes, cut in cubes
1 large onion, finely sliced
3 or 4 tomatoes, chopped
bayleaf
1 head of Florentine fennel, sliced, or 1 teaspoon fennel seeds
1 sprig of celery

slice of orange peel
3 or 4 sprigs of parsley
salt and pepper
boiling water
Cut the fish into uniform sizes. Take a large saucepan and put in the olive oil, crushed garlic, potatoes cut in small pieces, the onion, tomatoes, bayleaf, sliced fennel or seeds, celery, orange peel, parsley, salt and pepper. Cover with boiling water and boil fiercely over a high heat for 10 minutes, or until the potatoes are beginning to soften. Add the fish, bring back to the boil and continue cooking rapidly until the fish and potatoes are cooked – about 5 minutes. Put fish and potatoes on a dish, discard the extra fish heads and strain the soup into a tureen. Serve with bread and rouille in the same manner as for bouillabaisse.

Bourride
Like l'Aigo-sau, this Mediterranean fish stew uses only white fish, but no olive oil is added to the initial cooking stage, and it is simmered not boiled. It is thickened by adding aïoli enriched with extra egg yolks. For 4 people allow 1 kilo (2 lbs) mixed fish pieces using only white fish plus 1 or 2 extra heads.
1 onion, chopped
sprigs of thyme and parsley
1 teaspoon fennel seeds
bayleaf
slice of orange peel
water to cover or a mixture of half wine and half water
salt, pepper
aïoli (page 286) made with 4 crushed cloves garlic, 2 egg yolks and
    6 tablespoons olive oil
4 egg yolks
Use a large saucepan and put in the fish, onion, herbs, orange peel and enough water or mixture of wine and water just to cover. Bring just to boiling point, lower the heat and simmer for about 10 minutes. Meanwhile make an aïoli and stir in the 4 extra egg yolks. Carefully remove the cooked fish on to a warm dish. Discard the extra heads. Strain the stock. Stir some of the stock, a spoonful at a time, into the aïoli and when it has become quite liquid, stir the whole bowlful of aïoli into the soup. Put over a low heat and stir until the soup thickens, don't let it boil or it will curdle, it should become thick and

creamy. It is ready when it coats the back of a spoon. Serve with bread as for bouillabaisse.

Freshwater bouillabaisse

You can make a freshwater version of bouillabaisse if you happen to be suddenly presented with a variety of different fish by an angler in the family. Use fish like eels, small perch or pike, trout, etc. following the same procedure as the recipe on page 271–2.

On a typical, wet and damp English day it seems an impossible dream to evoke the atmosphere of summer holidays, so instead take the inspiration from the warming *cotriades* and *chaudrées* of western France made with those fish from the Atlantic easily obtained from our own fishmongers. You can use one or two different varieties, or several, the more the merrier, making a mixture of oily, flat and round fish and for good measure, and to increase the flavour, add one or two extra fish heads.

Choose from such fish as mackerel, sardine, John Dory, sea breams, cod, conger eel, hake, haddock, gurnard, monkfish, red mullet, whiting, snappers, etc.

Cotriade

1 kilo (2 lbs) of mixed fish cut in chunks
1 or 2 extra fish heads
4 tablespoons butter
2 or 3 onions, chopped
1–2 leeks, chopped
2 cloves garlic
1 kilo (2 lbs) potatoes, peeled and cut in quarters
½ teaspoon thyme, parsley and chervil (or used crushed fennel seeds)
bayleaf
1 can Italian tomatoes
salt, pepper
juice of half a lemon
a few threads of saffron or ½ teaspoon powdered saffron (or use turmeric)
1 litre (1¾ pints) water (or use fish stock, or a mixture of both)
Heat a large pan, when it is hot add the butter, let it sizzle and add the chopped onions and leeks, cook over a medium heat until they

are soft and golden, stirring them from time to time to prevent sticking. Add the chopped garlic, potatoes, thyme, parsley, chervil (or fennel) and bayleaf. Mix well and cook a few moments before adding the canned tomatoes, salt, pepper, saffron and the water or stock. Cover and simmer for 10–15 minutes until potatoes are softening. Add the fish and heads and cook rapidly for 5–10 minutes uncovered until the fish is cooked. Put the fish and potatoes on to a dish, discard the extra heads and squeeze over the lemon juice and dust with chopped parsley. Strain the liquid and serve it separately. This is nice with sliced French bread, rubbed with a cut clove of garlic and browned for 10 minutes in a hot oven; or with garlic bread. Eat it in shallow soup bowls which you have warmed very thoroughly.

Chaudrée is less of a stew more of a soup than *cotriade* and the word 'chowder' is a derivation of the name. The fish is cooked in a stock made from vegetables and white wine. If you feel it is extravagant to use nearly a whole bottle of white wine, use half wine and half water, or use ½ litre (1 pint) of dry cider instead.

First make a *court bouillon*: empty ½ litre of wine (or cider) and ½ litre of water into a pan, add chopped garlic and onion or a leek, a sprig of celery, thyme, parsley, 2 bayleaves, salt and 6–8 peppercorns and ½ kilo (1 lb) potatoes cut in quarters. Bring to the boil and simmer for 15 minutes, uncovered. Add ½ kilo assorted fish as for *cotriade* (page 274) plus an extra fish head or two. Boil 10 minutes and transfer fish and potatoes to a tureen. Discard the extra heads. Let the soup boil and reduce by about a third, then, off the heat, add about 25 g (1 oz) butter, cut in pieces, stirring so that it melts into the soup. Pour over the fish and you are ready to eat.

Fish pie
One of those unsophisticated dishes which involves several cooking operations and can cause a fair amount of washing-up. However, it is worth all the trouble it takes, because simple though it may be, it is also delicious and adored by children and people who associate fish with bones – there aren't any.
700 g (1½ lbs) fillets of fish, choose two or three kinds from a
   selection such as hake, cod, coley, haddock, whiting, pollack
1 litre (1½ pints) of fish stock (*see* page 302)
700 g (1½ lbs) potatoes, mashed with butter, salt, pepper and milk

50 g (2 oz) butter
50 g (2 oz) flour
salt, pepper
1 tablespoon chopped parsley
1 tablespoon chopped capers (optional)
pieces of butter
Poach the pieces of fish in the stock for three or four minutes. Take out the fish, let them cool a little, remove skin and bones and chop roughly. Peel potatoes and put into boiling, salted water, cover and lower the heat and let them simmer until cooked. Meanwhile in a small pan, melt the butter and stir in the flour. Cook stirring for two minutes, then gradually add 600 ml (1 pint) of the fish stock. Keep stirring until it thickens, then simmer for 20 minutes uncovered. It will reduce and thicken as well as increasing in flavour. Add salt, pepper, parsley and capers if using. Heat oven to Gas 5/375°F/190°C. Drain and mash the potatoes, seasoning them with salt and pepper and beating in a generous knob of butter and a tablespoon or so of milk. Put fish into a large pie dish, it must be big enough so that the sauce doesn't bubble over. Pour over the sauce. Top with the mashed potato. Make a pattern with a fork, dot with pieces of butter. Bake 20 minutes. Raise the heat to Gas 7/425°F/220°C for a further 5 minutes.

Fritto misto di mare – Mixed fried seafood
This Italian dish uses a selection of different fish, all roughly cut to the same size, dipped in batter and fried. It is served with a spicy sauce. It is far and away superior to the battered fish pieces sold from deep freezers. You can use a selection of all sorts of fish but it is more authentic if you include a few scallops or Dublin Bay prawns and it looks attractive garnished with whole, unpeeled prawns.
175 g (6 oz) lemon sole or plaice fillets
175 g (6 oz) cod fillets
175 g (6 oz) dogfish or catfish
4 scallops or Dublin Bay prawns, shelled
600 ml (1 pint) whole prawns in their shells
oil for frying, sufficient to come ½ cm (¼ in) up side of frying pan,
    or use a wok and have the oil about 2 cm (1 in) deep
chopped parsley and lemon wedges to garnish
tartare or green sauce *(la pommade verte)*
Make a batter as on page 297. Cut scallops in half, keep the corals

whole; or peel the Dublin Bay prawns and cut them in half lengthwise. Cut the fish fillets into pieces all roughly the same size, removing any bones and skin. Dip them in the batter. Heat the oven to Gas 3/325°F/160°C. Heat the oil and fry the fish in small batches, as they turn crisp and golden transfer them to a dish, keep it hot in the oven with the door ajar. When all the fish is fried, scoop out any blackened bits left in the pan. Add the whole, unpeeled prawns and toss them for 2–3 minutes. Transfer them to the dish, sprinkle over the parsley and surround with the lemon wedges. Serve with the sauce in a separate bowl on the table, finger bowls and napkins and lots of French bread to mop up the juices.

Matelote – freshwater fish cooked in red wine
This dish can be made with a single fish like freshwater eel or carp but is really best if you use a mixture of different varieties.
freshwater fish weighing around 675–900 g (1½–2 lbs)
2 tablespoons olive oil
1 onion, chopped
1 carrot, sliced
150 ml (¼ pint) red wine and the same of water
salt, pepper
4 whole cloves garlic
bayleaf, rosemary and thyme
100 g mushrooms, quartered
kneaded butter using 25 g (1 oz) each of butter and flour
chopped parsley
croûtons of bread, rubbed with garlic and dried in the oven
Heat the oil in a flameproof casserole. Add the onion and carrot and soften for a few minutes, add the fish cut in slices and brown it all over. Add wine, water, salt, pepper, the whole peeled cloves of garlic, and herbs. Simmer covered for 20 minutes. Add the quartered mushrooms, cook two or three minutes. Thicken the sauce with kneaded butter, adding it in small pieces and stirring to mix. Continue simmering 10 minutes. Put fish in the centre of a dish, sprinkle with parsley. Surround with the bread croûtons.

Waterzooi
This Flemish dish can be made using any freshwater fish or use firm-fleshed seafood such as turbot, brill, monkfish or halibut. It's nice eaten with boiled potatoes, especially if they are new.

Allow 1 kilo (2 lbs) of whole, ungutted fish – ask your fishmonger to clean, skin and fillet it for you; or buy ready-cut fillets weighing around 700 g (1½ lbs), ask him to skin them. (You could ask for the head and trimmings for your fish stock.)
1 carrot
1 leek
1 onion
2 stalks celery
50 g (2 oz) butter
450 ml (¾ pint) fish stock – see page 302
4 tablespoons dry white wine
thyme, bayleaf
salt, pepper
pinch of nutmeg
juice of half a lemon
1 small carton single or half cream
chopped parsley

Chop the vegetables very finely. Melt the butter in a wide pot and when it is foaming, add the vegetables. Turn them to mix, put on the lid and let them sweat over a medium heat for 5–10 minutes. Pour in the fish stock, white wine, add thyme, bayleaf, salt, pepper and nutmeg and bring to the boil. Cut the fish into serving chunks, quite big, about 5 cm (2 ins) across and add to the pan. As soon as it begins to bubble again, lower the heat and poach for 10 minutes. Carefully remove the fish to a serving dish. Add the lemon juice to the stock and stir in the cream, pour over the fish. Dust with chopped parsley.

Seafood platter

The most marvellous simple way of presenting a dish of seafood, all you need is a varied selection of shellfish and someone you love, because it is very expensive.

You need a long flat dish on which you arrange five or six different varieties of shellfish. Perhaps a cleaned crab in the centre, half a dozen oysters or small queens in the half shell, mussels, cockles and clams, all steamed open, a handful of shrimps and another of prawns, a small heap of winkles garnished with a couple of whole Dublin Bay prawns. The whole thing garnished with lemon wedges and hearts of lettuce or watercress. Serve with mayonnaise or aïoli. Have fingerbowls, a dish for all the bits you discard, napkins, cayenne pepper and salt, small forks and skewers to pick out the stubborn bits. Serve it with brown bread and butter, or slices of French bread and naturally a bottle of delectable, dry white wine.

Raw fish
Eating raw fish seems a strange idea to most of us but only up to a few years ago we thought it strange to eat raw vegetables. Salad vegetables yes, but raw mushrooms or cauliflower were to many an extraordinary idea and still are to quite a few. Once people have eaten raw fish, they usually find it not peculiar at all but something new and quite delicious.

Golden Rule: for raw fish dishes, the fish you use must be as fresh as possible; buy from a fish market or a fishmonger you can really trust and tell him you want to eat the fish raw.

Ceviche – a lovely starter to a meal
This method of preparing raw fish comes from the Pacific coast of central and South America. It often seems to be confused with *escabèche*, which is quite different, the fish being fried or grilled before being soaked in a spicy marinade. Choose fresh fillets of firm fish such as bass, brill, cod, hake, halibut, John Dory, sole, turbot, trout, salmon etc. Allow about 100 g (4 oz) per head. Tell your fishmonger you're going to eat it raw and ask his advice as to which are the freshest fish on his slab. Cut it into small cubes, put into a shallow china or glass dish and cover with lemon or lime juice, you'll need about 1 lemon or lime per 100 g (4 oz) fish. Cover and put in the fridge for 6–8 hours.

In a salad bowl, put a finely sliced onion, 2 or 3 quartered tomatoes and a green or red pepper sliced. Add some freshly milled pepper, the fish drained of its lemon juice and garnish with black olives and chopped parsley.

Sashimi – the Japanese way of preparing and eating raw fish is equally lovely as a starter to a meal.
Select two or three varieties which will contrast in colour and texture, allowing 100 g (4 oz) in total per head. You can use such fish as bass, salmon, fresh tuna, sea bream, red or grey mullet, trout, turbot, conger eel, brill, bonito, John Dory etc.
The fish should be filleted, boned and skinned. Some people

suggest you should put the fish into a colander, pour boiling water over it, then dip it immediately into cold water, thus killing any lingering germs. This is up to you, if the fish is really fresh, it shouldn't be necessary. The fish has to be sliced and it is easier to do if you first chill it for 30 minutes in the fridge or freezer. The slices should be around 1 cm (½ in) thick and about 5 cm (2 ins) wide, but slice them thinner if you prefer. Use a very sharp knife and cut fillets of white fish by holding the knife at an angle of about 30°. Cut dark, oily fish like tuna straight down.

Garnish individual plates with a salad vegetable like lettuce or curly endive, arrange the slices of fish in an overlapping pattern, contrasting colour and texture. Make it as pretty as possible. You can if you wish add a garnish of perhaps watercress or parsley sprigs; or shredded carrot or cucumber; or finely chopped leeks or spring onions. Make it prettier still by garnishing with 2 or 3 prawns in their shells.

Sashimi is served with soya sauce and wasabi.

The **soya sauce** should be good quality made from whole fermented soya beans and sold in Eastern or health shops under names such as Tamari or Shoyu. Some people like to add a little finely grated ginger to the sauce. It should be served in small individual bowls, allow about 2 tablespoons per person.

Wasabi is Japanese horseradish. It is a green powder available in tins from Japanese and Eastern shops. You mix it with sufficient water to form a paste, like mixing mustard. It should stand for 10 minutes for the taste to develop. It is very hot and strong. Everyone puts some of the wasabi paste into their soya sauce, begin with just a little on the point of a knife, then increase the amount depending on the degree of hotness that you like or can stand. Eat the pieces of fish, dipping them into your mixture of soya sauce and wasabi. Try it!

Fish cakes can be made from almost any leftover fish. Simply mix equal quantities of cooked, flaked fish (bones and skin removed) with an equal amount of mashed potato, add a teaspoon or so of finely chopped onion, salt, pepper, herbs such as chopped parsley or dill, a squeeze of lemon juice and mix with beaten egg. Dampen your hands to prevent the mixture sticking and form the mixture into flat cakes. Set them aside for half an hour to firm, then fry them, coated in flour or breadcrumbs, in oil or bacon fat until crisp and golden.

Pilaff
This is particularly good with meaty fish like bonito or tuna but you
could use cod, or haddock or any other firm fish.
225 g (8 oz) cooked bonito or tuna or other fish
2 tablespoons olive or peanut oil
1 onion, chopped
1 green or red pepper, chopped
1 teaspoon turmeric
1 cup rice
2 cups water
2 hard-boiled eggs
250 g (8 oz) tomatoes, sliced
oregano
salt, pepper
Heat the oil in the pan in which you are going to cook the rice. Add
the chopped onion and green or red pepper and let them soften for a
few minutes. Stir in the turmeric, add the rice and the two cups
water. Bring to the boil. Cover, lower and heat and simmer for
20 minutes. Meanwhile heat the oven to Gas 5/375°F/190°C and
hard-boil the eggs. When the rice is cooked, spread it over the base
of a shallow oven dish, season with salt and plenty of freshly milled
black pepper. Add the chopped eggs and flaked fish and mix lightly.
Cover with a layer of tomatoes, sprinkle with oregano, salt, pepper
and olive or peanut oil. Bake 15–20 minutes.

Le poupeton
This Provençal dish was created to use up the remains of a bouillabaisse instead of giving it to the cat. Poor cat, but give him a piece of
the finished dish to make him happy. You can make it when you
have cooked a large fish or you have fish left over from any fish
stew. It is a cross between a soufflé and a fish loaf and if that seems
an unlikely combination, try it. It makes a lovely supper dish, eaten
perhaps with a fresh green salad to which you have added a sliced
head of fennel.
butter
2 cups cooked fish from which all skin and bone has been removed
150 ml (5 fl oz) milk
½ cup breadcrumbs
50 g (2 oz) grated cheese
4 eggs, separated
salt, pepper

Heat the oven to Gas 5/375°F/190°C. Butter a 1 litre (2 pint) mould. Crush the fish and mix with the milk, add the breadcrumbs, grated cheese and mix in the egg yolks. Season with salt and pepper. Beat the egg whites until stiff and fold into the mixture. Pour into the mould and cook 30–40 minutes. Serve surrounded by grilled or baked tomatoes or with a tomato sauce (*see* page 292).

Roes
There are two sorts of roe, hard and soft. The soft belongs to the male fish and is known as milts; female roe consists of the eggs and it is the female roe of the sturgeon which is sold as caviare; that of the grey mullet forms the base of the Greek taramasalata, although in this country smoked cod's roe is used in its place. The roes of the herring and the shad are delicacies and it is really much a matter of taste as to whether the hard or soft is nicer. Soft roes almost melt in the mouth whilst the hard roes have a pleasing chewiness. Roes can be used as part of a stuffing or made into a simple dish in their own right. There are recipe ideas under the separate fish entries.

Sauces

A sauce can transform the simplest of fish dishes into something really quite special and hundreds of sauces have been created, enough to fill an encyclopaedia. This section is therefore limited to those already mentioned.

COLD SAUCES

Flavoured butters are lovely with grilled fish. Make more than you need for any one time and keep in the fridge either in a bowl, or better still in a roll wrapped in foil, like a sausage, and just cut off slices as you need them. There are two methods of making them:
1. Mix the flavourings directly into the softened butter using either a mortar and pestle, or a bowl and wooden spoon, or a food processor or:
2. Heat the buttter until it is just melted, mix in the flavourings, then pour into a bowl to set.
Below are some suggestions but you can of course invent lots of others.
Allow 100 g (4 oz) of unsalted butter

Anchovy	Two or three chopped and crushed anchovy fillets plus a few chopped basil leaves.
Capers and gherkins	1 teaspoon of each, chopped.
Chives	A tablespoon of snipped chives and 1 teaspoon of lemon juice.
Garlic	1 chopped clove of garlic, 1 tablespoon chopped parsley, salt, pepper, 1 teaspoon lemon juice.
Herbs	1 teaspoon of chopped dill and chervil; or thyme and rosemary.
Horseradish	1 tablespoon horseradish sauce.

Lemon	Zest and juice of half a lemon, salt, pepper.
Maître	1 teaspoon lemon juice, 1 tablespoon chopped
d'hôtel	parsley.
Mustard	1 tablespoon Dijon or herb mustard.
Tomato	2 tablespoons tomato purée.
Shellfish	*See* recipe for crayfish butter on page 67.
Spiced	½ teaspoon each of ground cumin and coriander seeds.

Flavoured oils
Olive oil or other good quality oil like walnut or peanut (ground nut) can be used in place of the butter. Simply add one of the above suggestions to 4 or 5 tablespoons of oil.

Flavoured oil for cooking fish or adding at the table
If you grill a lot of fish, it is not a bad idea to make a bottle of flavoured oil. You can use this to brush over the fish as you cook it, or you can add it at the table as a simple sauce. In the Midi they call this **Pilipili sauce**. Take a clean, glass bottle with a screw top and put in the following herbs and spices:
4 red chillies; 8 black peppercorns; 2 tablespoons coriander seeds; 4 chopped cloves of garlic; 4 tablespoons chopped parsley; sprigs of rosemary, marjoram, dill and fennel; 1 teaspoon salt; 1 tablespoon vinegar. Fill the bottle with peanut or olive oil. Put on the top and leave to infuse for several days. Use as required.

Pistou sauce is traditionally eaten with a vegetable-based soup or with pasta, but it is also delicious with simple baked fish like bass or grouper. Use a mortar and pestle, or a food processor. Crush 3 cloves of garlic, add a handful of chopped fresh basil leaves. Mix to a paste. Add 1 teaspoon tomato purée. Gradually beat in 150 ml (¼ pint) olive oil until you have a thick sauce. If you have no basil, use parsley, it won't be the same but is still delicious.

Vinaigrette sauces are lovely with grilled or poached fish, use a simple vinaigrette made with a good quality oil and lemon juice or vinegar, or add extra flavours. You can put all the ingredients into a screw-top jar and give it a good shake; but it will be thicker and better if you use a mortar and pestle.

Basic vinaigrette
Mix 1 teaspoon Dijon or herb mustard with 1 tablespoon of lemon juice (or use a wine or cider vinegar), salt and pepper. Beat in 5 or 6 tablespoons good quality oil such as olive. Below are some suggested variations:

Anchovy	Begin by crushing 1 clove of garlic, two or three anchovy fillets, then add all the other ingredients.
Caper	To the basic vinaigrette add 2 tablespoons capers.
Egg and gherkins	Begin by crushing a hard-boiled egg yolk, add the other ingredients and stir in 3 or 4 chopped gherkins and a tablespoon of chopped parsley.
Herbs	Add a tablespoon of chopped herbs, such as parsley, dill, chervil, thyme, lemon thyme, oregano or marjoram.
Olives	Add 3 or 4 chopped green or black olives.
Spices	Add 1 teaspoon of crushed spices such as cumin, coriander or fennel.

Mayonnaise sauces
These sauces can be eaten with many sorts of fish dishes both hot and cold and can be made ahead of time. All the ingredients should be at room temperature before you begin.

Basic mayonnaise
Use a mortar or a bowl with a rounded base. Put in 1 teaspoon Dijon or herb mustard, add 2 egg yolks and break them up with the pestle (or use a whisk or wooden spoon). Gradually begin to beat in oil (use olive, peanut, sunflower or any good quality vegetable oil), drop by drop; as the mixture begins to thicken you can add the oil more liberally, but never in a great splash. Keep beating and lifting the mixture and adding oil until it is very thick (2 egg yolks can absorb at least 300 ml [½ pint] oil). Add a tablespoon of lemon juice or wine vinegar, which will thin the mixture. If you wish you can then add more oil. Season it with salt and pepper.

Rémoulade
Add to a basic mayonnaise 1 tablespoon each of chopped capers, gherkins and parsley.

Tarragon mayonnaise
Pour boiling water over a handful of fresh tarragon leaves. Dry it well. Crush it, put it into a bowl and continue as for basic mayonnaise.

Tartare sauce
To a basic mayonnaise, add 1 teaspoon each of the following: chopped capers, green stoned olives, gherkins, chives and parsley.

Aïoli
This is a sauce for garlic lovers because ideally you should allow a clove of garlic for everyone. Begin by crushing them into a paste and then add one or two egg yolks and continue as the basic mayonnaise. Finish it off by adding a very little lemon juice, although this is an optional extra.

La Pommade verte – green sauce
Eat with grilled or poached fish such as salmon, sea trout, sea bass. It is simple to make if you have a food processor, otherwise you can do it by hand but it will take some energy and time.
handful of spinach and 1 of sorrel leaves, or use all spinach
boiling water
handful of mixed fresh green herbs such as parsley, chervil and
   tarragon
2 or 3 chopped anchovy fillets
1 tablespoon each of chopped gherkins and capers
3 hard-boiled egg yolks
a piece of dry bread, the size of a walnut, soaked in water then
   squeezed dry
olive oil
salt, pepper
1 teaspoon vinegar
Put spinach and sorrel leaves into a bowl and pour over enough boiling water to cover. Drain well. Add the herbs. Chop all the leaves finely or put into the food processor. Add the anchovy fillets, gherkins and capers. Mix well. Add the egg yolks and the bread and mix everything together until you have a paste. Gradually begin to add olive oil drop by drop and then as the sauce begins to thicken, add more oil until you have the consistency of a thick mayonnaise. Season with salt, pepper and mix in the vinegar.

Gribiche sauce
Like the above sauce, this one is made using hard-boiled egg yolks; it is good with cold poached fish.
   Crush two hard-boiled egg yolks, gradually beat in, drop by drop, 150 ml (¼ pint) olive oil, as it thickens add it a little more generously.

When it is thick, stir in 1 teaspoon wine vinegar, salt, pepper, one chopped gherkin, a teaspoon capers and a teaspoonful of chopped mixed herbs such as parsley, chives and tarragon.

Rouille

This is eaten with Provençal fish soups and stews and is not really a mayonnaise, although one version is made with egg yolks. It should be very hot and fiery and coloured a rust-red. You can make it in a food processor or blender or in a mortar and pestle; failing either of these use a bowl and a whisk. Below are three separate versions.

Madame Boeuf's rouille

Madame Boeuf is not ninety years old; she was about eighty when she made us all a bouillabaisse and gave me this recipe. You soak in water some small, hot chillies, about 7 or 8 if you want it very strong. After they have soaked for several hours, you crush them in the mortar. You crush also several cloves of garlic. In your *soupe de poisson*, you add a few slices of potato and when they are soft, take them out and crush them in your mortar with the chillies and the garlic. You then add a very little of the broth and gradually beat in olive oil to make a thick sauce. To serve, toast slices of bread at the top of a hot oven, spread with rouille, put a slice into each soup bowl and serve.

Monique's rouille

Her grandson's wife has a lighter version. Crush 2 red chillies and 2 cloves of garlic, mix in 1 teaspoon Dijon mustard, add an egg yolk and mix well. Gradually beat in olive oil, a few drops at a time until you have a thick sauce, stir in ½ teaspoon tomato purée.

Rouille made with bread

Yet another version uses bread as a thickener. You crush 2 red chillies and a clove of garlic per person. Soak a piece of stale bread as big as a walnut in water, squeeze it out and add to the mortar. Mix well and beat in 3 or 4 tablespoons olive oil. Everyone adds a teaspoon or two to their soup or bouillabaisse. Watch out, this one is quite concentrated and hot.

Walnut horseradish sauce

Delicious with cold poached salmon or sea trout. Whip a carton of double cream. Stir in 1 or 2 tablespoons of horseradish sauce, 1 tablespoon of yoghurt and 2 tablespoons of skinned, chopped walnuts. (Skin them by soaking for a minute or two in boiling water, the skins slip off paper-thin.)

Cucumber and yoghurt
Peel half a cucumber, chop and add to a cupful of thick yoghurt. Add freshly milled pepper and a squeeze of lemon juice. Make just when you are about to eat, otherwise the water in the cucumber will make the sauce runny.

HOT SAUCES

Beurre manié is not a sauce but a means of thickening a cooked sauce that is too runny. Mix equal quantities of softened butter and flour and stir small pieces into the hot, not boiling, sauce. As each one melts, so add another and in a matter of a few minutes your sauce is thickened.

Melted butter
The following sauces are all based on melted butter with different flavourings. They are mostly quick and simple to do and will give an instant fillip to plainly cooked fish whether it is fried, grilled, baked or steamed.

Beurre blanc
For poached freshwater fish like pike or those which tend to be dry. Chop two shallots, put them into a small pan with a heavy base and simmer them gently in 2 tablespoons wine vinegar, when the liquid has evaporated and the shallots are soft, add 1 tablespoon cold water. Set aside until the fish is ready. Take 100 g (4 oz) butter out of the fridge and slice it in thin slivers. When the fish is cooked, put the small pan on the lowest possible heat, let the mixture warm and then add the first piece of butter, whisking until it melts, then add a second and continue in this way until all the butter has been added. The sauce will be like thin Hollandaise, white and creamy.

Beurre noisette
This is a delicate mixture of melted butter and lemon juice which is delicious with fried or grilled flat fish of all kinds or poached fish like salmon or sea trout. Melt 100 g (4 oz) butter until it turns a pale nut-brown, squeeze in the juice of a lemon, add a handful of chopped parsley and pour over the fish.

Beurre noir
Not black at all but dark brown, traditionally served with skate and goes well with all cartilaginous fish such as dogfish and shark. Melt 100 g (4 oz) butter until it turns a dark brown but does not blacken. Put 2 tablespoons vinegar, 2 of capers and 2 of chopped parsley into a small jug, pour this mixture into the sides of the pan. Pour over the fish.

Anchovy sauce
A deliciously fishy way of adding flavour to some of the blander fish. Melt 100 g (4 oz) butter and add 2 or 3 crushed anchovies. Let them soften for a few minutes, then pour this over the fish.

Sauce au citron – lemon sauce
Serve this with baked or grilled fish. Peel one or two lemons, including the pith. Use a sharp knife and peel in a whorl like peeling an apple, using a sawing motion and you'll find it is quite easy. Cut the lemons into rings. Put them into a saucepan with 75 g (3 oz) butter, ½ teaspoon fennel seeds and 2 tablespoons white wine, let it cook gently for 15 minutes.

Hollandaise
Hollandaise is a warm sauce based on the mayonnaise theory but is made with butter not oil. Most recipes suggest using a *bain-marie* (one pan standing inside another which is half filled with hot, not boiling, water) and beating small pieces of butter into the egg yolks. The problem with this method is that the hot water can make the sauce too hot, the eggs begin to curdle and the butter separates into a ghastly oiliness. If the fish is already cooking, panic takes over and all is disaster. Margaret Costa in *Four Seasons Cook Book* makes the whole thing very simple and the following is based on her method. You must have a small, thick-bottomed pan and a balloon whisk.

Make your hollandaise before you cook your fish and keep it hot by standing the saucepan in a frying pan filled with hot water. Renew the hot water when it cools and give the sauce an occasional stir. It will remain perfect for well over an hour.
100 g (4 oz) concentrated or unsalted butter
2 egg yolks
lemon juice
1 tablespoon white wine or water
salt, pepper
Cut off 25 g (1 oz) butter and divide it into two thin slices; melt the

remaining 75 g (3 oz) gently until it is just melted, no more. Remove from heat. In a small saucepan with a thick bottom, put the egg yolks, 1 tablespoon of lemon juice, the wine or water, salt and pepper and beat until thoroughly mixed. Add one half of the 25 g (1 oz) butter and put the pan over a very low heat. Stir with a whisk until all the butter is melted and the eggs are beginning to thicken but not scramble, they will just begin to coat the wire of the whisk. Take off the heat, add the other half of 25 g (1 oz) piece of butter and beat it into the eggs. Then gradually, drop by drop, begin adding the melted butter, beating all the time. The sauce will begin to thicken until all the butter is added. Don't be impatient, add it drop by drop, beating constantly. If disaster strikes and it does separate, immediately beat in 1 tablespoon HOT water. You will end up with a thick, creamy, warm sauce, add to this lemon juice and salt and pepper to taste. Stand the saucepan in a frying pan filled with hot water until you are ready to eat. Give it a stir from time to time.

Béarnaise sauce
Made in the same way as a hollandaise but before you begin, put a finely chopped shallot, 4 tablespoons wine vinegar, 4 tablespoons dry wine or vermouth, ½ teaspoon dried tarragon, pepper and salt into your small, thick-based saucepan. Bring slowly to the boil and simmer gently until it has reduced to about 2 tablespoons. Let it cool. Then add the egg yolks, mix well and proceed as for the recipe for hollandaise. Finish off by adding 1 tablespoon chopped parsley and 1 of chopped fresh tarragon.

Cream sauces
Luxury sauces made with cream can be made in a matter of minutes.
Basic method Put 50 g (2 oz) butter into a small saucepan and let it just melt over a low heat. Stir in 4 tablespoons double, single or half-cream and let it reduce and thicken over a medium heat, stirring all the time, add 4 more tablespoons cream, a squeeze of lemon juice, salt and pepper. You can add a tablespoon or two of other flavourings such as capers; herbs; snipped chives; two or three chopped anchovy fillets.

Basic béchamel and velouté sauces

The method for these two sauces is the same, béchamel uses all milk
or a mixture of milk and cream, velouté a mixture of milk and fish
stock, or all fish stock. They can be plain or act as the base for all
sorts of additions.

25 g (1 oz) butter
2-3 tablespoons of flour – depending on whether you want a thin or
    thick sauce
300 ml (½ pint) liquid (either all milk, or a mixture of milk and
    cream, or a mixture of milk and fish stock or all fish stock)*
salt, pepper

Use a small, heavy-based pan, melt the butter and stir in the flour on
a low heat. Cook for a couple of minutes, stirring, then gradually
add the liquid, raising the heat to medium and keep stirring until it
thickens. Lower the heat, add salt and pepper and cook very gently
for about 20 minutes.

The flavour of the basic béchamel can be increased by first slowly
heating the milk with the addition of a bayleaf, piece of onion or
shallot, piece of carrot, pinch of nutmeg and a sprig of parsley or
other herb such as dill or fennel. Let it just simmer for 20 minutes,
then strain before using.

Béchamel is the base of many other sauces, below are some
variations to the basic recipe:

Caper   Add 1 tablespoon capers.
Cheese   Add 3 or 4 tablespoons grated hard cheese to
               cooked béchamel sauce and stir off the heat
               until the cheese melts.
Parsley   Add a handful of chopped parsley, the juice of half
               a lemon to a sauce made with half milk half
               cream.
Mushroom   Cook 100 g (4 oz) chopped mushrooms in the
               butter before adding the flour to the basic sauce,
               add a squeeze of lemon juice at the end of
               cooking time.
Mussel   Add a drained can of mussels (choose those in
               brine not vinegar) to the cooked sauce.

*If you want to make a *velouté* sauce but have no fish stock, use half milk and half
water and add 1 tablespoon of concentrated fish sauce which is found in many
Eastern and Oriental shops, see page 302.

Velouté sauces can be enriched by stirring in either a tablespoon of cream, or an egg yolk, or yoghurt, or a tablespoon or two of flavoured butter (*see* page 283) right at the last minute. Don't let them boil again as they will curdle.

Raïto is a light sauce made with red wine which comes from Provence. It is delicious with fried fish such as monkfish, skate, hake, dogfish, cod, salted cod or haddock.

2 tablespoons olive or peanut oil
1 onion, finely chopped
1 heaped tablespoon flour
150 ml (¼ pint) red wine and the same amount of hot water
1 tablespoon Eastern fish sauce (optional [*see* page 302])
1 tablespoon tomato purée
2 or 3 crushed cloves of garlic
sprigs of thyme, parsley and a bayleaf
salt, black pepper
1 tablespoon capers and/or the same of chopped, stoned black olives
Heat the oil in a small thick-based pan and fry the onion until golden. Stir in the flour, mix well, then gradually stir in the red wine, followed by the hot water. Add the fish sauce (if using), tomato purée, garlic, thyme, parsley and the bayleaf. Cook on a low heat, uncovered for 10–15 minutes. Season to taste with salt and pepper. Add the capers and/or black olives.

Tomato sauce
2 tablespoons olive or peanut oil
1 onion, chopped
1 carrot, sliced
1 or 2 cloves of chopped garlic
large can of Italian tomatoes
salt, pepper
parsley, thyme, oregano or marjoram – use sprigs of fresh herbs or
    ½ teaspoon each of dried
bayleaf
lump of sugar
Heat the oil in a small heavy-based pan, add the onion and carrot and cook about five minutes. Add all the other ingredients and simmer uncovered for 30–40 minutes.

Creole sauce
Made like the tomato sauce with the addition of 2 or 3 red peppers, chopped (or use a small can of pimentos), and two chopped stalks of celery. Cook them in 2 or 3 tablespoons peanut oil or butter with a chopped onion, then add a large can of tomatoes, some thyme and a bayleaf, a little salt, lots of black pepper and cook uncovered over a low heat for about 30 minutes. Add one or two crushed, hot chillies or ½ teaspoon chilli powder and a squeeze of lemon or lime juice.

Gooseberry or rhubarb sauce
225 g (½ lb) gooseberries or rhubarb
little water
sugar
25 g (1 oz) butter
Put whole gooseberries or the rhubarb cut into 5 cm (2 in) pieces into a small pan with a little water. Simmer gently until soft, press through a sieve. Taste and if necessary add a very little sugar, stir in 25 g (1 oz) butter.

Sorrel sauce
Wash and remove the leaves from 100 g (4 oz) sorrel. Melt 25 g (1 oz) butter in a saucepan, add the sorrel and let it reduce for two or three minutes. Stir in 1 teaspoonful of flour and still stirring cook for a couple of minutes, before gradually adding 300 ml (½ pint) single or half cream. Stir over a low flame until the sauce thickens, add salt and pepper.

Cooking Methods

1. Fish hardly needs any cooking time at all. Once it has reached the temperature which turns the raw flesh opaque, it is ready.
2. Cooking fish beyond this point will spoil it. It simply becomes dry and tough, loses flavour and goodness.
3. Because it needs such a short cooking time, flavours are often added before cooking begins. Hence marinading or cooking it in a *court bouillon,* or stock, which has been prepared beforehand.
4. Eat it as soon as it is ready. Keeping it hot means it simply carries on cooking. If you have to keep it warm for a few minutes, put it in a warm oven covered loosely in foil, with the door ajar.
5. Remember to heat serving dish and plates ready for the cooked fish.
6. Cooking times cannot be precise because they depend on thickness, size, etc., so always check to make sure you don't overcook.

BAKING

Suitable fish: most kinds, especially whole round fish, cutlets, fillets or steaks.
Pre-heat oven.

Method 1. Butter or oil an ovenproof dish, add the fish, dot with butter or sprinkle with oil. Add liquid in the form of a glass of dry wine, vermouth or cider, or the juice of a lemon; or lay strips of lemon along it. The skin of a whole fish may be pierced and slivers of garlic inserted. Lay a loose piece of foil or buttered paper (use the wrapping paper from a pack of butter) on top of the fish. Baste very frequently.

Method 2. En papillote Score whole fish two or three times on either side. Oil or butter a piece of foil large enough to wrap the fish.

Season the fish with herbs and spices, add a little chopped garlic or onion, perhaps some finely sliced mushroom or chopped tomato, chopped anchovy fillet or a rasher of bacon. Lemon adds flavour, either squeezed over the fish, or slices laid along it. Dot with butter or sprinkle with oil. Wrap the foil around to form a loose parcel but fold the centre join and the ends so as not to lose any of the juices. Put on a baking sheet and put in the oven. Cooking times vary with the type of fish and the heat of the oven.

BRAISING

Suitable fish: most whole fish, thick cutlets, fillets and steaks.
The fish is cooked on top of the stove or in the oven, which should be pre-heated. It is laid on a bed of vegetables which have been cooked in a little oil or butter, flavoured with herbs and other seasonings. Very little liquid is added and it is covered with foil or a close-fitting lid.

FRYING (SHALLOW)

Shallow frying is preferable to deep frying.
Suitable fish: small whole fish, cutlets, steaks, fillets, skate wings and shellfish.

1. To prevent wet fish coming into contact with hot fat or oil, it should be coated with flour before cooking or for a change try using cornmeal which gives a sweeter taste. Oily fish such as herring are good coated in oatmeal (*see* Coatings, page 297).
2. Heat a frying pan and when it is hot add enough oil or butter to a depth of about ½ cm (¼ in). Olive oil gives a good flavour but is expensive, otherwise use a good quality vegetable oil such as peanut/groundnut, rapeseed or corn. If using butter choose unsalted or concentrated butter, neither of which will burn as easily as salted butter; a little oil added to the pan also helps prevent burning.
3. As soon as the oil or butter sizzles add the fish and fry over a medium heat, turning the fish over when the underside is golden brown to fry the other side.

Frying à la meunière

Whole or filleted fish is delicious fried in this manner. It is coated in flour and fried in clarified butter, which is butter from which some of the water content has been removed. Put the cooked fish on a hot serving dish, wipe the pan clean, melt a generous knob of ordinary butter in the pan and as soon as it sizzles squeeze in the juice of half a lemon, pour over the fish and serve garnished with parsley and lemon wedges.

Clarified butter

Heat 100 g (4 oz) butter gently so that it separates becoming oily with a white foam on top. Strain through a muslin cloth into a bowl. Keep in the fridge and use as required.

FRYING (DEEP)

Suitable fish: small whole fish such as whitebait, sprats or trimmed flat fish, thin fillets or cuts of large fish.

1. Coat the fish in flour, batter or breadcrumbs (*see* opposite). If cutting up fish make sure all the pieces are roughly the same size.
2. Use either a deep fryer or a large, deep, heavy pan with a flat base and a frying basket. Or use a wok which is very economical on oil. Use a good quality vegetable oil such as peanut/groundnut, rapeseed or corn. Oil must be deep enough to immerse the fish completely. Heat over a medium heat to a temperature between 180–190°C/350–375°F. Test by dropping a small cube of bread, it should rise to the top and turn golden in one minute at 180°C/350°F.
3. If using a frying basket dip it in and out of the pan to oil it so the fish won't stick. Add the fish, not too much at a time. Raise the heat just for a minute because the fish will reduce the temperature a little.
4. The fish will be done when it turns golden and rises to the surface.
5. Drain the fish on kitchen or greaseproof paper, sprinkle with salt, lemon juice and dust with parsley.

The oil can be strained and kept in a cool place to be used once or twice more, but only for fish.

COATINGS

Flour or Cornmeal coating
Season the fish with salt and pepper and lay it in a plate of milk. Put flour or cornmeal on a second plate, dip both sides of the fish into it, sprinkling on extra if not completely covered. Lay each piece of fish on a cake cooling rack, this will help to dry the flour a little and make it stick better. (You may find it easier to coat the fish if you put the flour or cornmeal in a paper or plastic bag, add the fish, shake gently to cover both sides.)

Oatmeal Season fish with salt and pepper. Put oatmeal on a plate, lay the fish on it, sprinkle some more oatmeal on top, and pat firmly to make it stick.

Breadcrumbs Beat an egg yolk with 1 teaspoon of oil and 1 of water. Dip in the fish. Hold it up over the dish to drain it. Put breadcrumbs on a plate, lay the fish on it, sprinkle more breadcrumbs on top, and pat firmly to make them stick. Set aside for 30 minutes for the coating to firm.

To make breadcrumbs Use stale bread without crusts. Grate it or put it through a blender or food processor to make crumbs. Spread it on a baking tray, cover with paper and leave for 24 hours to dry in a warm place (such as over the stove, airing cupboard, plate warming drawer). Keep in an airtight jar.

Batter coatings
The following makes a crisp light coating:
100 g (4 oz) flour
salt, pepper
1 tablespoon olive, corn or peanut oil
200 ml (7 fl oz) mixture of milk or water, or beer or water
1 egg white
Sift the flour, salt and pepper into a bowl. Make a hollow in the centre and add oil and liquid gradually. (The yeast in beer helps to lighten the batter; if you use water, a teaspoon of dried yeast would have the same effect.) Beat the mixture just until it is smooth and frothy. Set it aside to rest for an hour. Just before using whisk the egg white until it is thick but still soft. Fold into the batter. Roll the fish in flour before coating, it will help the batter to stick better.

The following very light Japanese **tempura batter** is most suitable for small pieces of fish:

1 egg
100 g (4 oz) plain flour
250 ml (8 fl oz) water
Mix all the ingredients together using a whisk or fork. It doesn't matter if you don't get rid of all the lumps, this batter is best if it is not over-worked.

GRILLING

Suitable fish: steaks, fillets and small whole fish up to 500 g (about 1 lb).
You can use a conventional grill with rack, or use a flat, cast-iron grill pan like those made by Le Creuset which cooks over a hotplate.
Golden Rules
1. For better flavour marinade fish before cooking.
2. Pre-heat grill and pan for 5–10 minutes before you start to cook. (You can ease the washing-up by lining the pan with foil.)
3. Oil the grill rack, which need not be pre-heated, using a piece of kitchen paper or a pastry brush dipped in oil, this prevents fish sticking.
4. Be on hand during the whole of the cooking operation and baste frequently.

Table of approximate grilling times
Round fish:	4–8 minutes each side
Flat fish:	4–6 minutes each side
Steaks:	8–15 minutes, depending on thickness
Fillets:	3–4 minutes on cut side, 2 minutes on skin side
Kebabs:	About 12 minutes

Fish is cooked when flesh turns opaque and comes away from the bone, test with a skewer.

Whole round fish
1. Using a sharp knife, score the fish on either side, by cutting two or three diagonal slashes (though small fish like sardines don't need scoring) this helps the fish to cook evenly and you can insert slivers of garlic, herbs or other flavourings. Cooking fish with heads on adds to their flavour, so remove them after cooking either in the kitchen or at the table.

2. Put fish on grid in grill pan, brush with oil or melted butter or a mixture of oil, lemon juice, salt and pepper, or the marinade mixture. Put under the heat on a rung about 10 cm (4 in) away from the burners.
3. Turn the fish halfway through the cooking time, *see* table page 298 and brush again with more oil or melted butter.

Flat fish
1. You can remove heads before or after cooking, it's up to you, cut them off diagonally, black skin can be removed before or after cooking with most flat fish, though the thick skin of those like sole is usually removed before, scrape the white skin and score it lightly in a criss-cross pattern to prevent the fish curling.
2 and 3 as above: cooking times in table (page 298).

Steaks
Follow 2 above, steaks need not be turned but cook thick steaks over 3 cm (1½ ins) on a lower rung. Baste frequently. Cooking times (page 298).

Fillets and boned whole fish
Snip the edges two or three times to prevent curling. Follow 2 and 3 above, grilling cut side first, then turning to crisp the skin for 2 or 3 minutes. Cooking times (page 298).

Kebabs
Marinade cut pieces. Thread on oiled skewers, alternating with such things as pieces of onion, tomato, green or red pepper, bacon, mushrooms, bayleaves, etc. Brush with oil or melted butter, or with the marinade and grill first on a low rung, basting and turning every two minutes. Raise the pan to a higher rung for the last four or five minutes of the cooking time, basting and turning once more.

Marinades Always use a china or glass dish, never metal, for marinades. Marinade fish for at least 30 minutes. A basic marinade consists of 2 or 3 tablespoons of oil, use olive or peanut/groundnut oil, lemon juice or wine vinegar, pepper and herbs and spices to your choice. Some suggestions overleaf. Salt is best added later as it draws out the moisture and makes the fish dry, but this can be an advantage with some watery fish like plaice or cod.

SUGGESTED MARINADES
1. Olive oil, chopped chilli, teaspoon thyme, teaspoon crushed fennel seeds and lemon juice.
2. Peanut/groundnut oil, chopped parsley, chopped spring onion, lemon juice, pepper, 1 teaspoon finely chopped ginger.
3. *Moroccan chermoula:* olive oil, lemon juice, 2 tablespoons fresh coriander, chopped, 2 cloves of garlic, chopped, 2 teaspoons paprika, 1 teaspoon crushed cumin seeds, 1 red chilli, chopped.
4. *Harissa marinade:* olive oil, lemon juice, 1 teaspoon harissa (bought in tubes or tins from Middle Eastern shops), teaspoon each of crushed coriander and caraway seeds.
5. *Pilipili sauce (see* page 284): can be used to marinade fish; add some lemon juice.

Barbecued Fish
The charcoal should be glowing hot and red before you begin cooking. A hinged holder is useful for turning the fish. Sprinkle herbs over the fire, or used dried fennel twigs or vine cuttings. Fish can be wrapped in foil and baked on a grid over the barbecue.

POACHING

Suitable fish: large, whole fish, fillets and shellfish.
Golden Rule: Once the fish is added, the liquid must only simmer NEVER BOIL.
This is one of the simplest and most delicious ways of cooking fish, it remains moist and if you cook it in a *court bouillon* or stock made ahead of time, it will be full of flavour. There is no need to scale fish before poaching, as the skin is easily removed once it is cooked. Flat fish will be prevented from curling if you slit the dark skin down the length of the backbone.
   The slow heating from cold to hot is all part of the cooking process and is suitable for small and large fish. You can serve poached fish hot with a sauce like hollandaise, béarnaise or raïto, or cold with a mayonnaise-based sauce.

Method
1. Lay the fish in pan in which it can lie flat either on a grid or a piece of crumpled foil. (Large fish will be easier to remove if you

slip a long, folded strip of foil under grid and fish, long enough to provide you with lifting handles on each side.) Season the fish inside and out with salt and pepper.

2. Pour over sufficient cold or tepid liquid (stocks or *court bouillon*, see below) just to cover it.

3. Put on to a low heat and as soon as the first bubble appears, lower the heat so that the liquid just simmers.

4. If the fish is to be eaten cold, turn off the heat and let the fish cool in the liquid before lifting it out.

5. If to be eaten hot, approximate cooking times are as follows: check after the shortest time, the flesh should be opaque and a skewer inserted into the thickest part should go in easily.

Small fish and fillets from

225–450 g (½–1 lb) 2–5 minutes
450–700 g (1–1½ lbs) 5–7 minutes
700 g–1 kilo (1¼–2¼ lbs) 7–10 minutes
1–2 kilos (2¼–4½ lbs) 10–15 minutes
2–3 kilos (4½–6½ lbs) 15–20 minutes

Skinning a whole fish and serving

You'll find it easier to skin a fish if it is still warm. Lay it on a piece of foil or greaseproof paper so that it is easier to handle and turn over. Cut off head and fins. Slit the skin along back and peel it away. Turn the fish over and repeat. Carefully lay it on a serving dish, garnish, putting the head back in place if you wish. At table, cut along the centre line, ease and divide the first fillet; divide second fillet. Lift out bone by the tail and serve the lower half in the same way.

STOCKS

Court bouillon is simply the French name for a vegetable-flavoured stock. It often contains wine or cider, but you can make quite a good version without. Add more flavour by including the heads, bones, trimmings, etc. from filleted fish. You can ring the changes by using leaks intead of onions, celery instead of carrots.

1 onion, sliced
1 carrot, sliced
thyme, parsley and 2 bayleaves
2½ litres (4½ pints) water
2 tablespoons wine or cider vinegar
300 ml (½ pint) dry white wine or cider (failing either of these, add

extra water plus 2 more tablespoons of vinegar and 2 teaspoons
sugar)
salt
12 black peppercorns
Bring to the boil, simmer for 20–30 minutes, cool and then strain. If
you find this amount is insufficient for your particular fish, add
extra water.

Milk court bouillon This is ideal for delicate fish such as brill, cod,
smoked haddock, turbot. Allow ½ milk and ½ water, add salt,
pepper, bayleaf and peeled lemon slices. No need for preliminary
cooking.

Fish stock or fumet is useful for making sauces.
1. Use the *court bouillon* in which you have poached fish; boil it
   hard to reduce to one third by which time the flavour will be
   greatly intensified.
2. Or use same vegetables and flavourings as for a *court bouillon*
   but add 225–450 g (½–1 lb) fish trimmings, bones, heads, etc.
   (not oily fish like mackerel or herring) and only sufficient liquid
   just to cover, half water and wine if you can run to it. Simmer for
   20–30 minutes. Cool and then strain.

Fish stock with the minimum of effort Use the liquid from
tinned mussels or clams; or follow Colin Spencer's advice in his *Fish
Cookbook* and use 1 pint water (or water flavoured with wine or
cider) to which you add 1 tablespoon oriental fish sauce. The brand I
use is called Cá Sac, which, like the one he mentions, Nam Pla,
comes from Thailand. The sauce is made from concentrated, fermented fish juices. If choosing other brands, go for the colourless
kind, rather than those flavoured with caramel, or use Japanese
Dashi, which can be bought in powdered form from some health or
whole food shops.

SMOKING

This is a fun way of cooking fish. You'll need to buy a smoker which
will include its own set of instructions. The fish is hot-smoked over
smouldering sawdust and the result is delicious whether hot or cold.
It's wonderful if you have an angler in the family who brings home
a surfeit of trout or mackerel.

STEAMING

Suitable fish: small whole fish, cutlets and fillets
This under-rated method of cooking fish is usually associated with invalids, which is a pity because it can be delicious as well as easily digestible.

Golden Rules:
1. Fish must be steamed and not come into contact with the liquid.
2. The liquid must simmer not boil.
3. Don't let the fish overcook; test with a skewer.

Method 1
1. Put fish on a buttered plate, or a steamer over a pan of water; or use a wok and a Chinese steaming basket.
2. Season the fish with salt, pepper, lemon juice, herbs such as thyme, parsley, tarragon or dill. Add a few diced mushrooms, a flavouring of soya sauce, some chopped spring onions and perhaps a dollop of yoghurt.
3. Cover the fish with a lid or plate, bring water to the boil, lower the heat and simmer gently until the fish is cooked. It will turn opaque. For a fish weighing 450 g (1 lb) test after 5–7 minutes. Time will vary according to thickness of fish.

Method 2
The **Chinese Method** Rub the cleaned fish inside and out with salt, score it lightly and insert slivers of fresh ginger. Put it on a plate. Make a marinade using 1 teaspoon sugar, 1 teaspoon soya sauce, 1 teaspoon wine vinegar. Pour over the fish. Add two or three chopped spring onions, a green pepper cut in strips, and put slices of lemon on top. Set aside for an hour. Lift the fish carefully and put it into a steamer over a pan of boiling water, or into a steaming basket which fits over a wok. Steam, testing after 5–7 minutes, but it depends on the size of the fish and may take twice this time or longer.

This method can be used for all sorts of whole fish such as sea bass, grey mullet, carp, sea bream, perch, trout, parrotfish, rabbitfish, etc. Vary the flavourings using, for example, soaked dried mushrooms, pieces of bacon or chopped anchovies and adding chopped garlic, herbs such as parsley or dill and spices like chopped chillies or ground cumin, coriander or fennel.

BONES

We nearly all remember being warned as children to look out for bones and this must account for so many people's resistance to tackling a whole fish on their plates. Just to look at a fish is enough to make them imagine the feel of a bone stuck like a wire needle between their teeth, or, worse, caught in their throat; then the frantic gulpings of water or chewing of dry bread, the swallowing to find it still persists, followed by the relief to find it gone, only to begin worrying anew about where it's going to lodge itself inside. It's neurotic fantasies like this that makes us such fish finger eaters and turns us into lovers of everything filleted and pre-packaged.

The whole thing becomes less of a trauma if we stop panicking and understand where to look for the bones. It's fairly obvious that most fish with a bony skeleton, whether round or flat, have a central backbone which bears smaller bones on either side. But a fish has fins and the fins must attach themselves to the fish with something and of course the answer is with bones. So to eat a fish begin by cutting off the head. Flat fish have tasty flesh between the rays of their fins, so scrape this out with your fork. Slit a flat fish down the centre or lateral line, a round fish down the back. The fillets may then be eased off the bone and the flesh eaten, whilst at the same time you carefully remove the bones belonging to the fins. Having eaten one half, lift off the backbone and eat the lower half.

GADGETS

This is a list of the gadgets and pieces of cooking equipment mentioned, many will already be part of the kitchen.

Baking dish	Large oval or rectangular flat dish in china or glass for marinading and baking.
Fish kettle	Luxury items; two sorts available: one for long fish, the other diamond-shaped for flat fish called a turbotière.
Fish slice or spatula	
Frying pan	Large enough for cooking for several people; an oval shape is ideal.
Frying basket	To fit into a saucepan or a deep fat fryer.

Grill pan	Or cast iron Le Creuset flat pan for grilling on a hot plate.
Lemon juicer	
Kitchen shears or scissors	
Knives	Oyster knife or small blunt knife for opening shellfish and scaling.
	Sharp pointed heavy knife.
	Long thin filleting knife.
Lemon zester	
Mortar and pestle	
Pastry brush	For basting fish when grilling.
Saucepans	Large, for making *court bouillon*, soups, etc.
	Small, heavy-based for sauces.
Skewers	
Sieve or colander	
Steamer	To fit over saucepan or steaming basket to fit on wok.
Tongs	For turning fried and grilled fish.
Wire brush	For scaling.
Tweezers	For stubborn bones.
Whisk	Balloon for sauces.
Wire mesh holders	Square and fish-shaped for holding and turning fish on grill or barbecue.
Wok	
Wooden mallet	

QUANTITIES

Most of the quantities in the recipes are not absolutely precise, except for things like sauces or batters. They are meant as a guide, no more. The following tables show some useful conversions.

Weight

Ounces	Grams	Ounces	Grams
1	25	10	275
2	50	11	300
3	75	12	350
4	100	13	375
5	150	14	400
6	175	15	425
7	200	16	450
8	225	17	475
9	250	18	500

Liquids

Pint	ml
¼	150
½	300
¾	450
1	600
1½	900
1¾	1 litre

Temperatures

Gas	°F/°C	
¼	225/110	Very cool
½	250/120	
1	275/140	Cool
2	300/150	
3	325/160	Moderate
4	250/180	
5	375/190	Moderately hot
6	400/200	
7	425/220	Hot
8	450/230	
9	475/250	Very hot

Techniques

This section deals with some of the preparation techniques that you might need to do. Most of these can be done for you by your fishmonger and when possible ask him. It will save you a lot of time. There are other methods and techniques which I have not included simply because they are not relevant to the recipes I have given.

Lots of fish are displayed and weighed before they are cleaned (gutted) though those caught by deepwater trawler and flat fish are usually sold already gutted. Once you have selected your fish and it has been weighed and priced, your fishmonger will probably ask you if you want it cleaned and if you want the head removed. (If he doesn't, make sure you remember to ask him because it will save you a lot of trouble.) Definitely get him to clean it for you and if you don't like the idea of the head, get him to remove that too. If you decide to leave the head on, make sure he removes the gills because they can make the taste bitter. At the same time if it is a fish with sharp fins or hard scales, ask him to trim and scale it. Ask for head and trimmings for a sauce or soup.

If you ever have to do any of these jobs yourself, here is how to go about it.

CLEANING (OR GUTTING); SCALING AND TRIMMING

It can be messy, so put a newspaper on the draining board or work surface, tearing off each page as it becomes sodden. A tip before you begin: you can get rid of fish smells on your hands by rubbing them with lemon juice and then washing them. You can remove smells from knives, etc. by adding a dollop of vinegar to the washing-up water.

Work near the sink. Work in stages. Watch out you don't prick yourself, wear gloves if you like. Remember fish can easily be bruised, so handle with care.

ROUND FISH

Trimming Cut away any spiky fins, beginning with the dorsal (back) fins. Work upwards from the tail, they will fan open as you lift them. Use kitchen scissors. You may find a sharp knife is necessary to cut away stubborn bones beneath the flesh.

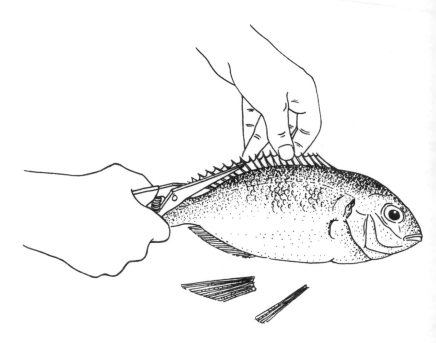

Scaling (Fish with smooth skin or small soft scales don't need scaling and you don't need to scale any fish you intend to poach, the whole skin can be easily removed after cooking [*see* page 301].)

It's easier to scale a wet fish so rinse it first under running water. Hold it by the tail and using the blunt side of a knife with the blade almost flat against the fish, scrape towards the head; make sure the scales don't lodge in the waste pipe. Finish the operation by rinsing the fish clear of any lingering scales.

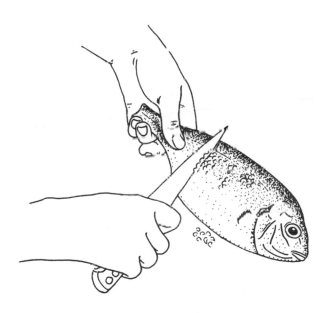

A few fish like perch have deeply embedded scales, you may find something stronger than a blunt knife is needed like the side of a cheese grater or even a horse comb. Some kitchen shops sell a gadget for scaling. Really stubborn scales can be loosened by immersing the fish for a few seconds in boiling water. Tough scales as they are loosened fly all over the place, to curb their flight, immerse the fish in water whilst you scale it.

Cleaning or gutting With the point of a knife, slit along the belly from the small hole or vent towards the centre to just below the gills. Scoop out the viscera (internal organs). Using the point of the knife, cut on either side of the backbone and remove any inner membrane, traces of blood or blackness. You can rub on salt to act as an abrasive if any bits refuse to budge. Make sure all innards get removed.

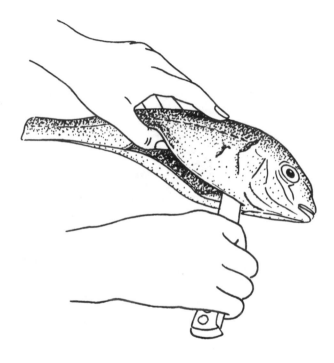

Cooking a fish with its head on adds to the flavour, but if this doesn't appeal to you, cut it off at this stage; otherwise remove the gills by pulling the head backwards, which opens the gill covers, pull out the gills or cut them out using either a knife or scissors.

Gutting small fish Fish like sardines are likely to distintegrate if you empty them through the belly. It is better to gut through the gills, make a curved cut just beneath the gill opening, pull the head backwards and pull out the viscera and the gills. Rinse under water making sure you have removed everything.

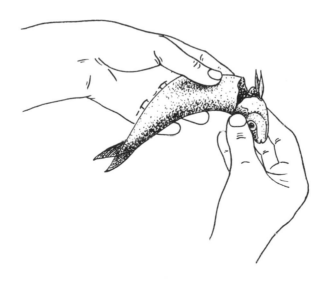

Wash under running water. Normally don't leave fish soaking; though certain freshwater kinds which are muddy, or fish like tuna which are very oily and can be bitter, benefit from being soaked in acidulated water (2 tablespoons of vinegar, 1 teaspoon of salt to 1 litre [1¾ pints] water). Details under individual fish.

Drying
Make sure the fish is thoroughly dried, use kitchen paper, before cooking.

FLAT FISH
Flat fish are normally sold gutted but if you have to do it cut a slit on the dark side just beneath the gills and pull out the innards which take up just a small place close to the head. Wash out thoroughly.

FILLETING

If a recipe specifies fillets but your fishmonger is only selling complete fish, ask him to fillet it for you and to give you the heads and trimmings for a basis for sauce or soup. If for some reason he won't do the filleting, at least make sure he cleans (guts) the fish for you, otherwise you will have two jobs to do. Filleting isn't difficult but it is time-consuming. If you have to do it, here is how to go about it.
Golden Rule: You must have a thin, sharp filleting knife.

Round fish
Each side yields 1 fillet.
1. To cut off the first fillet lay the cleaned fish on a board with its tail towards you, hold it steady and slice right down the back from head to tail to reveal the backbone.
2. Sever the fillet from the head, by cutting it away just under the gills.
3. Using short strokes with the knife flat against the bone, cut down the backbone, working to release the flesh, and lifting the fillet free with your other hand.
4. Carefully detach the second fillet using the flat of the knife and lifting the backbone clear with your other hand. Any tiny bones can be pulled out with tweezers.

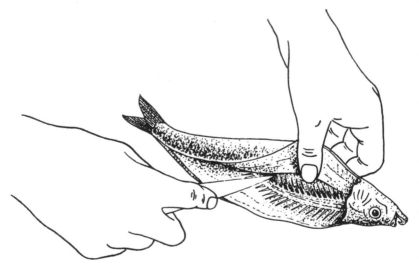

Flat fish

Each side yields 2 fillets.

1. Lay the cleaned fish on a board with its tail towards you.
2. Cut along the length of the backbone along the centre of the fish (not along the edge) to a depth of about ⅓ cm (¼ in).
3. Detach the first fillet by inserting the knife into this cut close to the head. Use short, slicing strokes, keeping the blade almost flat, working towards the tail so that you gradually ease the fillet clear, using your other hand to lift it. When you get to the tail, cut the fillet free.
4. Detach the second fillet in the same way.
5. Turn the fish over and detach the other two fillets.

The skeleton of the fish and trimmings can go into a *court bouillon* or stock pot.

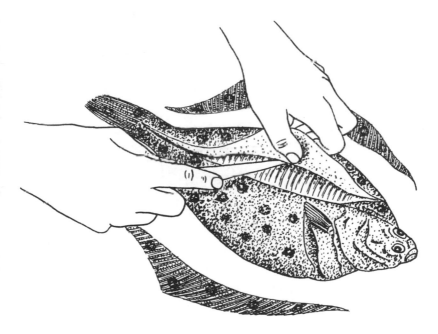

SKINNING

Most fish, especially round fish, don't need skinning before you cook them. If you don't like the idea of eating the skin, it is simple to remove it before serving. *See* page 301 for skinning a poached fish. Some flat fish like sole have a tough dark skin and this is usually removed before cooking. Get the fishmonger to do it for you. Otherwise you can do it yourself. To prevent your fingers slipping, dip them in salt first.

Fillets of fish
1. Lay the fillet on a board, skin side down.
2. Hold the tail end; keeping the blade of your knife almost flat, slip it between skin and flesh and gradually work towards the head end using a sawing motion.

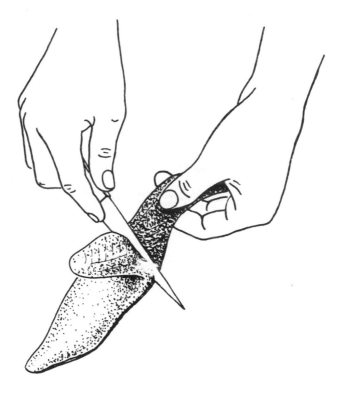

To skin a flat fish
1. Lay the trimmed fish dark side up on a board, the tail towards you.

2. Make a cut where the tail joins the body.
3. Carefully ease away sufficient skin for you to grip, using either the point of a knife or your fingernails.
4. Grip the skin firmly, holding the fish securely down with your other hand, rip away the skin in one motion, rather like removing surgical gloves.
5. The light skin simply needs to be scraped with the blade of a knife.

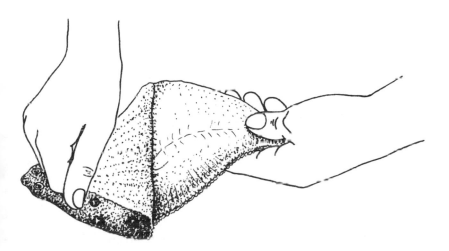

BONING

Fish have a better flavour if they are cooked on the bone, though sometimes you might want to bone fish like herring which have a lot of small bones and can cause misery at the table.
1. The fish should be cleaned and trimmed.
2. Slit the fish along the belly to the tail.
3. Lay the fish downwards on its belly and press all along the backbone with the ball of your thumbs, this will loosen the bone and flatten the fish.
4. Turn the fish over and using a knife and your fingers, ease away the spine with all the ribs attached.
5. Cut it free at head and tail, using scissors and lift out. Any stubborn bones remaining can be removed with tweezers. Drape

the fish over your hand, the bones will stick out like pins in a piece of material.

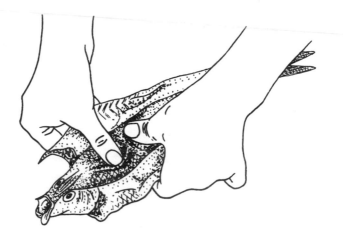

FROZEN FISH

This is a book about fresh fish so I have not given very much space to cooking frozen fish. Most have instructions on the packet. Whole fish are best thawed before cooking, either by leaving overnight in the fridge or at room temperature – allowing 3–4 hours per 450 g (1 lb) weight. Steaks and fillets can be cooked from frozen in which case as a general rule increase the cooking times given in recipes by a half.

Bibliography

Burgaud, Françoise, *Crustacés et Coquillages*, Librarie Générale Française, 1975

Burgess, G.H.O., Cutting, C.L. (in part), Lovern, J.A., Waterman, J.J. (Eds.), *Fish Handling and Processing*, Torry Research Station, HMSO Ministry of Technology, 1965

Christensen, J. Møller, *Fishes of the British and North European Seas*, Penguin, 1978

Čihař, Dr Jiří, *Freshwater Fishes*, Octopus, 1983

Davidson, Alan, *Mediterranean Seafood*, Penguin, 1981

Davidson, Alan, *North Atlantic Seafood*, Penguin, 1986

Davidson, Alan, *Seafood of South-East Asia*, Federal Publications, Singapore, 1976

Grigson, Jane, *Fish Cookery*, Penguin, 1975

Haas, W. de and Knorr, F., *Marine Life*, Burke Publishing, 1975

Hastings, Macdonald, and Walsh, Carole, *Wheelers Fish Cookery Book*, Michael Joseph, 1974

Lamb, Ted, *The Penguin Guide to Sea Fishing in Britain and Ireland*, Penguin, 1984

Larousse Gastronomique, English translation, Hamlyn, 1961

Lyon, Ninette, and Benton, Peggie, *Fish for all Seasons*, Faber and Faber, 1966

Lythgoe, John and Gillian, *Fishes of the Sea*, Blandford Press, 1971

MacMahon, A.F. Magri, *Fishlore*, Penguin, 1946

Midgalski, Edward C., and Fichter, George S., *The Fresh and Salt-Water Fish of the World*, Octopus, 1977

Muus, Bent J., and Dahlstrom, Preben, *Guide to the Sea Fishes of Britain and North-Western Europe*, Collins, 1974

Prunier, S.B. (Ed. Ambrose Heath), *Madame Prunier's Fish Cookery Book*, Hutchinson, 1967

Sharman, Fay, *The Taste of France*, Macmillan, 1982

Smith, Prof. J.L.B. and Margaret, *Fishes of Seychelles*, Dept. of Ichthyology, Rhodes University, Grahamstown, 1963

Smith, Margaret, and Heemstra, Phillip C. (Ed.), *Smith's Sea Fishes*, Springer-Verlag, 1986

SOPEXA and F.J.O.M., *Poissons et Fruits de Mer de France,* undated but recent
Spencer, Colin, *Colin Spencer's Fish Cookbook,* Pan, 1986
Tenison, Marika Hanbury, *New Fish Cookery,* Granada, 1979
Wheeler, Alwynne, *Freshwater Fishes of Britain and Europe,* Kingfisher Books,
    1983
Wheeler, Alwynne *The World Encyclopedia of Fishes,* Macdonald, 1985
Wood, Rev. Theodore, *The Sea-Shore,* T.C. & E.C. Jack Ltd, undated

Index